The Rule of Reciprocity
and
the Origin of Freedom

To David

Contents

Acknowledgments

I would like to thank Xlibris and Random House, Inc., for making this opportunity available to me and others. In the course of writing this book, I gave a great deal of thought as to how to bring the final piece to publication. My main concern is that the ideas contained here remain as disassociated as possible from any institution, political platform, philosophical position, or preexisting set of beliefs. In other words, intellectual independence is my paramount motivation. A book like this must stand (or fall) on its own. If the ideas presented here are wrong, then I'm wrong. If the book contains errors (either of omission or commission), then they are my errors alone, and not the product of any form of outside, editorial, or associative influence.

It has been over ten years since a beloved professor first introduced me to the basic principles that opened my eyes to the phenomenon and consequences I've described here. And over those ten-plus years, I have, through periods of greater and lesser effort and enthusiasm, been collecting the supportive material and compiling the notes that are now fully fleshed out in this book. As you read on, I think you'll quickly recognize that the spirit of independence I've chosen to pursue is not only of general value but also directly connected to many of the ideas contained herein. The existence of an independent-publishing option, as remarkably valuable (and rare in many parts of the world) as it may be, is not the product of fate or fortune; it is, instead, an extended effect of the phenomenon described in these pages.

Stephen Michael Strager
stephen.michael.strager@gmail.com

Introduction

Although this book can be read as philosophy, history, political science, or even, I suppose, a self-help book (a guide for your own daily dealings with others), it is none of these exclusively. Instead, it is a work that explores a single idea bearing relevance to each of those disciplines, an idea that in some ways I have dug out from between the cracks of the works of other thinkers then confirmed again and again through personal observation and research. In exploring the rule of Reciprocity, I draw in only the simplest ways from intellectuals such as Hegel, Hayek, Rousseau, and Foucault. And authors such as Havel, Sharansky, and Fukuyama, among others, have covered in greater detail (sometimes based on personal involvement) many of the larger historical movements upon which I only touch. What is original and valuable here (I hope) is the clarity with which the main idea is expressed.

My objective is simple: to expose and explain the rule of Reciprocity (which I will sometimes shorten to "Reciprocity") in a clear, concise, and vivid way. This introduction is already longer than the rule itself, which is stated—including key consequences—in four sentences. Following the statement of the rule, Reciprocity is explored in three sections that explicate its two main components (system, power) as well as the effective but nonessential element of broadcast. And numerous, real-world examples of Reciprocity-in-action are incorporated throughout.

Ultimately, I want to deal with facts because the rule of Reciprocity itself is a fact, one that I am simply describing, not creating. Reciprocity is a rule not of human nature or even human behavior per se, but of human interaction. That is to say, it is not necessarily in one's nature to be "reciprocal," and one cannot behave "reciprocally" in the sense I am using the term (just as one cannot behave "gravitationally"). But one's actions are affected, and can be guided, by an understanding of the rule of Reciprocity (just as one's actions are affected, and can be guided, by an understanding of the law of gravity).

The sections that follow the rule do, by virtue of their examination of specific examples, describe a different way of looking at the world. But the rule of Reciprocity itself provides more than a new perspective and a fresh vocabulary. Reciprocity is a verifiable phenomenon that operates in, on, and around us. And those who seek to influence the actions of others must understand this rule or risk ceding whatever power they may hold.

The Rule of Reciprocity

The rule of Reciprocity:

Power is transferred through its own exertion.

And from this rule, these consequences follow:

1. The point at which power is exerted is the point at which there exists the greatest potential for its transfer.
2. The people upon whom power is being exerted define its limits.
3. When the purpose of an exertion of power includes the maintenance of power, then power is maintained through calculated conservation, not unlimited exertion.

Exploring the
Rule of Reciprocity

The Observation

One Day on the Bus

It is difficult to choose a single opening example to illustrate the rule of Reciprocity because Reciprocity emerges everywhere in the web of human relations: from classrooms to class-action lawsuits, from marital interactions to martial law, from contained flash points such as police arrests to sweeping historical dramas.

So I'll start simply and build.

Once as I was sitting on the number 30 bus on Columbus Avenue in San Francisco, a woman and her young daughter ran up alongside trying to board before the bus pulled away. They made it right to the door just as it was closing, and the door did close . . . on the little girl. It was not clear whether the driver intentionally allowed the door to close on her or whether this was an honest accident. At any rate, the girl, who was probably six or seven years old, was not hurt, but her mother was clearly upset. As they boarded the bus, she proceeded to berate the driver, who apologized and seemed to take it all in relatively good stride *until*, at the peak of her passion, the mother declared that she wanted to file a report on him.

At that point (we had driven one block), the driver pulled the bus to the curb and said (actually shouted) something along the lines of, "OK, you want to file a report? We'll file a report." He then announced to everyone that the bus was now out of service. This was an electric bus attached to overhead cables by two poles, and the driver even went so far as to get out and detach the poles from the cables (thus seizing all power from the bus—literally and figuratively). Then he radioed his supervisor and declared to us that he'd have to wait until the supervisor arrived. Everybody (including the mother and her daughter) got off the bus and took the next one that came along. I walked.

All in all, this is not an event destined to be memorialized in the historical canon. So why even consider this inconsequential exchange? To answer that question, let's examine the incident from the perspective of Reciprocity. What, exactly, transpired there between the mother and the driver? To begin, it is unclear whether the door-closing was an intentional act on the part of the driver (an overt exertion of power), a covert/concealed exertion (an exertion concealed, in this case, behind the alibi that it was an accident), or actually an accident. While the concept of concealed exertion becomes profoundly important later, let's agree, for the sake of this discussion, that it was an intentional exertion. Then this is our starting point: the driver exerted his power to let the door close and keep the mother and daughter off the bus regardless of the harm it might have caused the girl. What we see next is the immediate transference of his power to the mother based *only* on the mother's determination that this exertion exceeded agreed-upon limits.

As a passenger, the mother has power. Even though the driver sits behind the wheel, the passenger also has a certain amount of control over the bus and the driver, a certain ability to influence their actions. Whether the mother viewed the door-closing as intentional or merely irresponsible, she defined the driver's act as being beyond acceptable limits, took the power he had transferred to her through his action, and exerted that power back on him in the form of a serious upbraiding; and she did influence his actions: he apologized. But then *she* went too far (in the eyes of the driver, who was now the one *upon whom* power was being exerted) by declaring that she wanted to report/broadcast this incident in which it was obvious no one was injured. She overexerted, transferred the power back to him, and we all got off the bus.

And here's where we are so far with regard to the rule of Reciprocity: power is transferred through its own exertion; the point at which power is exerted is the point at which there exists the greatest potential for its transfer; the people upon whom power is being exerted define its limits.

Most of the examples that I provide in the coming sections are of broader scope and greater complexity than that isolated incident, but here is the core concept of this study (and the reason why it is worthwhile to consider this inconsequential door-closing incident): What was at work on the bus that day is also at work in the world-at-large. The two fundamental elements of Reciprocity—system and power—along with the effective though not essential ingredient of broadcast are all present in the bus example and appear throughout the following illustrations as well.

The rule of Reciprocity and its consequences confirm a preexisting paradigm of power. This model holds that power is not fixed hierarchically, or as Michel

Foucault states in *The History of Sexuality Volume I,* that "power comes from below; . . . [that] there is no binary and all-encompassing opposition between rulers and ruled," that instead we see "manifold relationships" that "bring about redistributions, realignments, homogenizations, serial arrangements, and convergences."[1] Foucault's succinct and accurate statement that "power comes from below" leads logically to this conclusion: if power comes from below and also exists at the top, then power is infused throughout. The rule of Reciprocity simply explains the mechanism by which those "redistributions" and "realignments" (the transferences that we saw on the bus) take place.

It may be hard for some to accept the proposition that power is vested in all people. To select one obvious objection from among a myriad of possibilities, you might ask, "What about slaves? What power could they possibly have?" And yet, the institution of slavery is consistently destroyed wherever it emerges. Or to choose a more specific example: "what power did the American Indians have?" Apparently none: their lands were taken. So doesn't this disprove the rule at the outset? How can all people have power, and yet the Indians have none? This may seem intriguing, but it is not a contradiction. There are specific reasons why the American Indians did not have power in relation to Europeans when the Europeans invaded their lands, and there are specific reasons why they do today.

If you don't accept this premise regarding the distribution of power prima facie—and if the bus example didn't quite clinch it for you—I believe it will prove itself through this work's main inquiry. This study accepts the nonbinary model of power as its starting point and asks not "is power distributed?" but "if power resides everywhere in greater and lesser concentrations, then how is it transferred?" If power is in a state of constant negotiation, what is the mechanism of its exchange? My aim is to dissect Reciprocity, to explain why it exists, how it works, and what the implications are for those who understand the rule and those who don't. Foucault and others have tackled society's grand architecture, the development and consequences of our vast matrix of organizational machinery—the entire power grid, so to speak. I'm just going inside to expose a single wire.

System

Although Reciprocity is a rule regarding the exertion of power, we're not starting with power. We're starting with system. Why? Because system precedes power; it is power's prerequisite. That statement, "system is power's prerequisite," immediately begs for definitions of both power and system. So here they are. I'm defining *power* as the ability to influence another's actions. And I'm defining *system* quite simply as agreement.

A simple agreement, a single cooperative link between two individuals would stand as the most basic system. As agreements accumulate, expand, and endure, systems become more complex and mature. If power is the ability to influence another's actions, then what is the source of power? Quite simply: agreement creates power. To make *system* synonymous with *agreement* and then say that system is a prerequisite of power, or that power doesn't exist outside a system, is the same as saying that absent agreement, power doesn't exist. That is a true statement. Absent agreement, only force exists. And this leads to a key distinction, the necessary understanding that there is a difference between force and power.

Force v. Power

Here is the simple idea that forms the foundation of the force/power distinction: a punch in the face in an uncharted wilderness is different from a punch in the face on a city street.

A punch in the face in a wilderness that precedes or somehow stands separate from any system is an exertion of force subject to the rules of force relations (i.e., retaliation and resolution based solely on the determination of who is strongest or otherwise better fit for the challenge). On the other hand, a punch in the face in the city is an exertion of power subject to the laws of the system in which the punch is thrown, that is to say, subject to that system's organizational efforts, its accumulation of agreements. So if one caveman hits another caveman over the head with a club, that's an act of force. If a policeman hits someone over the head with a club, that's an act of power. Caveman, policeman, same act (hitting someone over the head with a club), different contexts, different consequences—different definitions. And here's why all of this is true . . .

There's no way to know what went on before record, but logically at some point, there had to be contact between individuals and—perhaps sooner rather than later—conflict as well. Human contact could have begun with cooperation, but we know there was conflict at some point because there is conflict today. There simply had to be contact and conflict. There's just no way to avoid this.

Let's imagine, then, contact and conflict between two men who meet under circumstances that preexist agreement of any sort. And without being completely ridiculous about it, let's call them cavemen.* Now, if one caveman hits the other caveman with a club, we can all agree that's an act of force both under the common definition (physical exertion) as well as my own: physical exertion outside a system (with *system* being defined as an accumulation of agreements). And let's say that he hits him with the club in

---

* I want to insert two disclaimers here. First, I promised I would deal with facts, not theories, and now I'm jumping into a theoretical account of the genealogy of system starting with two hypothetical cavemen. I'm doing this only because I want to show that the rule of Reciprocity is inscribed from the very start into the genetic material of human interaction. Since we have no record of first contact, I have to proceed hypothetically with an illustration based on logical explication. Second, there is a philosophical tradition of hypothesizing about "first men" (hence, my tongue-in-cheek cavemen), and I want briefly to acknowledge and differentiate my participation with regard to that pattern. The most prominent of "first men" experimenters, G. W. F. Hegel, posits that man's "fundamental passion" is the desire for recognition while Hobbes and Locke identify it as self-preservation (Fukuyama, 158-59). To be clear, I am not interested in the first man—I am interested in the first agreement. It may be true that the motivation for first conflict was recognition, and it may not. We really don't know. But we do know that there was a first conflict and a first agreement (because we have both today). By engaging in this "first agreement" thought-experiment, I only wish to make clear that the rule of Reciprocity (the fact that power is transferred through its own exertion) emerges immediately at the moment of agreement, even the very first agreement, and is not dependent on the development of a more mature system.

an effort to persuade this second caveman to perform in a certain way, for instance, to gather berries for him. To begin with, there is no guarantee that the caveman's club will influence the action of this other caveman; so if power is the ability to influence another's actions, then this clubbing is not at its essence an exertion of power. The aggressor caveman may simply accomplish nothing, or at worst, may club his victim to death, and that's not an influence of action. That's the exact opposite of influencing someone's actions; it's the elimination of action since death makes it impossible for the other man to act at all.

In the force relation that arises between these cavemen as long as the one who is exerting force has made an accurate calculation of his own fitness versus his adversary's, he can club away all he wants. He has nothing to lose. The caveman he's clubbing isn't bringing him berries today, and if he clubs the man to death, the dead caveman won't bring him berries tomorrow either. The dead caveman loses everything, but the clubber loses nothing. In this pure force relation, the rule of Reciprocity does not pertain.

But the entire arrangement transforms in a flash once the second caveman acquiesces to the first caveman's demands. Power is born at the instant of acquiescence. And the very next time the first caveman comes after his new berry bringer with a club, it will be an exertion of power subject to the rule of Reciprocity.

Here is an analysis of why force transforms to power at the moment of acquiescence:

"I'll bring you berries if you don't club me" establishes a simple system built on a single agreement. At that instant of acquiescence, in the moment when the agreement is formed, the *weaker* party is vested with the ability to influence the stronger party's actions, and power is immediately infused throughout the system. To begin with, the weaker caveman gets his assailant to cease clubbing, and in the future, he will avoid clubbing if he gathers berries. Thus, the one who acquiesces influences the other's actions on an immediate and ongoing basis. In this way, agreement can be seen as the initial element in the formation of power. But as we see, acquiescence is not purely a *granting* of power to the clubber (remember, the one exerting force has no influence over the other's actions until the other acquiesces)—it is really an *acceptance* of power. It is the acceptance of the opportunity to influence the clubber's actions by performing in an agreed-upon manner.

It is the weaker individual who actually creates power by submitting in agreement. The *potential* for power is found in the intention of the stronger party in a force relation—whether he is pursuing agreement or annihilation. But the power is actually created by the weaker party. Thus we see the truth in Foucault's statement, "Power comes from below." And because power is immediately vested in those with apparently less influence (those who are bringing the berries as opposed to those who are eating them), we also find in the moment of acquiescence a balancing movement (however slight).

Initially in force relations, limits are set by the party best fit for the conflict—"I choose not to kill you." Following acquiescence, the rule of Reciprocity emerges, and the limits are defined by those upon whom the exertion is being made—"I agree to bring you berries if you stop clubbing me." A first limit has been set. Of course, realistically, the first agreement could be, "I'll bring you berries if you don't kill me," and the clubbing could continue but to a reduced degree (so as not to lead to the death of the berry bringer and thus the end of berry harvests). Even if this were the case, even if the clubbing continues to a lesser degree, the berry bringer has still influenced the clubber's actions. A first limit is always set.

Thus, at the moment of the initial acquiescence/agreement, both parties are vested with the ability to influence the other's actions (power); and as the result of that infusion of power throughout the system, the party who is initially less influential does use its influence (however slight) to begin to define limits on the *future* exertions of the more influential party. This is how agreements accumulate. Prior to that first agreement, all exertions were acts of force subject solely to the rules of force relations, but with that single, simple agreement in place, any future attempt to influence the other's actions becomes an exertion of power. At the point of each new exertion, new agreements are reached (explicitly or implicitly), new limits are set, or the system disintegrates, and the parties return to force relations.

Let's assume an instance in which, following the first limit, we don't fall back to force relations and that, over time, new limits accumulate. This is not an outrageous assumption since it describes reality. The constant definition against the original agreement (whatever it is) requires subsequent agreements, and as more agreements are reached, the more able the berry bringer becomes to influence the clubber's actions. Consequently, the rule of Reciprocity predicts that the cause and effect surrounding the very act of clubbing will eventually reverse: clubbing will no longer be accepted as a technique for encouraging acquiescence but only as the (generally extreme) consequence of a breach of the accumulation of agreements. It becomes punishment, not persuasion.

To illustrate this, let's leave the caveman behind and fast-forward about thirty-five thousand years to meet the policeman.

Now, rather than a caveman clubbing his contemporary, we envision a policeman using his club to subdue a civilian. As stated above, it is the same act in a different context. For there even to be a policeman patrolling city streets, many, many agreements must have accumulated. Therefore, the clubbing is a power relation, not a force relation since both the civilian (who has agreed to abide by the law) and the policeman (who has agreed to abide by *and* enforce the law) are, either by choice or circumstance, operating under this accumulation of agreements and stand subject to the rule of Reciprocity.

I say "either by choice or circumstance" to highlight another change that has occurred since those cavemen met. Although the first agreement had to have occurred directly between the two individuals, as agreements accumulate and expand, people are incorporated into (and acquire power within) systems to which they did not explicitly agree. An individual who immigrates and takes citizenship under a set of agreements does so by choice. One who is born into these agreements, or travels temporarily under them, does so by circumstance. For example, I can't go to the United Kingdom and drive my car on the right-hand side of the road simply because I am a U.S. citizen. The circumstance of my being in England makes me subject to the agreements that the English have reached amongst themselves, and I must drive on the left-hand side. So although the agreement was not reached directly between the British government and me or between the two specific individuals in our example—the policeman and the civilian (who may not be a citizen of the policeman's country but is a citizen somewhere)—it was reached in such a way as to encompass them. In reality, this occurs through an accumulation of agreements culminating in the laws defining sovereignty and jurisdiction.

The policeman and the civilian are operating under a system, which, by the very nature of the accumulation of agreements, involves both permission and prohibition (returning to our theoretical example: the clubber is permitted to take the berries that are gathered but is prohibited from clubbing/killing the gatherer; the gatherer is permitted to live relatively free from the club but is prohibited from refusing to gather berries). Under the accumulation of agreements that currently exists in the United States, I am permitted to drive my car as long as I hold a valid license. However, I am prohibited from driving my car at a speed in excess of the agreed-upon limit. If I do exceed the speed limit, that breach raises the potential for the transfer of my power (my ability to influence the highway patrol *not* to pull me over and ticket me), and I become subject to apprehension and, depending upon the degree of my exertion (the speed at which I was traveling), various levels of penalty, usually imposed through fines but also including suspension and, following multiple infractions, revocation of my license. In other words, as my exertions increase, they transfer to the police an increase in power (an increased ability to influence my actions) at the same time that they decrease my own power (making me less able to influence the actions of the police). Power is transferred through its own exertion.

Of course, I am *capable* of driving my car at a hundred miles per hour whenever and wherever I want, but I am not allowed to—that is to say, I agree not to do this when I accept my driver's license, so we have moved from the rules of force relations (defined by fitness for a challenge) to the rules of power relations (defined by agreement).*

Similarly, I am prohibited from driving my car while under the influence of intoxicating substances. If I do, it is deemed an even greater exertion than simple speeding, and having transferred more power to those who have agreed to enforce the laws, I am subject to apprehension *and* incarceration. If I resist arrest, I transfer even more power, and I am then subject to the club. With each exertion, I transfer more power away from myself, handing others the increased ability to influence my actions.

On the other hand, if I acquiesce and the policeman uses the club against me, he is potentially transferring some or all of his own power to me (the point at which power is exerted is the point at which there exists the greatest potential for its transfer) if I deem it an overexertion (the people upon whom power is being exerted define its limits) and choose to expose the overexertion (broadcasting it myself with the supporting testimony of my injuries or through witnesses). The point is, depending upon the degree of the policeman's exertion (the amount of power he has transferred to me), I can seize that power and greatly influence *his* actions up to and including *his own* incarceration.

And here we have all the ingredients for Reciprocity—system (the agreements that developed to define acceptable police behavior) and power

---

* Once one accepts that we have moved from force relations (defined by fitness for a particular challenge) to power relations (defined by agreement), one must also recognize that a number of key points, stated above in theory, have now been illustrated in fact:
  1. There is a difference between force and power.
  2. The difference is defined by the presence/absence of agreement.
  3. If the presence/absence of agreement defines the distinction between force and power, then agreement creates power.

(the exertions on the part of both the police and the individual within the system)—as well as the effective though not essential ingredient of broadcast (the ability to expose those exertions).

This policeman example was not chosen at random.

In the early morning hours of March 3, 1991, a man named George Holliday went to his window and witnessed members of the Los Angeles Police Department surrounding an individual whom the highway patrol had trapped near the entrance to Hansen Dam Park. Awoken by the sounds of sirens from the police cars that continued to converge, as well as the staccato chops of the helicopter hovering above, Mr. Holliday went out onto his balcony and filmed the brutal beating of Rodney King with his new Sony camcorder.[2]

Before we fully embark on this more complex example of Reciprocity-in-action, it is worth emphasizing that the point here is not to rehash the Rodney King incident in an effort to assess or assign blame, but instead, to understand how the events played out with regard to the rule of Reciprocity, the idea that power (the ability to influence another's actions) is transferred through its own exertion. The main point I'm trying to make by using this familiar example of extremely violent, physical exertion is that having occurred within a system, even these forceful actions were acts of power—on the parts of both Mr. King and the police—and as such, they were subject to Reciprocity.

Here we will see that this force/power distinction is not merely a matter of semantics but an important difference that leads to a clearer understanding of the event itself. In the Rodney King tragedy, we experience the same back-and-forth transference of power that we saw in the simple bus incident. And we come to recognize that the very concept of the *escalation of force*, which sat at the heart of the consequent courtroom confrontation, reflects, and in fact rests on, the existence of the rule of Reciprocity.* All the events—the arrest, the verdict, the riots, and their aftermath—put the rule of Reciprocity on vivid display.

It is difficult to decide where to start with an event as complex as the Rodney King episode. But for our immediate purposes, let's start with the night of his arrest and recognize that on that night, Mr. King made the first exertion when he took the wheel in an intoxicated condition, an act defined as an overexertion under the accumulation of agreements that govern drivers

---

* What the LAPD refers to as the escalation of force we would call acting on an increasing transference of power since it occurs within a system. Having said this, I will be using the term *escalation of force* because that's what the police use, but the distinction is still present: what they refer to as force, we now see as power.

and police in the Los Angeles area. Mr. King's own defense attorneys stipulated that his blood-alcohol level was nearly two and a half times the legal limit at the time of his arrest, and there was circumstantial evidence, though no final proof, that he had ingested other intoxicating substances as well.[3]

By driving while intoxicated, Mr. King initiated the potential for the transfer of his power to the police. That is to say, as a result of his exertion, Mr. King would be less able to influence the actions of any police officer who might pull him over while the officer would be more able to influence his. But this particular overexertion also created the potential for an above-average transfer of power (the potential for the officers to influence his actions in a more severe and lasting manner) because Mr. King was on parole when these events took place. The parole violation is a second simultaneous exertion. Mr. King's third exertion occurred when he drove over the speed limit on the Foothill Freeway, again potentially transferring power away from himself and to the police, making him less able to influence their actions (i.e., get them to ignore him) and making them more able to influence his (i.e., pull him over). At every step of the way, Mr. King was transferring more power away from himself and to others. Then when Mr. King attempted to outrun Tim and Melanie Singer, the husband-wife highway patrol team who did try to pull him over, his evasive exertions transferred even more power away from him and to them. Rodney King led the officers on a 7.8-mile chase in which he drove 110 to 115 miles per hour on the Foothill Freeway and up to 85 through residential areas of Los Angeles before becoming cornered in front of the Lake View Terrace apartment building where Mr. Holliday was sleeping.[4]

Driving while intoxicated, violating parole, speeding and evading arrest had all been predefined as overexertions under the Los Angeles system, and as such, these acts transferred power away from Mr. King. Still, had he stepped from the car and cooperated with the arresting officers, it is unlikely he would have experienced the policeman's club. We know this because there were two individuals in the car with Mr. King—Bryant Allen and Freddie Helms—both of whom exited the car as instructed and complied with the demands of the police throughout. Neither man was hit even once.

Mr. King was struck fifty-six times.

Had Mr. King cooperated at the outset, assuming a prone position from the first request and then been struck fifty-six times (or once), this police overexertion would have created the even greater potential for the transfer of power back to Mr. King. Ultimately, the jury was faced with the task of unwinding a frantic, back-and-forth series of power exertions and transfers.

When it comes to the question of identifying exertions and transferences between Mr. King and the police that morning, there are two tapes that unspool before our eyes simultaneously. There is a tape of Mr. King exerting his power upward, attempting to stand again and again (not acquiescing) despite police instructions to assume a prone position and, thus, transferring power to the police; and there is a tape of the police exerting their power downward, striking and kicking Mr. King again and again even while he lay sprawled on the ground and, thus, transferring their power to him, making him more able to influence their actions (subsequently, through the mechanism of the legal system). Same tape, of course, but two different exertions of power. So the jury was asked this question (though it was not worded this way): did the police transfer their power to Mr. King, or did Mr. King transfer his power to the police? There was no doubt that Mr. King had violated the law. But did the police overexert in their efforts to apprehend him? And even more specifically, did the police continue their exertions following Mr. King's acquiescence?

Mr. King made numerous exertions (DUI, parole violation, speeding, evading police, resisting arrest) and, in the process, transferred much power to the police; the police deemed his actions an overexertion (the limits are set by those upon whom power is being exerted), and they took the power he had transferred to them and exerted it back onto him (attempted to influence his actions) by arresting him. He continued to exert and transfer even more of his power (his ability to influence their actions) to the officers by refusing to follow their instructions.

Under the accumulation of agreements that govern civilians in Los Angeles, an individual must comply with the instructions of a police officer, and any refusal to do so is, by definition, an overexertion that transfers more power to the police. On the other hand, a police instruction to assume a prone position is not necessarily an overexertion, and it does not, by definition, transfer power to a civilian. In a mature system, the law operates under an assumption of acquiescence—after all, the very presence of power in this instance stems from acquiescence/agreements into which all civilians and police officers in Los Angeles have entered (either by choice or circumstance). Exertions contrary to police instructions transfer power to the police, making the police more able to influence an individual's actions in escalating degrees of severity. That is how the jury decided this complex case. Again, those upon whom power is being exerted define its limits, and for the purpose of the resolution of disagreements such as the one between Mr. King and the police, the system establishes a jury to serve as proxy for the entire community and define limits on its behalf. This jury defined the police actions as within acceptable limits, deciding that Mr. King's extreme exertions had transferred an extreme amount of power to the police. And the jury's decision represents an express acknowledgment of the rule of Reciprocity.

However, had the jury in the King case ruled against the police, that verdict still would have stood as an acknowledgement of the fact that power (the ability to influence another's actions) is transferred through its own exertion.

Despite the fact that civilians are expected to acquiesce when interacting with police commands, Reciprocity predicts that as a history of interactions and agreements accumulate, laws defining limits on police exertions will also emerge. That is, of course, the case: the existence of the laws of unlawful arrest and police brutality stem from (and confirm the truth of) the rule that power is transferred through its own exertion. Under circumstances in which a civilian has made little or no exertion, the sudden, unexpected command to drop to the street and assume a prone position could easily be defined as an overexertion in itself, increasing the civilian's subsequent ability to influence the actions of the officers. Similarly, even if a civilian has broken the law, police exertions can only escalate in *response* to the suspect's exertions (escalating force) as an increased ability to influence the suspect's actions is transferred to the police. But even then, police exertions must fall within prescribed boundaries. For instance, even if a suspect were to resist arrest with deadly force, he could be killed, but not, for example, sodomized.

As stated earlier, if an individual who is arrested deems the arrest itself, or police behavior during the arrest, to be an overexertion (the people upon whom power is being exerted define its limits) and chooses to expose the overexertion, broadcasting it himself, with the supporting testimony of his injuries or through witnesses (with or without an accompanying videotape), then that individual could take the power transferred to him and use it to influence the actions of the arresting officers—up to and including *their own* incarceration.

This transfer of power from the police to the suspect is precisely what happened in the Abner Louima incident, when, on the morning of August 9, 1997, officer Justin Volpe used a broken broomstick to sodomize Mr. Louima in the bathroom of Brooklyn's Seventieth Precinct. As a result of Officer Volpe's actions, Mr. Louima suffered injuries—damage to his internal organs, including lacerations of his intestines and bladder—that could never be sustained in the course of an arrest without an overexertion of police power (as already defined by the agreements governing the police in Brooklyn).

Though there were no witnesses willing to testify regarding the assault (police silence was deemed by many to be an additional exertion on the part of the officers, thus transferring even more power to Mr. Louima), Mr. Louima did broadcast this sickening overexertion of power through the supporting testimony of his injuries. And on February 27, 1998—less than six months after the incident—a grand jury handed down a 12-count indictment against five officers in which Count One described the alleged actions of two officers under the heading "Overt Acts":

> On or about August 9, 1997, in a rest room at the 70th Precinct, the defendants JUSTIN VOLPE and CHARLES SCHWARZ hit and physically assaulted Abner Louima, by kicking him and by shoving a wooden stick into his rectum and mouth while his hands were handcuffed behind his back.[5]

The event began with Mr. Louima being taken into custody by the police. The final outcome of Mr. Louima's arrest: Officer Schwarz was sentenced to five years, and Officer Volpe was sent to prison for thirty years. Had Officer Volpe simply taken Mr. Louima into custody and not exerted power in the way he did, Mr. Louima would have had little influence over Officer Volpe's actions. Again, power is *transferred* through its own exertion. In this case, a tremendous amount of power was transferred from those officers to Mr. Louima through their own exertions.

Though the concepts of unlawful arrest and police brutality lead to a result opposite to the concepts of evading police and resisting arrest that we encountered in the King incident, they still represent an explicit acknowledgement of the rule of Reciprocity: if it is true that power is transferred through its own exertion, then it can be transferred *up* from less influential to more influential (resisting arrest) and *down* from more influential to less (unlawful arrest).

When Stacey Koon, the sergeant who was the supervising officer at the scene of Rodney King's arrest saw Mr. Holliday's tape, he was apparently unconcerned; in fact, he is quoted as saying, "This is great! They got it on tape! Now we'll have a live, in-the-field film to show police recruits. It can be a real-life example of how to use escalating force properly."[6] In Sergeant Koon's view, Mr. King's own exertions are transferring more and more power to the police, giving them more and more ability to influence his actions in escalating degrees of severity. Consistent with this view, at the trial of *CA v. Powell, et al.*, the officers who beat Mr. King proffered the defense that they had escalated and de-escalated force only in *response* to Mr. King's own exertions. On the stand, former LAPD captain Robert Michael testified on behalf of the officers, stating that "there were ten distinct uses of force rather than one single use of force. In each of those uses of force, there was an escalation and a de-escalation, an assessment period, and then an escalation and a de-escalation again. And another assessment period."[7]

Similarly, Michael Stone, defense attorney for Officer Powell made this statement: "Los Angeles police officers, like most other police officers in departments throughout the state, are trained in the escalation and de-escalation of force . . . As the suspect's movements and activities create an increase in the threat to the officer or an increase in the resistance to arrest or an increase in the attempt to escape, the officers are taught to escalate force. As the suspect becomes more compliant, or ceases the threat or ceases the resistance, the officers are taught to de-escalate the force."[8] Thus, even according to the police themselves (those to whom the Los Angeles system grants the most initial influence in an encounter with civilians), power is transferred through its own exertion. In fact, Darryl Mounger, defense attorney for Sergeant Koon, the senior officer at the scene, made the explicit assertion that Mr. King had power in this confrontation: "He [Sergeant Koon] is not in charge of this situation. There is only one person that's in charge of this situation, and that's Rodney Glenn King."[9]

Interestingly, prosecutor Terry White, acting on behalf of Mr. King, also implied that there was a relationship between the actions of the police and the actions of Mr. King while reaching the opposite conclusion of the attorneys for the officers: "Whatever Rodney King was or whatever he did, it did not justify what you saw on that videotape."[10] The fact that he is saying this at all, the fact that he is asserting that Rodney King's actions did not justify the actions of the police, implies that there is some correlation, that the actions of a suspect *can* justify police exertions. Again, the point here is neither to defend nor condemn the police or Mr. King. The point is to illustrate that physical exertions within a system are acts of power subject to the rule of Reciprocity and to highlight the fact that *both* sides are relying on the rule of Reciprocity (the fact that power is transferred through its own exertion) as they make their case to the jury. In short, Mr. King is asserting that the police transferred power to him; the police are asserting that Mr. King transferred power to them. And neither assertion could make any sense without the existence of Reciprocity.

Commander Michael Bostic, the highest ranking officer to testify at trial, explained the policy of escalation and de-escalation this way: "The theory of escalation de-escalation is a way of describing to police officers their responsibility for the minimum level of force possible to take an arrestee into custody . . . The theory basically states that an officer's use of force must be in direct response to some action by the suspect, and it must be a reasonable reaction to that, again with the idea in mind of using the minimum possible force available to an officer and at the same time prevent injury to the suspect and to the officers."[11]

This is the key point: the policy of escalation/de-escalation does not create Reciprocity; the rule of Reciprocity creates the policy.* Absent the underlying rule that power is transferred through its own exertion, it is not inherently logical that any police department would pursue a policy of minimum force, particularly the Los Angeles Police Department, whose officers, because they police such a large population, are regularly exposed to a variety of unpredictable and often deadly dangers. Why would the police handicap themselves with a policy that requires *minimum* force to be used only as a reasonable *reaction*? Or to invert the question, why wouldn't police policy always be to use overwhelming force? Wouldn't that be a more efficient and effective way for the police to protect the community from criminals and protect themselves from harm? Police officers are charged with the task of catching crooks while avoiding injury. Doesn't the use of minimum force make it less likely that they will fulfill either of those goals? If your objective is to apprehend criminals, wouldn't your policy be to act in such a way as to subdue them instantly and entirely? Then why is it that the police would develop this minimum-force policy?

It is unacceptably vague to say that such a policy exists because it is *humane, fair* or *just* although these statements gain accuracy once we recognize Reciprocity's impact on those concepts: justice itself, as we will see shortly, cannot be precisely defined without an express understanding of the fact that power is transferred through its own exertion. Similarly, the explanation for the existence of escalation/de-escalation can't be based entirely on some permutation of an "evolved understanding" or even the development of a more mature system. While the development of a system of agreements is necessary to reach certain ends in practice, the basic idea of escalation and de-escalation was there at the start—in the relationship between the clubber and the berry bringer. Thus, these police policies can only be explained by an acknowledgment of the basic, precedent rule that power is transferred through its own exertion.

Quite simply, the Los Angeles Police Department does not rely on overwhelming force because to do so would be to transfer power *away* from

---

* As will become clearer later, this same principle is also true for the *system* (accumulation of agreements) that produces this policy. The fact that power is transferred through its own exertion created this system, not vice versa.

itself, and the seed of such a policy is present at the moment of the first agreement. As we will see shortly, limits have been defined by prior victims among both civilians and police, and it is through those past negotiations (the ones which, as Foucault says, "bring about redistributions, realignments, homogenizations, serial arrangements, and convergences") that new agreements (limits on police and civilian exertions) were reached. While it might be satisfying to attribute the accumulation of agreements in Los Angeles to some vague concept of social, intellectual, or moral advancement—a general improvement in society—this would be imprecise. We would still need to ask from where this improvement arose.

The sad truth is there are societies today in which the police can more easily beat and even kill suspects without reprisal. Does that make the people in those societies somehow less human, less understanding, less advanced? No, it means their systems are less acknowledging of the rule of Reciprocity. In actuality, when you get right down to it, it means that someone somewhere in the system is making efforts to preempt balancing by diminishing the potential for transfer of power that their exertions necessarily create. We will cover that in greater detail in the "Power" section. But for now, suffice it to say that given enough police killings in such a society, or the wrong one at the wrong place and time, those upon whom power is being exerted will set new limits as the rule of Reciprocity surfaces quickly and with dramatic effect.

Following the verdict in *CA v. Powell*, the rioters in Los Angeles showed us one way by which such a redefinition of limits can be pursued. Obviously, significant segments of the Los Angeles population did not view Mr. Holliday's video from the same perspective as Sergeant Koon. They did not see the tape of Mr. King standing again and again. Instead, their eyes were drawn to the other far more dramatic image, the one that showed power being exerted downward and transferred to Mr. King. Their perspective rested firmly on the rule of Reciprocity as they saw the police officers transferring power not only to Mr. King but to segments of Los Angeles's African American community whom Mr. King came to represent. This perspective precipitated the riots that followed the verdict exonerating the police officers. However, I'm not going to cover the riots and their aftermath yet. The riots, I will argue, were a form of broadcast. So we'll return to them in that section.

For now, we'll leave the matter of force v. power behind to take a closer look at the development of system, which makes power possible in the first place. The rule of Reciprocity explains what happened between the LAPD and Rodney King as well as the NYPD and Abner Louima. With regard to the force-versus-power distinction ("a punch in the face in an uncharted wilderness is different from a punch in the face on a city street"), both the King and Louima events explicitly confirm that even extreme acts of violence occurring within a system are acts of power, not force, subject to—and confirming—the fact that power is transferred through its own exertion.

Just a final aside before we leave force v. power: Although I wasn't present when Mr. King received his driver's license, I can guarantee you that he was not hit with a club at the DMV in order to encourage acquiescence with the accumulation of agreements. Nobody is. As stated above, the rule of Reciprocity predicts that the cause and effect surrounding the act of clubbing will reverse as we move from caveman to policeman. Physical exertion will become only acceptable as the (generally extreme) effect of a breach of agreement. It transforms from persuasion to punishment. This transformation occurs not as the result of altruism on the part of clubbers but rather, as the necessary effect of the fact that power is transferred through its own exertion. Individuals who hold more influence within a system and who understand Reciprocity will restrain (though not necessarily refrain from) certain exertions and thus maintain more power longer, just as less influential individuals who understand the rule will pursue certain strategies that tend to draw power to them as opposed to transferring it away. As force transforms to power, all exertions increase the potential for redistribution, reduction, and even loss of the ability to influence others' actions. Thus, unnecessary exertions open up the possibility for unnecessary transfer and, ultimately, the redefinition of limits by those upon whom power is being exerted. This is true everywhere—in offices, in classrooms, in marriage, in politics, and so on. As we have seen (and will continue to see), what was in operation on the bus that day is also at work in the world-at-large, helping us to identify and understand significant historical developments including this recurrent pattern: those who are at first held in less influential positions within a system are consistently able to induce, pursue, and settle, by significant degrees, a certain balancing—a movement from disenfranchised victim to acknowledged participant (a movement from bondage to freedom)—based on the fact that, over time, Reciprocity enables them to leverage transferences and record their redefinitions of limits within the accumulation of agreements. But how exactly does this happen? That is the question I'll now begin to answer with greater specificity.

The Victim's Doctrine

As we continue this examination of the development of system, it is probably clear by now that what I refer to as the accumulation of agreements is often equivalent to what we more commonly call the law. But the accumulation of agreements is not always equivalent to the law because every agreement does not always have to be or become law (but every agreement will always create power and manifest the rule of Reciprocity).

Also, of course, every law is not "agreed" to in the sense that we would normally use that word. But for the sake of simplicity, I am using the term *agreement* to cover everything from naked acquiescence to more consensual, harmonious accords. At this point, however, whether we're talking about submission or consensus is irrelevant—once two or more parties begin participating in a system, no matter how that participation arises, the rule of Reciprocity comes into play. Now, in order to better understand the important relationship between the law and Reciprocity, we must first consider what the law is (and is not).

First, let's look at what the law is not. There is nothing in its nature that says the law must *acknowledge* Reciprocity. In reality, you can have a rule of law that vehemently and violently attempts to deny or diminish the rule of Reciprocity—a law that attempts to exert power without opening up the possibility for its transfer. Thus it has been observed that "Chinese leaders want rule *by* law, not rule of law" because "[u]nder rule *by* law, the law can serve as a mere tool for a government that suppresses in a legalistic fashion [emphasis added]."[12] The distinction between *rule by law* and *rule of law* can become quite blurry. In the subsequent section on power, we will cover the techniques by which rulers attempt to deny or diminish the rule of Reciprocity—such techniques being, in the end, always attempts to reduce the potential for the transfer or loss of power. But for now this is a crucial point: *the rule of law* is not just another way of saying *the rule of Reciprocity*. To make the relationship perfectly clear: the rule of Reciprocity precedes and leads to the rule of law (and rule by law as well).

In the end, all laws operate under the rule of Reciprocity; not all laws acknowledge it. Still, it is important to define this relationship between what we call the law and Reciprocity itself because the real-world examples I will draw from as I continue to explore the cause and consequences of system do deal with the creation and/or existence of specific laws. So we must not mistake *law* as a shorthand for Reciprocity (or vice versa) even though the existence of many laws do arise out of (and prove) the rule that power is transferred through its own exertion.

Regarding what the law is, we must begin by disabusing ourselves of the popular perception that the law is handed down from above—carved in stone and delivered from the mountaintop—always flowing from stronger to weaker. If that were true, it would immediately undermine the proposition that power comes from below and significantly weaken the rule of Reciprocity. In fact, nothing could be further from the truth. In reality, the law is the victim's doctrine.

Here is the simplest way to prove the point: the prohibition against theft was not written by the thief. Prohibitions against theft were sponsored by the victims (or potential victims) of theft and their allies. Or as Rousseau wrote regarding the death penalty, "It is in order to avoid becoming the victim of a murderer that one consents to die if one becomes a murderer oneself."[13]

But what of those laws that *are* imposed by kings and dictators? The law is at its essence the victim's doctrine even when it is handed down from above (even when it attempts to deny the fact that power is transferred through its own exertion). A king who imposes a law does so only (and always) to protect his reign. Thus, he is projecting himself into the lowered position of victim in an attempt to preempt his own vulnerability. Of course, all laws are an exertion of power subject to the rule of Reciprocity (whether the system acknowledges this or not), and the king, by passing such laws to protect himself, does in fact transfer power to those whose actions he seeks to influence (his people) even if his intention is to do the exact opposite. Thus, if those upon whom this power is being exerted define this exertion (the enactment of these laws protecting the king) as beyond acceptable limits, then the king, in seeking to discourage insurrection, only inspires it.

While a king may make preemptive proclamations with relative ease, in systems where Reciprocity is actively acknowledged, laws almost always *require* victims, and preemption becomes problematic. To cite an extreme example, one would have had a difficult time establishing no-fly zones over Washington DC prior to the attacks of September 11, 2001. Or to make the point even more obvious, if a lawmaker had suggested placing antiaircraft guns atop the World Trade Center for the purpose of shooting down passenger planes, he'd have been laughed (and voted) out of office. Why? No exertions. No victims. No transference of power to justify such extreme actions. Preemptive measures are difficult in systems that acknowledge Reciprocity because Reciprocity requires exertion for transference.

Here's an example of two opposite acts leading to the conclusion that the law is the victim's doctrine: In free societies, the right of assembly is established by the people who seek to avoid falling victim to oppression. In fear societies, prohibitions against assembly are put forward by dictators who seek to avoid falling victim to revolt. These are completely opposite laws with opposite purposes, yet both are inspired by the victim. The law is always the victim's doctrine.*

So we see by this example of opposite laws that the law and Reciprocity are distinct (in fact, systems that attempt to diminish Reciprocity can have laws that are designed to deny Reciprocity), but that regardless of whether or not any given law (or system) acknowledges or attempts to deny Reciprocity, all laws are sponsored by victims or potential victims.

One could rightly say that the policy of escalation/de-escalation and the laws governing police brutality that we encountered in the King and Louima cases exist not simply to help the police maintain their power (reduce the possibility of transference by limiting police exertions) but also to protect suspects from injury. And this would not be inconsistent with the fact that the law is the victim's doctrine or that power is transferred through its own exertion. People *have* been victims of police brutality, and this is precisely from where the laws limiting police behavior have arisen. Those laws exist to minimize the possibility that others will be victimized. Here's the process by which Reciprocity inspires a victim's doctrine with regard to limiting police exertions: people were victimized by excessive exertions on the part of the

---

* The distinction between a *free society* and *fear society* is taken from Natan Sharansky, who defines the difference clearly: "A society is free if people have a right to express their views without fear of arrest, imprisonment, or physical harm . . . a society that does not protect the right of dissent . . . will inevitably turn into a fear society" (Sharansky, 40). "The right of dissent" itself is an acknowledgement of the rule of Reciprocity: that a government's exertion transfers to the people an increased ability to influence the government's actions (an increase of power). Denial of the right of dissent is an attempt to diminish the rule of Reciprocity, an attempt to impede the transference of power. Given the distinction made in the previous subsection (force v. power), it is also notable that Mr. Sharansky (who struggled under Soviet oppression) chooses to say that such regimes rule by "fear," not by "force" as is often suggested. As Francis Fukuyama correctly points out: "There is no such thing as a dictator who rules purely by 'force'" (Fukuyama, 15). First, it is simply impossible logistically to restrain/control every civilian physically. Second, to govern, one must have some system in place; therefore, force becomes power, and to govern purely by exertion is to increase constantly the potential for the transference of power from oneself. Thus, as we will see in the "Power" section, dictators engage in a number of strategies designed to *conceal* their exertions and diminish the effects of Reciprocity, and in so doing, they merely prove the truth of the rule.

police; these excessive exertions transferred power to those victims and their allies who redefined limits, and those limits were subsequently recorded as law/policy (the victim's doctrine).

In effect, saying that the policy of escalation/de-escalation exists to help police maintain their power is the same as saying that the policy is there to help avoid civilian victims because an increase in civilian victims will equal a transference of/decrease in police power.

You could also easily envision a society in which the police were never allowed to kill a suspect, but this, in turn, would lead to more victims among police ranks; police officers *have* been killed in the line of duty, and consequently, the laws allowing police to use deadly force in certain circumstances arose from the power that was transferred to those victims (and their allies). Here's the process by which Reciprocity inspires a victim's doctrine with regard to protecting the police: police officers were victimized by excessive exertions on the part of civilians; these excessive exertions transferred power to those victims and their allies who redefined limits, and those limits were subsequently recorded as law/policy (the victim's doctrine).

In effect, saying that policies regarding the use of deadly force exist to help avoid future police deaths is the same as saying they are there to help civilians maintain their power because an increase in police deaths will equal a transference of/decrease in civilian power.

Whether the limits are set on behalf of more influential individuals or less influential individuals, the rule of Reciprocity delivers justice for history's victims.

To return to our traffic law examples, even a simple regulation such as "cross on green and wait on red" rests on the need for protection—protecting pedestrians (potential victims) from being run over by cars. The stop light was not invented until long after the car; traffic laws weren't instituted until the dangers became apparent (until enough victims had piled up). If I asked you whether Mr. King was right to drive drunk, you would say no. If I asked you why, you'd say, "Because he could hurt somebody." The laws that defined the limits on Mr. King's actions emerged from the victims of drunk drivers in an effort to protect future victims (as did the laws that defined the limits on the acts of officers Schwarz and Volpe in the Louima incident). And the reality is that those restrictions against drinking and driving were not brought into existence at the whim of a judge who sat on high handing down edicts upon intoxicated motorists. In fact there was, in the United States, a long history of leniency toward drunk drivers. Why? Because the victims had not yet spoken. But when they did, the power came from below, not from judges, but from mothers.

In May 1980, thirteen-year-old Cari Lightner was walking to a carnival when she was struck from behind and killed by a drunk driver. This driver had been convicted of drunk driving two times prior to the incident, had plea-bargained a third arrest, and was currently out on bail following an even more recent arrest for hit-and-run drunk driving.[14] That grotesquely poor definition of limits, the fact that the system permitted this man to drive again following so many extreme exertions, sparked a movement that continues to this day. Later that same year, Candace Lightner, Cari's mother, founded the group Mothers Against Drunk Drivers (subsequently changed to Mothers Against Drunk Driving) or MADD. Many changes to drunk-driving laws have followed, and though they can't all be attributed solely to MADD's efforts, we can say for certain that they are not in any way attributable to the judge who released the driver that killed Cari Lightner. Power comes from below.

Much of MADD's efforts and impact involve the act of broadcast—in this instance, the exposure of the exertions and effects of drunk drivers—which we will cover later. But here are some salient facts regarding the rapid development of the victim's doctrine following the founding of MADD: Before the end of 1980, MADD held its first national press conference (broadcast) in Washington DC with members of Congress (those who negotiate and record the accumulation of agreements at the federal level on behalf of the citizens of the United States). In 1982, President Reagan formed the Presidential Commission on Drunk Driving on which MADD was invited to serve. Also in 1982, Congress enacted into law a resolution backed by MADD establishing the first National Drunk and Drugged Driving Awareness Week. Again in 1982, the Howard-Barnes bill was passed by Congress, which earmarked federal highway funds to support state efforts against drunk driving. And in 1984, President Reagan signed the National Minimum Drinking Age Act, requiring all states to establish 21 as the minimum age for the purchase and public possession of alcohol.[15]

It is theoretically possible that Mrs. Lightner might not have regarded her daughter's death to be the result of an unacceptable definition of limits on the part of the system, in which case she would not have sought a redefinition, and the world would have waited for another inevitable exertion and transference to spark the change in agreements. It is also possible that an individual who had not suffered the tragedy that Mrs. Lightner did might have gone to Capitol Hill to demand the same changes—and it is unlikely he or she would have succeeded. Such a person though very much in the right would not have possessed the necessary power (the ability to influence others' actions) that was transferred to Mrs. Lightner by the event of her daughter's death. Again, preemptive measures are difficult in systems that acknowledge Reciprocity because Reciprocity requires exertions for transference.

MADD's success at redefining limits describes in fact the process that was first presented in theory: the excessive exertion transferred power to the victim's allies who redefined limits, and those limits were subsequently recorded as law/policy (the victim's doctrine). Mrs. Lightner's successful redefinition of limits not only provides a clear example of the process by which Reciprocity inspires a victim's doctrine but also illustrates the rule of Reciprocity itself—power is transferred through its own exertion—along with these key consequences: the point at which power is exerted is the point at which there exists the greatest potential for its transfer; the people upon whom power is being exerted define its limits.

In addition, it is worth noting that not only did new drunk-driving laws emerge as the *result* of the rule of Reciprocity, but each stiffening of the drunk-driving laws is at its essence a codification *of* the rule of Reciprocity, meaning that each change makes it ever more clear that drunk drivers transfer power away from themselves through their own exertions. Candace Lightner took the power that was transferred to her and used that power (her ability to influence others' actions) to persuade lawmakers to rewrite the agreements, which judges now enforce. Because the law is the victim's doctrine, Mrs. Lightner's influence extended beyond the adjudication of her daughter's case and exerted an influence on all drunk drivers in order to protect future victims. *

Having recognized that Mrs. Lightner's influence extended beyond the adjudication of her daughter's case, let's now return to the Louima matter to take up an issue that we did not consider before. The power transfer between the police and Mr. Louima raises an interesting question. At no point in the process did any officer have the power to put Mr. Louima in prison for five years (let alone thirty!)—he was arrested for allegedly participating in a scuffle outside a nightclub. Yet the police exertions were so extreme—so far beyond the limits defined by the accumulation of agreements—that those actions transferred to Mr. Louima even more power than the police themselves had. So here's the question: where did this power come from? How is it possible

---

* As was mentioned before, MADD began as Mother's Against Drunk *Drivers*, but then, in a move that reflects strategic insight into the rule of Reciprocity, revised its name to Mother's Against Drunk *Driving*. Why do this? To make exertions against drivers is to potentially transfer power to those drivers. But you can't transfer power to *driving*.

for the police officers to transfer more power away from themselves than they held in the first place?

In this instance, Mr. Louima was able to draw power from a preexisting victim's doctrine put in place as the result of the transferences of power to *previous* victims of police overexertions. Had Mr. Louima been the first to experience police brutality, then he and his allies would have had to take a different path toward the redefinition of limits, one that would certainly have included broadcast and might even have incited a systematic refusal to abide by other agreements (civil disobedience) or even a return to force relations (revolution).* But Mr. Louima was not the first person in New York City to be abused by the police. Agreements arose out of, and limits were redefined as a consequence of, previous police exertions. Relying on the rule of Reciprocity, others had already cleared the path and instituted the agreements Mr. Louima and his allies would follow. So although it may have looked like the power exerted against the officers came from judges and prosecutors, it came from below, from previous victims.

In a mature system, the victim's doctrine has already defined the limits for many common exertions such as arrests, speeding, or even murder; in fact, murder has several different definitions based on the severity of the exertion, generally: involuntary manslaughter, voluntary manslaughter, first-degree murder, and second-degree murder. But death is death, so why have these different definitions? Reciprocity explains why: each increase in the killer's degree of exertion transfers more power *away* from the killer and *to* the victim (or allies of the victim); as the exertions of a killer increase, as he transfers more power away from himself, he gives others the greater ability to influence his actions up to and including *his own* death (if the death penalty exists under the accumulation of agreements that hold authority over his act).

---

* It is precisely the sort of exertion against Mr. Louima, a single catalytic act, which can lead to the (often significant) redefinition of limits. As Francis Fukuyama has aptly observed: "It is a curious characteristic of revolutionary situations that the events which provoke people to take the greatest risks and set in motion the crumbling of governments are seldom the large ones that historians later describe as fundamental causes, but rather small and seemingly incidental ones" (Fukuyama, 177). Reciprocity cannot predict when, where, or by whom limits will begin to be redefined; it can only predict that in situations where Reciprocity is not acknowledged (or acknowledged inconsistently) such dramatic redefinitions will occur as a result of the facts that power is transferred through its own exertion and those upon whom power is being exerted define its limits.

Today, most definitions of limits no longer have to be made from scratch on a case-by-case basis. Living in an era long after the days of our cavemen and their first lone agreement, Mr. Louima drew his power from the accumulation of agreements itself, an accumulation that had emerged from and was shaped by the rule of Reciprocity and which, at the time of the assault, had been codified and accepted as an external authority.

The Emergence of External Authority

Returning to our policeman for a moment, we have seen that police have power over suspects, that suspects have power over police, and that, in either case, this power is transferred through its own exertion. And we have seen that this transference is not a function of mature mechanisms of adjudication but that, in fact, the development of mature mechanisms of adjudication are results/functions of the fact that power is transferred through its own exertion.

But how does this happen? How do we move from that first caveman contact and conflict (that must have occurred somewhere sometime), to the condition of mature systems and mechanisms of adjudication? *

As we saw with our caveman, power is created at the point of the first agreement, and the rule of Reciprocity emerges there. At the moment of the creation of power, there is the clubber and the berry bringer (more influential and less influential), and there is also the agreement that they reach. By pursuing agreement, the winner of the initial force relation allows power (at first unknowingly) to become vested in his counterpart. But here's a consequence implicit in the foregoing, which we can now make explicit,

---

* I have used the term *mature system* a number of times now, so in the interest of clarity, I think it may be helpful to define what I mean by *mature*. I don't mean "old." A mature system is not just an older system, but is, instead, a system that has developed an ability to handle problems it has already faced. A child who cries when its mother leaves the room is immature. As the child faces this problem again and again, it learns how to handle it and stops crying. It has matured. Yes, since time has passed during this interval, the child has also aged, but it is possible to age without maturing. If at eighteen years old, that same individual still cries when his mother leaves the room, we would say he is now even *more* immature (although even more time has passed). Therefore, maturity is not age. Maturity is the ability to handle problems one has faced before. Facing problems one has not yet faced, and learning how to handle them, is the process of maturing.

a fact that serves as the underlying ultimately unavoidable impetus in the movement from caveman contact to the sort of policeman contact we saw in the King and Louima cases: as a result of the fact that the clubber allows the agreement to influence his own actions (he stops, or reduces the severity of, his clubbing), he immediately places himself *below* the agreement. He appears to place only the berry bringer below the agreement, but in fact, both parties to the agreement are being influenced by it (whether the clubber chooses to acknowledge this at the outset or not). When the berry bringer acquiesces, the clubber accedes.

Although we have returned to that world of theory inhabited by the clubber and the berry bringer, in reality, this slow, painful awakening, the movement toward the moment when the ruler accepts the inevitable truth that not only has he subordinated himself to the accumulation of agreements but that to deny this fact would be to transfer power *away* from himself (because it would risk the dissolution of the entire system), constitutes the primary plotline of the interaction between rulers and those they rule.

In short, every revolution centers around this movement: the effort to place the ruler below the rules.

Of course, many revolutions simply replace one dictator with another. But that is a consequence of dissemblance on the part of the rebel/revolutionary who, upon seizing power, simply discards the promises he made or redefines them to fit the fact that he will continue to deny/diminish the rule of Reciprocity. That is to say, he will diminish the potential for the people to take the power *he* subsequently transfers to them through his own authoritarian exertions. The recipe for replacing one dictator with another and subsequently diminishing Reciprocity is always the same: Utilizing broadcast techniques, the aspiring dictator exposes the exertions of the outgoing regime then takes the power transferred by those exertions and uses it against that regime and/or the revolution's opponents. He then co-opts the people into new agreements that diminish/deny Reciprocity under the pretense that these agreements are necessitated by the current, unsettled circumstances. Vladimir Ilyich Lenin did it to Russia in 1917 (taking the power transferred by the exertions of the tsars); Ho Chi Minh did it to Vietnam in 1945 (taking the power transferred by a mess of exertions on the parts of Emperor Bao Dai as well as Japanese and French occupiers); Mao Zedong did it to China in 1949 (taking the power transferred by the exertions of Chiang Kai-shek); Fidel Castro did it to Cuba in 1959 (taking the power transferred by the exertions of Fulgencio Batista).

Lenin: "There can be no avoiding the arrest of the *entire* Kadet party and its near-Kadet supporters so as to *preempt* conspiracies. They're capable—the whole bunch—of giving assistance to the conspirators [i.e., they're capable of unsettling current circumstances even further]. It's criminal not to arrest them [i.e., their exertions justify our actions]. It's better for dozens and hundreds of intellectuals to serve days and weeks in prison than that 10,000 should take a beating [emphasis added]."[16]

Minh: "[F]or more than eighty years, the French imperialists, abusing the standard of Liberty, Equality, and Fraternity, have violated our Fatherland and oppressed our fellow citizens [i.e., exerted against us]. They have acted contrary to the ideals of humanity and justice. In the field of politics, they have deprived our people of every democratic liberty [i.e., exerted against us] . . . They have built more prisons than schools [i.e., exerted against us]. They have mercilessly slain our patriots [i.e., exerted against us]; they have drowned our uprisings in rivers of blood [i.e., exerted against us]. They have fettered public opinion [i.e., exerted against us *and* inhibited our ability to expose their exertions*] . . . To weaken our race they have forced us to use opium and alcohol [i.e., exerted against us]. In the field of economics *they have fleeced us to the backbone, impoverished our people*, and devastated our land [i.e., exerted against us] . . . In the autumn of 1940, when the Japanese fascists violated Indo-China's territory . . . the French imperialists went down on their bended knees and handed over our country to them. Thus, from that date, our people were subjected to the double yoke of the French and the Japanese . . . The truth is that we have wrested our independence from the Japanese and not from the French. The French have fled, the Japanese have capitulated, Emperor Bao Dai has abdicated. Our people have broken the chains which for nearly a century have fettered them [emphasis added]."[17]

(Declaration of Independence of the Democratic Republic of Viet Nam, September 2, 1945)

"Thanks to the sacrifice in struggle of our compatriots all over the country . . . we have succeeded in building up our freedom and independence [i.e., exercised the power transferred to us by our oppressors' numerous exertions]. To-day we need to consolidate this freedom and independence . . . [which] requires the sacrifice in struggle of our compatriots all over the country, but [owing to unsettled circumstances] we are also badly in need of donations . . . *mainly from well-to-do families*. This is the meaning of 'Gold Week.' 'Gold Week' will collect the gold given . . . *mainly by the well-off families* to devote it to our most pressing and important task [emphasis added]."[18]

("On the Occasion of the 'Gold Week,'" fifteen days following Minh's Declaration of Independence)

"At first, patriotism, not yet communism, led me to have confidence in Lenin . . . Step by step, along the struggle, by studying Marxism-Leninism *parallel with participation in practical activities*,* I gradually came upon the fact that only socialism and communism can liberate the oppressed nations and the working people throughout the world from slavery [emphasis added]."[19]

("The Path Which Led Me to Leninism," fifteen years after "Gold Week")

Mao: "[N]ot a single task in the interest of the people can be resolved together with the running dogs of imperialism—Chiang Kai-shek's Kuomintang and their accomplices [i.e., those who have exerted against us]. Even if resolutions were reluctantly adopted, they would be useless, because [the Kuomintang and its accomplices] would tear up all the resolutions the moment the opportunity ripened and would launch a ruthless war against the people [i.e., abandon the system and fall back to force relations] . . . Within a period of just over three years, the Chinese people, led by the Communist Party of China, have quickly awakened and organized themselves into [i.e., formed agreements in order to create] a nationwide united front to fight against [i.e., exercise the power transferred by] imperialism [i.e., exertions], feudalism [i.e., exertions], bureaucratic capitalism [i.e., exertions], and the Kuomintang reactionary government [i.e., the exerters], which represents these things in a concentrated form . . . The present Chinese People's Political Consultative Conference is convened on an entirely new foundation. It is representative of the people

---

*   "Participation in practical activities" certainly included collecting the wealth of the "well-to-do" during "Gold Week" (and after).

of the whole country and enjoys their confidence and support. Therefore, the Chinese People's Political Consultative Conference declares that *it* exercises the functions and powers of a National People's Congress. According to *its* agenda the Chinese People's Political Consultative Conference will formulate the organic law of the Central People's Government of the People's Republic of China . . . *It* will elect the National Committee of the Chinese People's Political Consultative Conference, elect the Council of the Central People's Government of the People's Republic of China, adopt the national flag and the national emblem of the People's Republic of China, [and] decide on the site of the Capital of the People's Republic of China [emphasis added]."[20]

Castro: "The revolution stands above everything! This is the party of the country. The spectacle that would most please our enemies is any division in the labor congress . . . This [i.e., the current unsettled circumstance] means that it is the duty of all of us to see that the congress is an example of revolutionary unity. Against the attacks of our enemies there must be discipline."[21]

Thus, dictatorships are born. And we see here specific illustrations of what was stated more generally above—utilizing broadcast, the aspiring dictator exposes the exertions of the outgoing regime then takes the power transferred by those exertions and uses it against that regime and/or the revolution's opponents. He then co-opts the people into new agreements that diminish/deny Reciprocity under the pretense that these agreements are necessitated by the current unsettled circumstances ("Against the attacks of our enemies there must be discipline").

Still, that all of this is true in no way refutes, but actually supports, the assertion that every revolution revolves around the effort to place rulers below the rules. In point of fact, there is simply no example of a revolution in which the aspiring leader has succeeded by broadcasting this self-revealing report: "I just want to be a dictator myself." Instead, the prospective regime moves forward on the exposure of the current regime's exertions coupled with promises of returning power to the people—i.e., placing the rulers below the rules. (Castro: "Don't worry about elections . . . The person most worried about this is myself. I'm not interested in being in power one minute more than necessary."[22])

The fact that many revolutions fail at the stated goal of placing the rulers below the rules does not mean that this wasn't their *driving force* in the first place (even if the dictator used that driving force to mask his personal ambitions). The difference between Lenin, Minh, Mao, and Castro on the one hand and George Washington, Mohandas Gandhi, Nelson Mandela, and Václav Havel on the other is that while both groups relied on Reciprocity to effectuate change, the dictators relied on Reciprocity to *seize* the power that was transferred to them as representatives of the people upon whom power was being exerted; alternatively, the liberators relied on Reciprocity in order to institute agreements that acknowledged Reciprocity.

Washington: "This government, the offspring of our own choice uninfluenced and unawed, adopted upon full investigation and mature deliberation, completely free in its principles, in the distribution of its powers, uniting security with energy, and *containing within itself a provision for its own amendment*, has a just claim to your confidence and support [emphasis added]."[23]

Gandhi: "The Congress has come to have a tradition of its own. For years—for more than sixty years—it has fought the British Government . . . But what is the condition of the Congress now? Congressmen think that now it is their Government . . . The real power is in your hands."[24]

Mandela: "Ours has been a quest for a constitution freely adopted by the people of South Africa, reflecting their wishes and their aspirations . . . a democracy in which the government, *whomever that government may be*, will be *bound by a higher set of rules*, embodied in a constitution, and will *not be able to govern the country as it pleases* [emphasis added]."[25]

Havel: "There must be structures that in principle place no limits on the genesis of different structures . . . These structures should naturally arise from *below* [emphasis in original]."[26]

Of course, we can find the liberators' *words* spoken by dictators as well (Ho Chi Minh recited portions of the U.S. Declaration of Independence when he took power). But those words are a disguise, an act of concealment, and the fact that these tyrants mask their motives simply shows that they understand Reciprocity even as they set themselves upon a lifetime of effort to deny/diminish it. On the other hand, none among the second group—Washington, Gandhi,

Mandela, Havel—established themselves as dictator following the liberation of their country. Instead, they each relied on Reciprocity to lead a revolution that placed the leaders within systems designed to be capable of accomplishing the inevitable redefinitions (such future redefinitions being made inevitable precisely by Reciprocity and its consequences).

Many significant conflicts revolve around the unequal application of the rules, or the application of unjust rules, but every revolution concerns the placing of rulers below the rules. This may seem, at first blush, like an overly broad claim. Does it now require a survey of every revolution on record? No. The statement that every revolution is about placing the rulers below the rules is logically irrefutable for one simple reason: once you get the rulers below the rules, you no longer need revolution to effect change.

Now, before we move forward, consider this: just as it is not inherently logical for the LAPD to institute its policy of minimum force to apprehend criminals (but Reciprocity explains why it does), it is also not inherently logical that the tsars, Chiang Kai-Shek, Bao Dai, and Batista would *lose* power over time (but Reciprocity explains why they do). Why wouldn't dictators simply become stronger and stronger until the world was ruled by few or one? The ongoing loss of power can only be explained by the fact that power is transferred through its own exertion. Posit the inverse of Reciprocity for a moment—power is not transferred through its own exertion; power is maintained through its own exertion. In that instance, descendants of the first clubber, or whoever happens to accumulate the most power at any given time, would continuously exert, maintain, and consolidate power as their territories expanded to encompass the earth. But that is not a description of reality. Instead, we see various systems (at various stages) moved by Reciprocity in the direction of acknowledging Reciprocity. Some dictators do succeed in maintaining their positions for their entire lives, but the systems they oversee cannot (and do not) easily continue while those systems that acknowledge Reciprocity can (and do). As Reciprocity is acknowledged, the leaders become temporary while the systems gain permanence.

In the end, the fact that power is transferred through its own exertion helps us understand how and why liberators succeed as well as the techniques by which dictators survive—and the reason why dictatorships fail—all of which will be addressed more directly in the section on Power. For now, the task is to illuminate the process by which Reciprocity leads to that moment when the clubber acknowledges the fact that power is infused throughout the system and that the agreements hold authority over his own actions as well.

To recap, at creation, agreements begin to separate from the individuals who initiated them and establish an external authority that exists as a control on the behavior of all parties. What is the difference between *power* and *authority*? *Power* is the ability to influence another's actions. *Authority* is the agreement from which that power is drawn. As we saw most explicitly in the Louima case, extant agreements (emerging out of prior exertions and transferences) form an external authority from which we can draw the ability to influence others' actions even though we weren't personally parties to those preexisting agreements or the events (exertions/transferences) that inspired them. The fact that power is transferred through its own exertion explains the interactions between the mother and the driver on the bus, the events of both the Louima and King cases, as well as the success MADD has had at redefining limits. That is to say, Reciprocity enables us to understand why these events transpired the way they did. But Reciprocity also explains how we *arrived* at the agreements that facilitated those events (i.e., how such a system was formed). In addition to helping us understand the dynamics of those individual incidents, the rule of Reciprocity also helps us recognize broad historical patterns that have emerged from the interactions of rulers and ruled.

The fact that the first agreement precipitates further agreements and that the accumulation of agreements eventually emerges (explicitly) as an external authority placing a control on the behavior of both the ruler and the ruled is neither fantasy nor theory. It is a precise description of reality. And we can identify historically, many moments when the berry bringers (less influential individuals) met their clubber (more influential individual) face-to-face to explicitly assert that the ruler was below the rules.

On one particular day (June 15, 1215) the berry bringers were called barons and the clubber was called king, and they met in a meadow named Runnymede. The agreement they reached, the charter they signed, was called the Magna Carta.

Why was this document called the Magna Carta (Great Charter) as opposed to just simply the charter? Because it was not the first. The Magna Carta followed many others, including the Laws of Edward the Confessor (1042-1066), Charter of King Henry I (1100-1135), Stephen's Charter (1135-1154), the Charter Granted by Henry II (1154-1189), and the Charter of King John (1199-1216), King John being the ruler who signed the Magna Carta as well. In other words, agreements had accumulated.

And therefore, Reciprocity was not born at Runnymede; Reciprocity is what brought the British there.

If an accumulation of agreements had not vested power in both the king and the barons and if that power was not transferable through its own exertion, then we would not witness Foucault's "redistributions, realignments, homogenizations, serial arrangements, and convergences," the exertions and transferences that led up to the signing of the document. Obviously, it is not possible to detail the specific exertions and transferences that took place over the course of centuries, but there is also no need. Neither the *emergence* nor the *effects* of the Magna Carta can be attributed exclusively to the historical details that led to or followed its creation. While the berry bringers did not jump up and shout "Magna Carta" immediately following acquiescence and accession, the rule of Reciprocity and its consequences explain the inevitable process that leads from the moment of that first agreement (that had to happen sometime somewhere) to the moment when King John signed a charter in a meadow.

With regard to the emergence of the Magna Carta, it is of limited usefulness to attribute the appearance of the charter exclusively to the events that led to it. To say that the principles embodied in that document emerged only as a consequence of the specific, nonreproducible, historical events that preceded it is the same as saying that such an advancement could never occur again anywhere else unless the same precise precedents (the Laws of Edward the Confessor, Stephen's Charter, etc.) were to recur. Obviously, not every system that acknowledges Reciprocity passed directly through the meadow at Runnymede.*

With regard to the effects of the Magna Carta, to say that the Magna Carta is the cause of all subsequent liberation as opposed to one of many

---

* Václav Havel did not lead the Velvet Revolution across Runnymede, nor were Nicolae and Elena Ceausescu executed on that field, and the barons did not march forth from that meadow to end apartheid in South Africa—but one phenomenon did move all these events forward. And it can't be fully explained by poesy such as "man's thirst for freedom" since without a mechanism of change—without the fact that power is transferred through its own exertion—such a thirst could not be quenched. Without the rule of Reciprocity and its consequences, we would not experience progressive liberation, only the endless substitution of one oppressive system with another. But Václav Havel did not develop a totalitarian superpower state to pull down the iron curtain, and Nelson Mandela's skin didn't suddenly turn white. So how do such liberators succeed in their respective revolutions without commandeering the mechanisms of oppression/position of oppressor themselves, and absent such commandeering, why doesn't the oppression they experienced simply continue *ad infinitum*? We have seen the answer: rather than out-oppressing their oppressors, these liberators took the power (the ability to influence others' actions) that was transferred to them by virtue of their oppressors' exertions and used that very power to enact revolutionary redefinitions in the systems—redefinitions which themselves acknowledge Reciprocity.

consequences (both small and large) of Reciprocity is to overstate the importance of that important document. In fact, direct descendants of those very barons who demanded the Magna Carta from King John later went around the world imposing systems that denied/diminished Reciprocity; and in each and every instance, they (the British) subsequently experienced the same process of exertion and transference leading to redefinition of limits and, ultimately, the failure of colonialism. Had this particular instance of acquiescence/accession (the Magna Carta) not occurred at this particular time and place, then, just as we said with regard to Mrs. Lightner and the creation of MADD, the world would have waited for another inevitable exertion and transference to spark the change in agreements.

So instead of halting on the precise historical details to find causation or dwelling on the Magna Carta as cause in itself, we should take the invaluable data provided by accounts of the Magna Carta's emergence as our starting point in order to examine them for evidence of the underlying phenomenon of Reciprocity and its consequences.

We've traveled a long way from the clearly defined opening example of the interaction between the mother and the bus driver and the exertions and transferences that occurred between them, but there is nothing in this Magna Carta example that does not stem (directly or indirectly) from the fact that power is transferred through its own exertion. What was at work on the bus that day is at work here as well, and what happened between the mother and the driver is the same as what happened between the barons and their king. Therefore, we can ask, with regard to the interactions between the barons and the king, what was the "door-closing" event (e.g., the police beating, the tragic death of a young girl) that prompted the redefinition of limits? We can then examine the nature of those new limits to recognize not only that these particular redefinitions placed the ruler below the rules but that they relied on Reciprocity in order to codify Reciprocity.

So what was the "door-closing" event, the reactive agent that sparked the emergence of the Magna Carta? In short: "The document was the product of concessions forced upon King John by rebellious barons interested in protecting themselves from onerous exaction by the King to finance his losing war effort in France."[27]

Or:

The document [agreement] was the product of concessions [consequences of transferences] forced upon King John [clubber] by rebellious barons [berry bringers] interested in protecting themselves from [redefining limits following] onerous exaction [exertions] to finance [make more fit for the challenge] his losing war effort [force relations] in France.

King John's reign was acrimonious from the outset, and the barons gained power (the ability to influence the king's actions) as a direct result of the king's own exertions.

Here's how events transpired.

Almost immediately upon his accession to the throne in 1199, King John entered into force relations with France and soon found himself simultaneously entangled in a series of exertions and transferences with Pope Innocent III, a conflict that finally ended with the king's acquiescence to the pope's demands. The king's continuous exertions—or in this case, exactions—transferred power to the barons and

> By 1214, when John returned in total defeat from France, he found that discontent had ripened into active agreement [power] among his opponents that the time was at hand for redress of their grievances [exertions they defined as beyond acceptable limits].
>
> The barons agreed [created power] among themselves that unless the King confirmed their liberties [redefined the limits of his exertions] by charter [a new agreement], they would withdraw their allegiance [refuse to gather berries], and they began preparations for war [a falling back to force relations]. In Easter week of 1215 they presented their demands [redefinition of limits], which were peremptorily refused . . . In May the barons formally renounced their allegiance [dissolved the system] . . . and marched on London [began to fall back to force relations]. The capitulation [acquiescence/accession] came with John's message to the barons that he would "freely accede to the laws [victim's doctrines] and liberties [redefinitions of limits] which they asked" if they would set a date and place to meet. The date they fixed was June 15, the place, Runnymede . . . The Charter [agreement] to which John agreed is an intensely practical document . . . Far from being a philosophical tract dealing in lofty generalities, it is keyed to the problems [exertions] at hand, spelling out one by one concrete remedies [new limits] for actual abuses [previous exertions].[28]

This example of Reciprocity-in-action shines a spotlight on the consequence that power is maintained through calculated conservation, not unlimited exertion as once again we see in fact what was first presented in theory: In an attempt to preempt his own vulnerability, the king passed certain laws (in this case, exacted taxes). Of course, all laws/exactions are exertions of power subject to the rule of Reciprocity, and the king, by passing such laws to protect himself, did in fact transfer power to those whose actions he sought to influence (his people) even if his intention was to do the exact opposite (i.e., to draw power *from* them). Thus, when those upon whom this power was being exerted defined this exertion (the enactment of these laws protecting the king) as beyond acceptable limits, the king, in seeking to discourage insurrection, only inspired it.

Reciprocity brought the British to Runnymede, and the phenomenon that we observe in this particular example is no different in its elements than the others we have examined before. Importantly, just as with the MADD example, it is worth noting that not only did the Magna Carta emerge as the *result* of the rule of Reciprocity but the terms outlined in it are in essence a codification *of* the rule of Reciprocity. It was Clause 39 that most explicitly codified Reciprocity:

> No free man shall be taken, imprisoned, disseised, outlawed, banished, or in any way destroyed, nor will We proceed against or prosecute him, except by the lawful judgment of his peers and by the law of the land.[29]

In other words:

> No free man shall be taken [exerted against], imprisoned [exerted against], disseised [exerted against], outlawed [exerted against], banished [exerted against], or in any way destroyed [exerted against], nor will We proceed [exert] against or prosecute [exert against] him, except by the lawful judgment of his peers [power comes from below] and by the law of the land [victim's doctrine].

It has long been acknowledged that the Magna Carta confirmed the rules are above the ruler. As Sir Edward Coke stated (perhaps a bit prematurely): "Magna Charta is such a Fellow, he will have no Sovereign."[30] Similarly, Henry Bracton is attributed as the author of these words in *On The Laws and Customs of England*, written shortly after the signing of the Magna Carta between 1250 and 1256: "[H]e is a king as long as he rules well but a tyrant when he oppresses by violent domination the people entrusted to his care. Let him, therefore, temper his power by law, which is the bridle of power, that he may live according to the laws, for the law of mankind has decreed that his own laws bind the lawgiver."[31] And as Arthur Hogue states in his study *Origins of the Common Law*, "Repeated confirmations of Magna Carta, when demanded by the community and granted by the monarchs, reiterated the idea that the king, like his subjects, was under the law."[32]

But the placing of the rulers below the rules is not the only inevitable consequence of the fact that power is transferred through its own exertion. Once the reality of external authority is acknowledged, we also witness a key development, part of the increasing control *of* the clubber and a slight almost imperceptible hint at a whole new kind of agreement.

Let's look again at Clause 39:

> No free man shall be taken, imprisoned, disseised, outlawed, banished, or in any way destroyed, nor will We proceed against or prosecute him, *except by* the lawful judgment of his peers and by the law of the land [emphasis added].

The words *except by* are the key to this passage because they open the door to the beginnings of a process. The king cannot prosecute the people unless he does it "by the lawful judgment of his peers and by the law of the land." Thus, this short clause states the *only* way the government can exert against an individual within the English jurisdiction. Here is the net effect when viewed within the overarching context of Reciprocity: it will be left to the judgment of the defendant's peers (the originators and ongoing arbiters of power) whether he transferred power away from himself or whether power was transferred to him, whether his actions will be influenced or whether he will influence the actions of others.

In his study of the history of the rule of law, Brian Z. Tamanaha makes this statement regarding the effect of the Magna Carta:

> In addition to subordinating the king to law, the Magna Carta has been credited with promoting the notion of due process of law . . . Although these words are not actually used in clause 39, the phrase "due process of law" was used in a statute in 1354, and came to be identified with the phrase "the law of the land." Over

time it acquired the connotation that at least a minimal degree of legal procedures—those that insure a fair hearing, especially the opportunity to be heard before a neutral decision-maker—must be accorded in the context of the judicial process.[33]

Here we see the very seed of an important development brought forward by the constant back-and-forth transferences that Reciprocity describes. As a system matures, as it develops the ability to handle problems it has already faced, new agreements are instituted, setting forth at first in general and then with more and more detail the specific procedures for handling problems in the future. In this way, a transformative form of agreement emerges—agreements that regulate the resolution of disagreements.

Agreements that Regulate the Resolution of Disagreements

"Bring me berries and I won't club you" is not an agreement that regulates the resolution of disagreements; neither is "don't drive drunk," "obey the speed limit," "cooperate with police," or "don't sodomize suspects." Even mandatory sentencing guidelines are not agreements that regulate the resolution of disagreements. However, "innocent until proven guilty" is. "No double jeopardy" is. Hearsay is. No matter how compelling a piece of testimony may be, a judge in the U.S. court system cannot (with a few exceptions) admit it into evidence if it's hearsay. In attempting to resolve any disagreement brought before his bench, the judge's own actions are being regulated (made regular) by agreements. Every rule of evidence is an agreement that regulates the resolution of disagreements.

The very existence of the grand jury that handed down the indictment against officers Schwarz and Volpe reveals the presence of agreements that regulate the resolution of disagreements: the state must proceed in a defined manner in order to pursue a prosecution. In this way, agreements that regulate the resolution of disagreements take the administration of justice out of the hands (the whim) of the more influential individual(s) in a system and place it within the parameters of a prescribed process. This type of agreement stands out as a significant step forward toward a system that acknowledges Reciprocity, a system that recognizes and *allows for* the fact that power is transferred through its own exertion. And this particular effect of the rule of Reciprocity—agreements that regulate the resolution of disagreements—furthers the effort to place rulers below the rules. Again, Clause 39 of the Magna Carta is an agreement that regulates the resolution of disagreements in that it tells the ruler the only way by which a free man may be prosecuted.

In short, agreements that regulate the resolution of disagreements are agreements that enclose retributive exertions and control rulers.

As systems are established, the first form of agreements will necessarily be of the permission/prohibition, quid pro quo variety (you can't have an agreement regarding how to resolve a disagreement until you first have an agreement over which a disagreement can arise). And permission/prohibition agreements will always exist, though, as new victims emerge, the specific permissions/prohibitions that constitute any given system will be redefined. Just as Reciprocity is at work in the formation of permission/prohibition agreements, it also works in the formation of agreements that regulate the resolution of disagreements. If rulers (i.e., those who render rulings—be they judges, kings, etc.) overexert, and if their rulings create victims, then those victims will take up the power that was transferred to them and use it to influence the actions of those judges/rulers. As disagreements are resolved, exertions and transferences will occur within the process of reaching those resolutions, and through that negotiatory activity—the exertions, transferences, and redefinitions of limits—certain parties to disagreements will be victimized by procedural overexertions; these excessive exertions will transfer power to those victims and their allies who will redefine limits, and those new limits (those new approaches to resolution) will be codified as agreements that regulate the resolution of disagreements. So Reciprocity tells us not only that limits will be redefined, but it also predicts that the processes by which those redefinitions are accomplished will be redefined as well.

The oldest recovered code of laws—the Code of Hammurabi, king of Babylon—comprises 282 statutes dictating resolutions to disagreements that (we can assume) had arisen within the kingdom at one time or another. For example:

> §1. If a man bring an accusation against a man, and charge him with a (capital) crime, but cannot prove it, he, the accuser, shall be put to death.[34]

> §108. If a wine-seller do not receive grain as the price of drink, but if she receive money by the great stone, or make the measure for drink smaller than the measure for corn, they shall call that wine-seller to account, and they shall throw her into the water.[35]

§278. If a man sell a male or female slave, and the slave have not completed his month, and the bennu fever fall upon him, he (the purchaser) shall return him to the seller and he shall receive the money which he paid.[36]

Clearly, some very specific exertions and transferences led to this equally specific codification of limits. But the most obvious problem arising from these laws—this voluminous victim's doctrine—is that it is utterly impossible to predict and prescribe a resolution for every potential problem that may arise in Babylon. While the Code of Hammurabi does impose specific resolutions for certain disagreements that may likely arise in the kingdom (in essence, mandatory sentencing guidelines), it does not clearly delineate any process by which those resolutions will be reached. In other words, under the first statute, if an accuser fails to prove his capital allegations, he himself will be put to death. But how *does* the accuser prove the capital offense? To whom must he prove it? Who holds the burden of proof? What is the standard of proof—preponderance of the evidence, reasonable doubt? And what is the process which he must follow?

Of course, there is little doubt as to how fresh disagreements will ultimately be resolved. You'll find the answer among the seven hundred lines celebrating the greatness of the king himself inscribed alongside those 282 laws on the black diorite block:

Hammurabi, the perfect king, am I . . . The king, who is preeminent among city kings, am I. My words are precious, my wisdom is unrivaled. By the command of Shamash, the great judge of heaven and earth, may I make righteousness to shine forth on the land.[37]

Obviously, this is not a system wherein the ruler operates below the rules. And in the end, the king (who is still considered above the law) will regulate the resolution of disagreements through his "wisdom" within a system that contends power comes from above ("Shamash"). In his code, Hammurabi—the dictator—dictates resolutions to disagreements. On the other hand, agreements that regulate the resolution of disagreements don't prescribe the resolutions themselves; instead, they define the process by which resolutions will be reached.

To see this distinction, flash-forward a few thousand years, stroll into the Assembly Room of the Pennsylvania State House in Philadelphia, and you'll find George Washington, Thomas Jefferson, Benjamin Franklin and the rest of the fifty-five drafters of the U.S. Constitution inscribing a very different set of agreements on the parchment before them:

Article I., Section 2. The House of Representatives shall choose their Speaker and other Officers; and shall have the sole Power of Impeachment.[38]

Article I., Section 3. The Senate shall have the sole Power to try all Impeachments. When sitting for that Purpose, they shall be on Oath or Affirmation. When the President of the United States is tried, the Chief Justice shall preside: And no Person shall be convicted without the Concurrence of two thirds of the Members present.

Judgment in Cases of Impeachment shall not extend further than to removal from Office, and disqualification to hold and enjoy any Office of honor, Trust or Profit under the United States: but the Party convicted shall nevertheless be liable and subject to Indictment, Trial, Judgment and Punishment, according to Law.[39]

Article II., Section 4. The President, Vice President and all civil Officers of the United States, shall be removed from Office on Impeachment for, and Conviction of, Treason, Bribery, or other high Crimes and Misdemeanors.[40]

Here, among the opening articles of the U.S. Constitution, we witness the convergence of the two concepts we most recently encountered—not only is the ruler placed below the rules, but there is also put in place a clearly delineated process for removing the ruler, a process that is itself an agreement that regulates the resolution of disagreements. In point of fact, "the final draft of the Constitution devoted more space to the rules for electing or removing the president than to delineating the powers of the office itself."[41]

Clearly, this is a system wherein the ruler operates below the rules. And in the end, preexisting agreements will regulate the resolution of disagreements within a system that acknowledges the president's power comes from below (i.e., from the people). Under the articles of the U.S. Constitution, agreements that regulate the resolution of disagreements don't prescribe the resolutions themselves; instead, they define the process by which resolutions will be reached.

To see this point illustrated, project forward another 187 years to the evening of August 8, 1974, walk into your living room, turn on the television, and no matter what network you tune to, this is what you'll hear:

Good evening. This is the 37th time I have spoken to you from this office, where so many decisions have been made that shaped the history of this Nation. Each time I have done so to discuss with you some matter that I believe affected the national interest. In all the decisions I have made in my public life, I have always tried to do what was best for the Nation. Throughout the long and difficult period of Watergate, I have felt it was my duty to persevere, to make every possible effort to complete the term of office to which you elected me. In the past few days, however, it has become evident to me that I no longer have a strong enough political base in the Congress to justify continuing that effort. As long as there was such a base, I felt strongly that it was necessary to see the constitutional process through to its conclusion . . . But with the disappearance of that base, I now believe that the constitutional purpose has been served . . . Therefore, I shall resign the Presidency effective at noon tomorrow. Vice President Ford will be sworn in as President at that hour in this office.[42]

Reciprocity reveals the Watergate scandal and President Nixon's resignation as an example of overexertion exposed through broadcast leading to the consequent transference/loss of power. The most powerful (influential) man in the world lost his ability to influence others' actions as the direct result of his own exertions when those upon whom the exertions were made defined those exertions as beyond acceptable limits and (using broadcast) exposed the president's exertions to the people (power comes from below) of the United States, and Congress (elected by the people and subject to their influence) passed the articles of impeachment (began to follow the process spelled out in the agreements that regulate the resolution of disagreements concerning conduct of the president). President Nixon resigned (acquiesced) before the process was completed, and in so doing, drew the slightest power (ability to influence others' actions) back to himself—he preempted impeachment and received a pardon. So we find in fact what was first presented in theory: agreements that regulate the resolution of disagreements are agreements that enclose retributive exertions and control rulers. In other words, Congress, and the Democratic Party in particular, could only proceed along a specified path (their retributive exertions were enclosed), and President Nixon could only go so far in his own defense (his actions were controlled). Once the president's power, his influence, his "base," was gone, he went as well. Again, agreements that regulate the resolution of disagreements take the administration of justice out of the hands (the whim) of the more influential individual(s) in a system and place it within the parameters of a prescribed process.

So as stated above in theory and now illustrated in reality, Reciprocity tells us not only that the limits themselves will be redefined, but it also predicts that the processes by which those redefinitions are accomplished will be redefined as well. And perhaps even more importantly, we see clear confirmation of this earlier assertion: once the ruler is placed below the rules, you no longer need revolution to effect change ("I now believe that the constitutional purpose has been served . . . Therefore, I shall resign the Presidency effective at noon tomorrow").

As stated earlier, this particular effect of the rule of Reciprocity—agreements that regulate the resolution of disagreements—follows and furthers the effort to place rulers below the rules because, as we now see, once you place the ruler below the rules, agreements that regulate the resolution of disagreements become a necessity. How else would you resolve such disagreements? For example, while President Nixon was not impeached, Presidents Andrew Johnson and William Jefferson Clinton were. Without agreements that regulate the resolution of disagreements, both leaders would have had to "impeach" themselves. The notion is absurd, but it underscores the point: once the ruler is placed below the rules, the traditional dictatorial mechanism of resolution is removed, and a new one *must* take its place.*

Interestingly, President Clinton was impeached for violating an agreement that regulates the resolution of disagreements. It is not against the law to lie in one's daily life—to your wife, your family, your friends, coworkers, and your boss. But once you enter the resolution of a disagreement (once you're testifying under oath), lying becomes illegal. While the law defining perjury

---

* This is not meant to imply that agreements that regulate the resolution of disagreements follow in precise chronological order from the moment that the ruler falls below the rules. In reality, agreements that regulate the resolution of disagreements can, and do, appear under dictatorships before the fact of external authority is finally fully accepted. But there are two distinctions to be made with regard to that phenomenon. First, agreements that regulate the resolution of disagreements can serve as one of the many masks behind which the ruler attempts to conceal his own exertions as he continues to rule on whim. Second, even if agreements that regulate the resolution of disagreements are in place (and sometimes fairly enforced), as long as the ruler remains above the rules, those agreements will ultimately be abrogated. Why keep yourself above the rules except to avoid being bound by them?

appears to be a permission/prohibition agreement ("you are prohibited from lying"), it is really an agreement that regulates the resolution of disagreements since lying is not a crime unless one is providing testimony under oath during the resolution of a disagreement. Similarly, in the Louima case, Officer Schwarz was sent to prison for five years not for his alleged participation in the underlying assault, but for perjury. Lying under oath is an exertion that transfers power away from the liar and to those who are attempting to resolve the disagreement. In addition to being impeached by the U.S. Congress, President Clinton was held in contempt of court by the Arkansas judge presiding over the resolution of the underlying disagreement between Paula Jones and the president. The concept of contempt of court also emerges from agreements that regulate the resolution of disagreements.

Now, to be clear, I am not attempting to draw a historical line of causation from the Code of Hammurabi to President Nixon's resignation and President Clinton's impeachment. In truth, George Washington, Thomas Jefferson, Benjamin Franklin, *et al.*, knew nothing of King Hammurabi. But I *am* saying that the phenomenon that inspired Hammurabi's code—exertion, transference, redefinition—is the same that inspired the U.S. Constitution. While the founding fathers did not know King Hammurabi or his code, they did know King George III, and the vast majority of the agreements they reached in establishing their more perfect union (the system they formed) came in direct response to specific exertions that that king had made. The Declaration of Independence dedicates approximately ten lines to the flowing poetics with which we are most familiar—"When in the course of human events . . . We hold these truths to be self-evident."[43]—and almost thirty lines to an unflinching itemized indictment of the king, broadcasting the "long train of abuses and usurpations,"[44] the specific list of royal exertions that these men (upon whom the king's power was being exerted) defined as beyond acceptable limits. Here are only a few of the charges against the king enumerated in the Declaration of Independence, specific exertions that were subsequently redressed by the redefinition of limits within the U.S. Constitution:

Quartering large bodies of armed troops among us.[45]

> Subsequently redressed and defined as beyond acceptable limits by the Third Amendment to the U.S. Constitution: "No Soldier shall, in time of peace be quartered in any house, without the consent of the Owner, nor in time of war, but in a manner to be prescribed by law."[46]

Imposing Taxes on us without our Consent.[47]

> Subsequently redressed and defined as beyond acceptable limits
> by Article I. Section 8. of the U.S. Constitution: "The Congress
> [elected and, therefore, acting at the consent of the people] shall
> have Power To lay and collect Taxes."[48]

Depriving us in many cases, of the benefit of Trial by Jury.[49]

> Subsequently redressed and defined as beyond acceptable limits by
> Article III. Section 2. of the U.S. Constitution: "The Trial of all
> Crimes, except in Cases of Impeachment, shall be by Jury."[50]

The United States Constitution was drafted in direct response to the
king's exertions, exertions that led to transferences and subsequently to
these, and other, specific redefinitions of limits. Clearly, the point at which
power is exerted is the point at which there exists the greatest potential
for its transfer; the people upon whom power is being exerted define its
limits; when the purpose of an exertion of power includes the maintenance
of power, then power is maintained through calculated conservation, not
unlimited exertion.

Sometimes, when we ponder the course of human events such as the
American Revolution and the drafting of the country's Constitution, those
events are so dramatic in effect and variegated in detail, and the individuals
who produced them (the people who redefined the limits of power) seem
so utterly extraordinary that we feel compelled to fall back on providence,
destiny, and other mysterious forces for the explanations we otherwise
cannot provide. But in the end, the phenomenon that guided the American
Revolution (exertion, transference, redefinition) is no different than the
phenomenon that guided the founding of MADD: the excessive exertion
transferred power to the victims and their allies (the founding fathers and
their fighting forces) who redefined limits, and those limits were subsequently
recorded as law/policy (the U.S. Constitution). So with regard to the nature
of the individuals who accomplish these redefinitions, to ask what brought
forth a George Washington is the same as asking why Candace Lightner
reacted the way she did. This simplifies the mystery, brings it closer to home,
and in the clean light of familiarity, we are perhaps less inclined to look to
providence/destiny for the answer to the riddle of Candace Lightner and

more able to admit that we simply cannot know why these *specific* individuals do what they do when they do it. If you want to try to untangle nature, nurture, timing, temperament, chemical causation, spiritual inspiration, and everything else that would have to be taken into account to finalize a precise theory of the causes of individual human behavior or, more broadly, human nature—please do.

But Reciprocity is not a theory of human nature. It appears in our nature to be both fearful and fearless; selfish and selfless; greedy and generous; in short, malevolent and benevolent. And gradations of these opposite traits can be seen running in a sort of spectrum (more and less present) across crowds of people. Thus as Viktor Frankl observed, "man is that being who invented the gas chambers of Auschwitz . . . He is also that being who entered those gas chambers upright."[51] But each quality can also emerge by degrees at any given time in any one individual. Reciprocity is a rule of human interaction that accommodates all of the traits manifested across that spectrum of human behavior. Whether greedy people interact with generous people or fellow misers, whether fearless people interact with fearful people or their fearless fellows, patterns of exertion and transference, acquiescence and redefinition will occur. In the end, the George Washingtons and Candace Lightners of the world do not create Reciprocity. Instead, their successes are created by the fact that power is transferred through its own exertion. Because without the fact that power is transferred through its own exertion, the exposure of such exertions wouldn't matter; transference and redefinition wouldn't exist, and there would be no balancing. The rule of Reciprocity has enabled Candace Lightner (and countless others in greater and lesser degrees) to create change, not vice versa. This is a difficult distinction and is in no way intended to eliminate the agency (or diminish the accomplishments) of those who act to redefine limits—I only mean to show that they all relied on the same phenomenon in doing so. Again, the rule of Reciprocity is not a theory of human nature, but it is a rule of human interaction. And as such, it is also a rule of human action (to interact, one must act). Some will act as Candace Lightner did. And other's will not. Why? That's the question Reciprocity cannot answer. Reciprocity cannot predict when, where, or (precisely) why the next George Washington or Mohandas Gandhi will emerge from the crowd of victims, that is to say, when the next great redefinition will occur; but it can tell us exactly how such individuals and their allies will effect change when they do: expose exertions, take the power transferred by those exertions, and use it to institute agreements that recognize Reciprocity.

It is a sad truth that Hammurabis still exist today. Kim Jong Il can't be impeached. He is a ruler above the rules, and if North Koreans want to replace their Dear Leader ("the perfect king am I") they must resort to force relations because they have no agreements to regulate disagreements with their ruler. Fidel Castro can't be impeached. He is a ruler above the rules, and if Cubans want to replace their Commandante ("the perfect king am I"), they must resort to force relations because they have no agreements to regulate the resolution of a disagreement with their ruler. You can continue this exercise ad nauseam, simply replacing one dictator's name (and nickname) with another. Kim, Castro, Gadhafi (Brother Leader), Swaziland's King Mswati III (the Lion of Swaziland), the additional dictators across Africa, and others around the world continue the ageless charade that power comes from above. Dictators not only place themselves above the law, but in doing so, they also maintain ultimate control over the resolution of disagreements. We have already established the fact that once the ruler is below the rules, revolution is unnecessary, but if we invert this to consider the condition wherein the ruler remains above the rules, we see that under those circumstances revolution/coup is the *only* choice for people seeking to replace a ruler.

As stated above, agreements that regulate the resolution of disagreements take the administration of justice out of the hands (the whim) of the more influential individual(s) in a system and place it within the parameters of a prescribed process. This establishment of process is part of a larger phenomenon: the measurable, "downward" pressure on power that comes as a natural consequence of the fact that power originates from below. Is this too theoretical? The effects of this natural downward pressure (the inclination to return power to its source) is experienced firsthand by any U.S. citizen summoned to jury duty.

Within the U.S. court system, the final decision of guilt and innocence is placed in the hands of ordinary people selected out of a pool drawn at random from the community. The system of judge/jury adjudication in the United States was established as a direct result of the exertions, transferences, and redefinitions that manifest the natural inclination to return power to its source. And though the trial is always presided over by a judge, the division of responsibility between judge and jury is clear: a judge judges the law; a jury judges the facts. Why? Because you need specialized knowledge of the agreements that regulate the resolution of disagreements (rules of evidence, procedure, motions, etc.) in order to preside over the resolution of a disagreement (a trial). But you don't need specialized education to listen to two stories, decide which one you believe, and carry out justice.

It is at the point when Reciprocity leads the ruler below the rules and agreements that regulate the resolution of disagreements emerge that we see "just" systems begin to take effect. After the ruler cedes dominion to the system, any agreement that regulates the resolution of disagreements will have justice in its sights. This is what we're really talking about when we consider the general phenomenon of exertion, transference, and redefinition and particularly when we isolate agreements that regulate the resolution of disagreements from the vast taxonomy of laws that constitute the world's numerous systems. We're talking about the pursuit of justice—a concept that cannot be accurately defined without an understanding of the fact that power is transferred through its own exertion.

Justice

As established earlier, a punch in the face in an uncharted wilderness is different from a punch in the face on a city street. That punch thrown in the wilderness is an act of force resolved through force relations (by whomever is best fit for the challenge), and justice is no more an element there than it is in any conflict between animals in the wild. But what of the punch that's thrown on the city street, that physical exertion—the act of power—occurring within the vast matrix of agreements that has arisen out of the previous exertions, transferences, and redefinitions (the human interactions) that created the system? How is justice measured in that scenario? The answer can only follow from another more basic question: what is *justice*?

Reciprocity supplies a definition:

Justice is the instance in which the power (the ability to influence another's actions) that is transferred through exertion from one individual or group to another individual or group is allowed to be exercised in turn by those upon whom power was initially exerted.

While this definition of justice—with its focus on transference—may be expressed in new terms, the concept itself is familiar. The phenomenon of exertion and transference is central to even our most basic vision of justice. It is no coincidence that the goddess of justice holds the scales in her hand. She stands as the symbol of transference, as the ability to influence another's actions is shifted from pan to pan in an act that is not balance, but *balancing*.

Now, of course, that's metaphor. So let's find fact.

To begin our journey away from theory, we'll start by summoning another simple scene into our mind's eye: a child at recess who has a toy snatched from her hand.

The snatching of the toy is an exertion of power and, as such, transfers power away from the snatcher and to the child who was playing with the toy to begin with. Assuming that she wants the toy back, and depending on a number of factors including the age of the child who has the toy snatched away (and her experience with or understanding of the fact that power is transferred through its own exertion), the victim of this snatching will do one of two things: she will either attempt to snatch the toy back, or she will broadcast the exertion—either indirectly by crying or directly by approaching a teacher (judge) to report the incident.

Let's assume an instance in which the child who has the toy snatched away doesn't simply snatch the toy back and consider the scenario in which she runs and tells on the other child. What is her expectation in reporting the exertion? Simply, she expects that the other child's actions will be influenced—the other child will at least be made to return the toy and may even be placed on a time-out. Whether or not the child who snatched the toy is placed on a time-out may depend on the severity of her exertion and whether or how often this child has snatched toys (or engaged in similar exertions) before. In other words, the toy-snatcher's exertions will continue to transfer more power away from her up to and including suspension and even expulsion from school. But we already know this. Sticking with our lone snatching incident and its relationship to justice, as the toy-snatcher's actions are influenced, as she is made to return the toy and sit out recess, the child upon whom the power was initially exerted feels that justice has been served. Why? Because the system has acknowledged that the toy-snatcher's actions transferred power to the victim and has allowed that transferred power to be exercised. Thus, justice is the instance in which the power that is transferred through exertion from one individual or group to another individual or group is allowed to be exercised in turn by those upon whom power was initially exerted.

Now, consider the inverted scenario in which the power transferred by the toy-snatcher's actions is not allowed to be exercised, a scenario in which she gets away with it. This opposite outcome leads to the opposite definition: injustice. *Injustice* is the instance in which the power that is transferred through exertion from one individual or group to another individual or group is *not* allowed to be exercised by those upon whom power was initially exerted.

So whether we come at it from the perspective of justice or injustice, we see that Reciprocity provides us with a relevant and useful definition.

At recess, the teacher dictates the resolution, and (to a certain extent) justice remains reliant on the whim of that individual.* In the legal system, the teacher position is held by a judge whose judgment is expected to be guided by an accumulation of agreements (authority), and the more those agreements account for and preserve the fact that power is transferred through its own exertion, the more able the system will be to facilitate justice. Taking it one step further, the more a system institutes agreements that regulate the resolution of disagreements (removing resolution from the hands of a dictator), the more able it will be to engage in the sort of balancing that reflects the fact that power is transferred through its own exertion. Thus, agreements that regulate the resolution of disagreements are an important step toward, and essential component of, a just system. To fall back on our metaphor for a moment, agreements that regulate the resolution of disagreements are the stable fulcrum upon which the balancing occurs.

One minor aside: obviously, the enforcement of agreements that regulate the resolution of disagreements does not guarantee justice. There are still unjust outcomes under just systems. A guilty suspect who gets off on a

---

* Of course, the teacher is operating within an accumulation of agreements (including agreements that regulate the resolution of disagreements), and if a student or students define the teacher's own actions as beyond acceptable limits (or if the students' parents do so by proxy), then the teacher can certainly transfer some (or all) of his power to the students and their allies. It is impossible to have a school without having an accumulation of agreements and, consequently, power. Therefore, it is impossible to have a teacher whose actions aren't subject to Reciprocity. But again, we already know this. What is important to note now is not that the teacher's interactions with the students are subject to Reciprocity, but that the ability to influence the other's actions is not equally distributed within the teacher-student relationship. Reciprocity produces *balancing*, not balance. Returning to the opening interaction between the mother and the driver on the bus: while the mother had power (a certain ability to influence the actions of the driver and, consequently, the bus), the driver had *more* power. The mother couldn't make the driver get off the bus. But the driver could make us all disembark. Again, Reciprocity produces balancing, not balance. Drivers will always have more power than passengers on buses because the accumulation of agreements distributes it that way. But the law (victim's doctrine) limits the driver's actions, and the rule of Reciprocity (the fact that power is transferred through its own exertion) leads to balancing when necessary.

technicality has benefited from an agreement that regulates the resolution of disagreements (that is precisely what a *technicality* is), and injustice has prevailed. Similarly, a guilty suspect who is acquitted by a jury that fails to discern the truth at trial has also benefited from agreements that regulate the resolution of disagreements, and injustice has prevailed.

As for the way in which agreements that regulate the resolution of disagreements do lead toward, and become essential components of, just systems, let's look back at Hammurabi's statutes to ask a series of definitive questions: Were they laws? Yes. Were they a victim's doctrine? Obviously (sometime, somewhere, someone in Babylon bought a slave who had the bennu fever!). Was the ruler placed below the rules? No. Were they agreements that regulated the resolution of disagreements? No. Was this a system that acknowledged Reciprocity? No. Was this a just system? No.

Now, certainly there is a sense of retributive justice in Hammurabi's code. If someone exerts against someone else, then the one who is exerted against can draw power from the king's code to influence the actions of the exerter if those initial actions were predefined as beyond acceptable limits. But Reciprocity is neither retribution nor revenge. During Hammurabi's reign, human beings were interacting and forming agreements, and Reciprocity was at work there. But Hammurabi's code attempts to *impose* balance, and the problem with that is, absent an impartial adjudicative process, the imposition of balance raises the likelihood that injustice will be perpetuated. Again, how exactly was the case against the wine seller to be proven before she was thrown into the water? How was the falsity of a capital accusation to be established before the accuser himself was put to death?

Notice that the solution to the toy-snatching disagreement was not that the victim was allowed to snatch a toy out of the snatcher's hands. The berry bringer did not club the clubber. Abner Louima did not subsequently sodomize Officer Volpe. Candace Lightner did not run over her daughter's killer with a car. Reciprocity does not lead to an eye-for-an-eye, a tooth-for-a-tooth symmetry, resulting in the infinite parade of exertion and transference without a lasting redefinition of limits. Instead, Reciprocity explains how and why systems engage in the balancing of exertions (i.e., justice) while *reducing* both persuasive and retributive eye-gouging/tooth-pulling actions (i.e., violence).

Regarding the reduction of *persuasive* violence, we saw earlier how and why the act of clubbing moves from persuasion to punishment as the diminishment of clubbing reduces the likelihood of victims and, thus, lowers the potential for loss of police power. Regarding the reduction of *retributive* violence, we also saw earlier that in a system that acknowledges Reciprocity, a killer's actions can be influenced to a degree that correlates with the degree of his own exertion, up to and including his own death. And in some instances, execution brings justice. Ultimately, Reciprocity cannot define the acceptability or unacceptability of a death penalty in any given system (only the people upon whom power is being exerted can do that). But this rule of human interaction—the fact that power is transferred through its own exertion—does lead to just systems, and just systems (which facilitate the balancing of power rather than the imposition of retribution and revenge) naturally discourage "eye-gouging" behaviors as the primary mechanisms of control and resolution.

Why do systems that acknowledge Reciprocity tend to discourage violence as the mechanism of resolution? Here's one reason: because violent acts once done cannot be undone. If a convicted thief has his hand cut off, the hand cannot be reattached if it is later proven that the convict was innocent. Justice (by definition) cannot lead to injustice (otherwise it would not be justice), thus violent resolutions are discouraged in order to reduce the likelihood of such final injustice. But there is another basic phenomenon at work here: violent exertions are discouraged because, again, we have moved from force to power. As a punitive system (accumulation of agreements) is formed, the emphasis will naturally shift from force to power (influencing the convict's actions through various degrees/techniques of incarceration as opposed to those forceful exertions that will tend to transfer power away from the individuals imposing punishment). Remember, the laws defining the limits on interactions between jailers and prisoners are also created as the result of exertions, transferences, and redefinitions of limits by victims (and their allies) from among both parties.

With regard to the development of just systems and their general discouragement of violence as the mechanism of resolution, one obvious high-profile example springs immediately to mind: the vote. As we move beyond our hypothetical toy-snatching illustration to scrutinize a real-world example, we see that the vote—which is both created by and acknowledging of the fact that power is transferred through its own exertion—provides real-life data describing Reciprocity's relationship to justice and just systems.

As mentioned earlier, Natan Sharansky defines a free society as one in which anyone can express a dissenting opinion in the town square. But he also exposes the limitation of his own definition: "According to the town square test, societies where women are not allowed to vote, where discrimination is rampant, or where the economy is rigidly controlled can still be free. This valid criticism demonstrates that every society that meets the definition of 'free' is not necessarily *just* [emphasis in original]."[52]

But why isn't it *just* that women be denied a vote?

In brief, denying women a vote is an exertion of power (it influences their actions), which transfers power to those women. If those upon whom that power is being exerted define the exertion (in this case, the denial of the vote) as beyond acceptable limits, and if the power transferred by virtue of that exertion is not then allowed to be exercised in turn, it is an injustice.

But there is a broader context to be examined here. Throughout history, unelected leaders have exerted and transferred power to their people; over time as agreements accumulate and more power becomes vested in those who are initially less influential, those initially less-influential individuals take the power transferred to them through their leaders' exertions and attempt to redefine limits on those exertions. In the majority of instances, these attempts at redefinition trigger a falling back to force relations (in addition, the progress of the accumulation of agreements is often interrupted by the introduction of force relations from outside). But falling back to force relations simply starts the process over: a new "first" agreement is formed; power is created, and the balancing begins anew.* At some point, rather than perpetually falling back to force relations, the vote finally emerges as an essential redefinition of limits put forward by victims (or potential victims) on both sides: those who are governed *and* those who govern. In this way, the vote replaces violence as the mechanism for resolving disputes between rulers and ruled, and it endures as the method by which those upon whom power is being exerted (the citizens of a system) are allowed to take the power transferred to them and exert it back on (use it to influence the actions of) their leaders.

I wish I could state a precise formula for when critical mass is reached, force relations are avoided and agreements that acknowledge Reciprocity are instituted, but none exists (or if such a threshold does exist, I am not able to define it). While the underlying and causative principle—power is transferred through its own exertion—is always the same, this essential transformation of system (from violence to vote) can only proceed on a case-by-case basis. The precise details of George Washington's success are different from the precise

---

* This describes and explains, in a broad manner, the history of Greece as it has stuttered forward, through advances and reversals, from one of the world's earliest democratic systems (5th century BC) into various incarnations of monarchy, military rule, and force-relation conflagrations to the country's present-day democratic republic, reestablished three-quarters of the way through the 20th century AD (1974).

details of Mohandas Gandhi's, yet both relied on Reciprocity to establish systems that acknowledge the fact that power is transferred through its own exertion. Interestingly, Gandhi *refused* to fall back to force relations—using the strategy of Satyagraha (which manifests itself, in part, through nonviolent civil disobedience) to draw power to himself rather than transfer it away as he led India toward democracy. Today, the world awaits other individuals (subjects of disparate yet similar systems around the world) to pursue, under different circumstances, the path that leads to liberation: expose the rulers' excessive exertions and use the power transferred through those exertions in order to redefine limits and establish enduring systems that acknowledge Reciprocity.

The vote, which is really not one agreement but an accumulation of both permission/prohibition agreements as well as agreements that regulate the resolution of disagreements, is itself a system that allows for the power that is transferred through exertion from the ruler to the people to be exercised in turn by the people.

Let's now take those questions that we applied to Hammurabi's code and apply them to the vote: Is the vote a law? Yes. Is it a victim's doctrine? Obviously (again, the vote is a redefinition of limits put forward by the victims and their allies from among the ranks of *both* rulers and ruled). Does the vote place the ruler below the rules? Yes. Is it an agreement that regulates the resolution of disagreements? Yes. Is it a system that acknowledges Reciprocity? Yes. Is it a just system? Yes.

Returning to the question of why it is unjust to segregate certain citizens from the voting rolls: Once the vote is established, in a system where leaders are elected, the leaders are given the ability to influence the actions of all the subjects/citizens of that system—be they men, women, members of a majority, or members of a minority. Consequently, to allow the leaders to influence these individuals' actions but not allow the power that is transferred by the leaders' exertions to be exercised in turn by any of those groups is an injustice.

Is it now necessary to review the various suffrage movements the world over in order to explicate this final non-theoretical illustration of Reciprocity's relationship to justice and the development of just systems? No. While one may not be personally familiar with the precise details of every suffrage movement on record, a basic understanding of Reciprocity enables one to outline how each moved forward: the disenfranchised group (e.g., women) led by an individual or individuals who innately understood Reciprocity/justice and how to pursue it (e.g., suffragists) used various forms of broadcast (e.g., protest marches) and possibly systematic refusal to abide by other agreements (e.g., strikes/civil disobedience) to expose the power being exerted against and transferred to them and increase their ability to exercise that power. In pursuing these tactics, the victims and their allies demanded that a redefinition of limits (a redress of the exclusionary exertions) be expressed in a victim's doctrine (law) allowing them to vote. Following acquiescence/accession, this new definition of limits (e.g., a constitutional amendment, parliamentary resolution, etc.) was codified.

So we see in fact what was first presented in theory: Reciprocity explains how and why systems engage in the balancing of exertions (i.e., justice) while *reducing* both persuasive and retributive eye-for-an-eye, tooth-for-a-tooth actions (i.e., violence). The fact that power is transferred through its own exertion leads to just (balancing) systems, and just systems generally discourage violence as the primary mechanism of control and resolution. The vote, an agreement that emerges from and supports the fact that power is transferred through its own exertion, replaces violence as the ultimate mechanism of resolution in systems that acknowledge Reciprocity.

But the fact that once some citizens have the vote, all must have it (for injustice to be avoided), carries with it a broader implication. Woven invisibly throughout this example is something beyond yet another illustration of the process (and product) of exertion, transference, and redefinition. As we have seen, agreements that regulate the resolution of disagreements allow equal access to the possibility of just resolution. But interestingly, equal access to the possibility of just resolution also leads (backward, in a way) to the rendering of just laws in the first place. For justice (and a just system) is found not only in the final resolution of disagreements but in the initial application of the laws as well. In short, equal access to just resolution *requires* just laws underneath.

How do just resolutions of disagreements lead (backward) to just laws? First, theory:

Here's a premise implicit in the rule that power is transferred through its own exertion, which we can now state explicitly: Reciprocity, while acknowledging the unavoidable correspondence between the more and less influential parties in a system, stands on a basis of inequality. Quite simply, power could not be transferred if it were distributed equally. Equal distribution of power would equal equilibrium—"a state of rest or balance due to the equal action of opposing forces."[53] By definition, the equal action of opposing forces creates a balance; and equal actions abutting each other preclude transference. Clearly, Reciprocity does not describe or produce this "state of rest;" instead, as was stated above, Reciprocity produces *balancing*.

Once we make this basic inequality explicit, we see that agreements are inevitably going to be applied unequally as a system develops. One party (the clubber) will have more power (more ability to influence the other's actions) at the outset, and an imbalance will remain throughout, although the more influential and less influential parties may switch places (repeatedly) as power is transferred through exertion, agreements accumulate, and systems mature. At the moment of that first agreement, balancing (however slight) begins, and if we trace the effects of Reciprocity following that first agreement through the accumulation of agreements to the emergence of external authority and agreements that regulate the resolution of disagreements, we see balancing occurring throughout.

Remember, you can't have an agreement that regulates the resolution of disagreements unless you have an underlying agreement over which that disagreement has arisen. Working backward—if a balancing is to occur within the process of resolving disagreements, then justice must become present in the underlying agreements themselves. That is to say, if the resolution of a disagreement (the pursuit of justice) uncovers an unjust agreement, an agreement that creates new victims, then the consequent balancing will have to lead backward to the modification/nullification of that underlying agreement. Otherwise, *two separate systems* would need to develop.

Now, fact:

In 1952, Oliver Brown had a disagreement with the Board of Education of Topeka, Kansas, over the fact that his daughter, who was in third grade, was required to walk an unreasonable distance to a Negro school while there was another (white) school much closer to their home. Consequently, he and his allies pursued the resolution of this disagreement through the regular channels of the U.S. judicial system (availing themselves along the way of agreements that regulate the resolution of disagreements) from the United States District Court for the District of Kansas (which ruled against him) to the U.S. Supreme Court (which ruled in his favor by overturning the doctrine of "separate but equal").

Brown v. Board of Education is interesting not because it outlines yet *another* example of Reciprocity-in-action (exertions by white segregationists, transference to black citizens and redefinition of the limits by those upon whom power was being exerted) as well as at least one of Reciprocity's key consequences: the point at which power is exerted (Oliver Brown and his daughter) is the point at which there exists the greatest potential for its transfer. Instead, it is most interesting because it illustrates the principle stated above—if the resolution of a disagreement (the pursuit of justice) uncovers an unjust agreement, a victim's doctrine that *creates* victims, then that unjust agreement will have to be remedied. Otherwise, two separate systems will need to develop.

Why must two separate systems develop? The U.S. government (itself an accumulation of agreements) was providing the education to Mr. Brown's daughter within the U.S. school system (a subset accumulation of agreements). It was also allowing Mr. Brown to participate in the court system (another subset accumulation of agreements). To say that Mr. Brown (and his family) could participate in the same U.S. court system as whites, but not the same school system would be to create an unsustainable dichotomy. Had the court continued to refuse to remedy the underlying injustices (lack of balancing) created by segregation, then the consequent, ongoing existence of a black school system would have, over time, required the establishment of a separate set of black agreements to regulate the resolution of disagreements arising within that system; then as additional, separate (but "equal") systems developed, a separate subset legal system would have required separate judges and lawmakers, a separate judiciary, Congress, president, a separate electoral system, a separate system of taxation, and so on until, finally, a fully separate black government appeared, and *two separate systems* existed parallel to each other. The Fourteenth Amendment, with its equal protection clause, was ratified in 1868; *Plessy v. Ferguson*, establishing the doctrine of separate but equal, was decided in 1896; *Brown v. Board of Education* came before the court in 1952. Clearly, this issue was not going to go away because those upon whom power was being exerted were going to continue to use their ongoing acquisition of power to influence the actions of the exerters and ultimately redefine limits.*

Ultimately, *Plessy v. Ferguson* and its doctrine of separate but equal was merely the legal means (and strategy of concealment—a way of masking the essence of the underlying exertion) employed by the group with more power (white segregationists) in order to avoid balancing. In the end, *Brown v.*

---

* As an aside, we see here why agreements that regulate the resolution of disagreements must be in place for this "backward" remedial process to work systematically. A dictator who projects himself into the lowered position of victim and passes a law to preempt his own vulnerability will certainly create victims along the way. But as long as he retains final say regarding the resolution of disagreements (as long as he maintains his own "separate" system for himself and his cohorts), relatively little can be done without conflict, coup, or revolution. Once the ruler falls below rules and agreements that regulate the resolution of disagreements are put in place, such unjust laws can be undone. And finally, as will become more important in the "Power" section when we consider the relationship of centralized political systems to decentralized economic systems, we also see here that one cannot acknowledge Reciprocity in one subsystem (e.g., the court system) and deny it in another (e.g., the school system) because citizens participate in each, and therefore, the entire system must align in recognition of or resistance to Reciprocity.

Board of Education did rule that the law, the victim's doctrine of separate but equal, created victims—"to separate them [Negro students] from others of similar age and qualifications solely because of their race generates a feeling of inferiority"[54]—and found it to be in violation of the equal protection clause of the Fourteenth Amendment. This, as well as the subsequent (and ongoing) history of the application of the Fourteenth Amendment, gives us valuable data confirming what was stated above—if the resolution of a disagreement (the pursuit of justice) uncovers an unjust agreement underneath, an agreement that creates new victims, then that unjust agreement will have to be modified/nullified. Otherwise, two separate systems will need to develop.

While it is relatively easy to look back and employ Reciprocity to help explain developments such as the *Brown v. Board of Education* decision or the broader effects of the Fourteenth Amendment, a complicated contemporary example of the consequence we're currently examining (the fact that Reciprocity defines justice, and justice leads either backward to just agreements or forward to two separate systems) can be found today in the controversy surrounding India's uniform civil code. Here we have neither the perspective nor the closure provided by our previous examples. But if the rule of Reciprocity has validity it can't only be explicated and illustrated historically but must also be applicable to current systems and their present controversies.

Here's the situation:

Article 44 of the Indian Constitution makes this provision: "The State shall endeavour to secure for the citizens a uniform civil code throughout the territory of India."[55]

This sounds pretty straightforward in theory. Article 44 is saying in effect that the State will work to make sure that the citizens of India all live under the same laws. The problem arises from the reality that such a uniform civil code conflicts with the obligations of various religious adherents across India, particularly those who are bound by faith to abide by Muslim Personal Law. So what does Reciprocity tell us with regard to this conflict? Well, in India, agreements have accumulated. External authority has been recognized. Agreements that regulate the resolution of agreements are in place. And justice (balancing) is available to the country's citizens. Therefore, if just resolution under the Indian system uncovers unjust laws, those laws will have to be modified/nullified or else an entirely separate system must develop. If all the citizens of India are being given the advantage of balancing in the resolution of disagreements, they must also be given the advantage of just agreements (agreements that do not *create* victims) underneath.

The salient question becomes, are Muslims being victimized by Muslim Personal Law, or will Muslims be more victimized if Muslim Personal Law is replaced by a uniform civil code? And the answer is, the people upon whom power is being exerted define its limits. In the end, the uniform civil code promised by the Indian Constitution either will or will not be implemented. The various vicissitudes, convulsions, "redistributions, realignments, homogenizations, serial arrangements, and convergences" that might occur between now and some future conclusion cannot be predicted (because human behavior cannot be predicted). But here we can introduce a relevant new truth and consequence revealed by Reciprocity: if a system recognizes the fact that power is transferred through its own exertion, then it can and will engage in the balancing and consequent progress that stems from such an acknowledgement. However, if a system does not recognize Reciprocity and does not allow for such balancing, then the system must (there is logically no other option) attempt to impose equilibrium—that "state of rest." Thus, inscribed in any accumulation of agreements, you will find either a systemic state of motion or a systemic state of rest. And in this context, both the stagnatory nature of a state of rest and the progressive nature of a state of motion have significant consequences for the future.

As we saw with the Magna Carta, it is not random historical chance, the non-reproducible chronology of specific events, but the action of an underlying phenomenon that enables systems to move forward toward justice (balancing). Any system that is not destined to fall back to force relations must become capable of balancing the power held by all the separate factions operating within it. The systems that acknowledge Reciprocity do provide for such balancing, and as a result, they are capable of something that the other systems are not: they are capable of *expanding*. Not simply incorporating outsiders, but expanding to encompass new definitions of limits and thus enabling more/diverse factions to acquire more power within them. The United States constitutional system has allowed individuals who began as slaves to acquire increasing amounts of power and, finally, full participation within the system. Similarly, the Indian system has allowed individuals who began as untouchables to acquire increasing amounts of power as well.

Once a system acknowledges Reciprocity, its underlying agreements can do more than accumulate, they can also expand—without being imposed—allowing diverse factions to acquire power. This phenomenon of expansion (and its consequences) is the topic we will now take up.

The Expansion of Agreements

What do I mean by *the expansion of agreements*? I don't mean merely the incorporation of more people into a system; expansion of agreements does not refer to the expansion of territory or the growth of a population, and it is not meant to imply the imposition of a system upon outsiders. Instead, expansion means the opportunity for individuals to *acquire* more power within a system. It is this distinction—the differentiation of imposition from acquisition—that is central to the contrast between the simple incorporation of more individuals into a system and the actual expansion of agreements.

Almost any system can be temporarily imposed, and I will take up imposition and its implications at greater length in the "Power" section. There was the potential for imposition even in the Code of Hammurabi. As the king conquered more land, he could potentially impose his code on a greater number of people. But that's not expansion. Hammurabi's agreements simply could not expand because they did not allow for the requisite balancing; they attempted to impose balance instead.

Of course, the expandability of agreements (the ability for subjects of laws to acquire more power under the exact same laws) *can* lead to the incorporation of more individuals because those who do acquire power may also have been, at one time, completely excluded. In truth, while expansion does not equal incorporation, the expansion of agreements does raise the likelihood that more people will be incorporated into a system over time because to the extent expansion is present, systems must become more or less permeable. Why? To hold people out is to hold people in. To hold people out is to restrict those who are in the system from interacting with those who are outside the system. And people living within a system that acknowledges Reciprocity will not allow themselves to be held in. They will redefine such limits on interaction. Thus, in reality, the United States of America is a country of immigrants who remain able to come and go at will, and the only problem America faces with regard to the permeability of its system is the heightened desire among subjects of other systems to enter and acquire power within the United States.*

---

*   Consequently, Reciprocity shows that the source of the immigration "problem" in the United States is not to be found in *its* system but in the systems from which the immigrants are fleeing. This is an issue of emigration, not immigration. People climbed over a wall to get *out of* East Germany (because its oppressive system did not acknowledge Reciprocity); and they climb over walls to get *into* the United States (because its system does). If one drills down to the very foundation of U.S. immigration, it is not wealth or opportunity that attracts outsiders—wealth and opportunity are consequences of the system, not vice versa. Therefore, at base, it is the system itself—a system caused by and acknowledging Reciprocity—that creates such attraction.

Taking the inverse for a moment, if the prerequisites for expansion (justice, etc.) are not in place, then Reciprocity predicts that the people will not be allowed to move freely. Why? A system that does not enable agreements to expand is a system that does not acknowledge Reciprocity, does not allow for balancing, and is, by definition, an unjust one. And an unjust system must seal its borders to avoid inevitable defections. Of course, this is not an all-or-nothing proposition but exists in degrees. The more a system acknowledges Reciprocity, the more it will allow its people to come and go. The less it does, the less it will allow such movement. As long as the clubber continues the lifelong effort of propping up an unjust system by denying/diminishing Reciprocity, the people within that system have only two choices for change—revolution or defection (fight or flight). All this, of course, is also borne out in reality. The iron curtain rose to enclose an unjust system (one that was incapable of engaging in balancing); and even at this writing, Castro's Cuba remains a prison: Cubans cannot come and go at will. They must be held within that system or else they flee—often to the United States.

Having clarified what is meant by the *expansion of agreements*—the ability for agreements to broaden to allow people to acquire more power within them—the logical questions are, Why and how do agreements expand?

First, why:

We understand why agreements accumulate—agreement spawns agreement as each new exertion is either defined as being within previous limits or inspires new ones. But why do agreements expand? Part of the answer to this question has been implied throughout the foregoing: agreements expand because the process of balancing (justice) that emerges from the fact that power is transferred through its own exertion allows new victims to draw broader definitions of limits. Is this all too theoretical? We've already seen the reality of this expansion in *Brown v. Board of Education*. The justices of the Supreme Court did not revise the Fourteenth Amendment when they overturned the doctrine of separate but equal; they simply allowed its equal protection clause to broaden to encompass the education of Negroes by eradicating the evasive tactic of "separate but equal." Thus, the agreement didn't *change*—it (or its application) expanded.

And yes, the passive voice is appropriate—the Supreme Court *allowed* the amendment to expand. The justices did not wake up one morning and say to themselves, "Hmmm, maybe we should expand our application of the equal protection clause of the Fourteenth Amendment to encompass Negroes by eliminating that 'separate but equal' evasion." Again, power (the ability to influence others' actions) comes from below. And in this case, individuals against whom an effort to deny/diminish Reciprocity was being made, individuals who were being partially excluded from this agreement, were able to influence the justices to let the agreement expand. Oliver Brown and his allies were able to influence the actions of the Supreme Court in a way that the parties in *Plessy v. Ferguson* were not because they (as victims) had acquired more power in the interim (from 1896 to 1952). Over time, they took the power transferred to them through the exertions of white segregationists and used it to influence the actions of those segregationists via the U.S. Supreme Court.

In sum, sometimes limits are redefined in the form of an entirely new agreement—e.g., the ratification of the Fourteenth Amendment, which allowed blacks to become citizens in the first place. And sometimes limits are redefined in the form of the expansion of existing agreements—e.g., *Brown v. Board of Education*, which expanded the amendment's equal protection clause to encompass black citizens without exception. Agreements expand when it is discovered that previous parameters set by preexisting practices were insufficient for justice to be served.

As an aside, there is an ironic, though important, twist that becomes apparent here. In a system that has placed the ruler below the rules—a system that says, "No one is above the law"—everyone is above the law since the law comes from below, and thus, everyone has the potential to change it. Candace Lightner changed it. Oliver Brown changed it. And the law books memorialize countless plaintiffs and defendants who were able to take the power transferred to them by others' exertions and use that power to influence the actions of others, sometimes redefining limits, expanding agreements, or changing laws along the way.

Earlier, I made this statement: at that instant of acquiescence, in the moment when the agreement is formed, the *weaker* party is vested with the ability to influence the stronger party's actions, and power is immediately infused throughout the system. Thus, I did, and continue to, equate agreement with acquiescence. Oliver Brown and his allies were able to exercise the power transferred to them because they were acquiescing in the broader scope; they were participating in the system. Once an individual acquiesces to a system, there is no such thing as nonparticipation. In the dynamic we're describing here, you either have acquiescence/agreement or you don't. The berry bringer either brings the berries, or he doesn't. Anything short of a falling back to force relations is participation. Even opposition is participation. Oliver Brown and his allies who took their case through the system were participating in the system; they were even co-operating (operating with the system to change the system), but they were also resisting. Redefinition relies on resistance. And in the same way that systems mature—developing the ability to handle problems they've previously faced—resistance matures as well. At the outset, as the less influential individual resists, he is relying solely on his own power (the fact that he can influence the more influential individual's actions) to redefine limits. Later, once agreements that regulate the resolution of disagreements are in place, the less influential individuals draw power not only from the exertions made against them but also from existing laws.

Why do agreements expand? Because as the less influential individuals in a system resist, the process of balancing (justice) that emerges from the fact that power is transferred through its own exertion allows those individuals to acquire more power under the agreements that already constitute the system.

Now, how:

Reciprocity (and its effects) explains how systems progress toward the expansion of agreements: the fact that power is transferred through its own exertion leads to the accumulation of agreements, which leads to the emergence/acknowledgement of external authority, which leads to agreements that regulate the resolution of disagreements, which lead to justice (systematic balancing), which leads (backward) to the remedy of unjust (or unjust application of) laws, which leads to expansion; therefore, the expansion of agreements is an (extended) effect of Reciprocity.

Once external authority emerges from below and is acknowledged by all, the system that facilitates balancing (the just system) begins to be codified, which is simply another way of saying that its agreements are remembered and recorded. This codification (memory) of agreements perpetuates authority and bestows the ability to influence others' actions, which is itself in perpetual negotiation/balancing. The expansion of agreements simply describes one pattern that occurs within that negotiation/balancing.

The examples of the expansion of agreements that I have touched on so far—*Brown v. Board of Education*, suffrage movements, the increased acquisition of power on the part of slaves/untouchables—are all also examples of integration, instances in which subjects of a system were further integrated into that system. But the phenomenon of expansion reveals itself in more ways than this ongoing integration. In fact, expansion is revealed in one particularly profound way: as human interaction proceeds, people begin to recognize recurrent patterns of exertion, transference, and resistance. As the system that facilitates Reciprocity is put in place, such a system recognizes those high-profile, recurring patterns and a new form of agreement emerges, an agreement that privileges certain prior resistances by "locking in" the resultant redefinitions and applying them in the most expansive manner possible. These new agreements are known as rights. In pursuit of an answer to "how do agreements expand?", rights (which come to encompass everyone within a system) emerge as a significant mechanism.

What are rights? Volume upon volume has been written on this question already, and not surprisingly, the definition (or perception) changes as more data (more record of human interaction) emerges. Hammurabi had less data than Aristotle; Aristotle had less data than Hobbes; Hobbes had less data than Jefferson; and Jefferson had less data than we have. So I will refrain from a (basically irrelevant) review of all that has gone before and instead stay within this study to focus only on the answer to which Reciprocity leads because, just as with justice, Reciprocity does uncover its own definition.

Here it is: Rights are agreements that codify resistance and control rulers, extended universally within a system and insulated from redefinition by custodial arrangement.

Now let's unwind that.

First: *Rights are agreements.* Sometimes rights are simple permission/prohibition agreements: e.g., the government and the people come to agree (through the negotiative process of exertion, transference, and redefinition) that the people are permitted to own guns, and the right to bear arms is defined. And sometimes, rights are agreements that regulate the resolution of disagreements: e.g., the government and the people come to agree (through the negotiative process of exertion, transference, and redefinition) that the guilt of an accused shall be determined in a court of law by average members of the community, and various rights including the right to trial by jury and the right against self-incrimination are defined. But in either instance, a right is obviously an agreement.

Rights are agreements. Agreements create power. Power comes from below. Therefore, rights come from below. This is true. Rights do not "spring directly from an understanding of what man is"[56] or any other noumenal origin. Instead, they emerge from the rule of Reciprocity, *produced* by the process of exertion, transference, and resistance/redefinition. And this leads us to the next part of the definition.

Rights are agreements *that codify resistance.* If a restriction on speech had never occurred, then the right to free speech would not have been defined (this is also obvious). But you can't understand how resistance translates into rights unless you understand the underlying rule that power is transferred through its own exertion, the resultant process of exertion, transference, and redefinition as well as the consequent, overarching pattern of human interaction we have traced—from force (no agreement) through the emergence of external authority to the expansion of agreements. Once you have agreement (system), then you have Reciprocity, transference, and the potential for the exercise of the power that is transferred (resistance).* Before that, you have only conflict.

Now, as we have seen, almost all laws are the codification of resistance. Going back even to our simple traffic-law examples, traffic laws weren't instituted until the dangers became apparent (until enough victims had piled up). The victims of car accidents resisted the onslaught and created their victim's doctrine to control drivers, and the traffic light was invented as one mechanism to facilitate the reduction of victims. Thus, "go on green, stop on red" is the codification of resistance. But "go on green" is not a right. In other words, I have a right to free speech, but I don't have a *right* to drive through an intersection when the light is green. Yet free speech and "go on green" are both permission/prohibition agreements that arose out of resistance. So what's the difference?

The difference is found first in the target of the resistance. The victim's doctrine establishing the "go on green" regulation arose from accidents that occurred in the normal course of interaction between drivers and the world around them. Thus, the resistance was not against the government, and "go on green" does not control rulers. There are a number of factors inscribed throughout the remainder of our definition of right that differentiate "go on green" and other similar agreements—not defined as rights—from free speech and those agreements that are. But for now, we come to this: rights are agreements that codify resistance *and control rulers.* And it is worth looking again at how we arrived at this point.

---

*   Resistance, as it's broadly defined, can exist outside a system. I am using the term here to describe a specific phenomenon: the exercise of transferred power in order to influence the actions of those whose exertions transferred that power. Resistance outside a system takes shape only in the actions that characterize force relations: fight or flight.

Following the emergence of external authority (placing the rulers below the rules) and the appearance of agreements that regulate the resolution of disagreements, we saw how the balancing (justice) that Reciprocity requires leads backward to the creation of just laws and/or just application. Clearly, you can't have rights until you've placed the rulers below the rules. Starting from the initial acknowledgement that the ruler is below the rules, we advance toward these agreements that are aimed directly at rulers. Whereas the very first agreement (unclearly) placed the ruler below the rules, rights are agreements that clearly direct the ruler's behavior. And this is where the distinction between rights and other agreements begins to take definite shape. A right is always aimed at a ruler. For instance, the right to bear arms is not intended to prohibit me from stealing your gun. It is aimed at the government to prohibit it from confiscating all guns. To go back to basics, the right to bear arms exists to ensure that clubbers aren't the only ones with clubs. Similarly, the rights of free speech and free assembly are not intended to stop me from telling you to shut up and quit hanging around. They are aimed at the rulers to preempt the imprisonment of dissidents. So whether rights are prescriptive, proscriptive, or procedural, they control rulers.*

The negotiative process that emerges from the fact that power is transferred through its own exertion eventually highlights certain limits that are required for balancing to occur. Rights attempt to hold those privileged limits in place. Consequently, we can see that rights both emerge from *and protect* the fact that power is transferred through its own exertion. The systems that do not allow for this protection either stagnate or fall back to force relations (or both). And we see again how the stagnatory nature of a state of rest (within systems that attempt to deny Reciprocity) and the progressive nature of a state of motion (within systems that acknowledge Reciprocity) have significant consequences for the future of any system. The concept of right is a consequence of the same process of balancing and tracing back that we have already covered. This means that rights are not the creators of justice. Instead, the justice (balancing) that Reciprocity requires creates rights as part of the pattern of the expansion of agreements. And expansion, the concept that brought us to this point to begin with, brings us to the next portion of the definition.

---

* Of course, once rights are established, one individual can violate another individual's rights, but the initial impetus and ongoing rationale for the establishment and maintenance of rights (as opposed to simple permission/prohibition agreements) is to control the rulers, not each other.

Rights are agreements that codify resistance and control rulers, *extended universally within a system*. Again, we have more data today than our predecessors had. Thomas Jefferson had no way of knowing that the rights he helped inscribe in the U.S. Constitution would one day expand to encompass the descendants of those he held as slaves. Therefore, he would not have given us this clause—"extended universally within a system"—as an accurate description of reality.* Today we have the data at hand (both from the United States and many other systems) to conclude that such universality does eventually emerge from the fact that power is transferred through its own exertion.

Here at this clause, "extended universally within a system," we add another reason why rights are distinct from "go on green" agreements. They are not posited on any affirmative act on the part of a citizen. "Go on green" is not a right because driving is not a right; it is a privilege. Driving is a privilege that is earned upon successful completion of a predefined process. Through the pattern of exertion, transference, and redefinition, the victim's doctrine has settled on the principle that people should not be allowed to drive until they can prove their competence. Thus, the driving privilege is not extended to anyone. It is *earned* by all who possess it. And even after that, the privilege can be revoked if an individual subsequently exhibits incompetence.

But this presents two problems: within the United States system, the right to vote is not completely universal and neither is the right to bear arms. So what are we to make of this?

With regard to the right to vote, the restriction is age based. Citizens (be they men, women, members of a majority or members of a minority) must have reached at least eighteen years of age before they can vote. Seventeen-year-olds can't vote. But doesn't this poke a hole in the definition "extended universally within a system"? No. Everyone ages. The prior restrictions on voting (exerted against women and minorities) guaranteed that some citizens would *never* vote. A woman does not naturally metamorphose into a man, and a black man's skin doesn't fade to white over time. But aging is universal; therefore, the right is

---

* The prosaic proclamation "all men are created equal" was conveniently circumvented in practice through a number of strategies, including the fact that slaves were not defined as men. By agreement (among the more influential individuals in the system), a slave was first defined as three-fifths of a man, and thus exempted from America's transcendent vision of equality. Of course, that exertion transferred power; the people upon whom power was being exerted (and their allies) defined the exertion as beyond acceptable limits, and redefinition (both of *man* and of the limits on such future exertions) followed.

extended universally. As an aside, depending on the jurisdiction and the crime, some convicts can't vote either. This is not an exception to the rule—the right was still extended to them. They simply forfeited it (as part of their loss of freedom) when they were convicted. All rights can be forfeited. An individual who is convicted of a capital offense will obviously forfeit all rights if the death penalty is imposed. But the rights were extended to that person to begin with.

Now, what about the right to bear arms? To recap, you need a license to drive (not universal); you don't need a license to speak freely (universal); however, you do need a license to own certain guns—yet "bearing arms" is still considered a right. So *now* is the definition faulty? This is an interesting question. And Reciprocity points to what may (or may not) be a surprising answer. First, it is necessary to understand the unique nature of the right to bear arms. Guns lend themselves to extreme exertions, and consequently, we would expect their use to trigger extreme transferences and redefinitions—which is precisely what has happened. In addition, *arms* have changed dramatically since Madison drafted the Bill of Rights, and consequently, so have the restrictions on ownership (e.g., it is not legal to *bear* a nuclear warhead). As a result of exertions, transferences, and redefinitions, a blanket right to bear arms is not extended universally. Does that make the definition wrong? No, it means that the right to bear arms may not actually be a right any longer. It may have morphed (through exertion, transference, and redefinition) into a highly protected privilege. It has certainly entered a grey area.*

This consideration of whether the right to bear arms remains a right leads to the final phrase—*and insulated from redefinition by custodial arrangement.* Rights can be redefined, but they enjoy a presumption of protection, a certain insulation from redefinition.

Again, despite the inherently severe nature of arms exertions, the ability to own a gun has been (and continues to be) insulated from redefinition. Guns have killed many more people than drunk drivers, yet the restrictions on drunk driving were imposed rapidly and with relatively little resistance while restrictions on the right to bear arms face an uphill battle within the U.S. system. There is

---

* I have intentionally left aside the controversy regarding the phrasing of the U.S. Constitution's Second Amendment—"*A well regulated Militia, being necessary to the security of a free State*, the right of the people to bear Arms, shall not be infringed [emphasis added]"—because regardless of what the Supreme Court rules regarding that introductory clause, the right to bear arms has been and will continue to be infringed (redefined) as ongoing exertions (including the development of new arms) and transferences lead to new limits.

a reason why this is so, and we will see it in a moment. But for now, the point is that rights are only insulated, not completely immune, from redefinition.

To illustrate, from inception to today the limits on the right to free speech have been (re)defined by the following landmark cases (among others):

> *Schenck v. United States*
> (Establishing the "clear and present danger" doctrine)

> *Brandenburg v. Ohio*
> (Narrowing "clear and present danger" via the "imminent lawless action" test)

> *Chaplinsky v. New Hampshire*
> (Introducing the "fighting words" doctrine)

> *Roth v. United States*
> (Obscene material not protected)

> *New York Times v. Sullivan*
> (Malicious intent must be proven in libel cases against public officials)

> *Miller v. California*
> (Upholding the "average person, applying contemporary community standards" guideline to determine obscenity)

So we see from this varied collection of exertions, transferences, and redefinitions that a right is only insulated from redefinition not fully protected.

Now, although rights are able to be redefined—as exertions and transferences lead to new limits—they are kept in a condition of privileged custody. Why? Why is this custodial arrangement created? The answer brings us back to the definition of justice that led us to expansion in the first place: these agreements (rights) are protected because, by controlling rulers, they protect the balancing (justice) that Reciprocity requires. Why is it that drunk-driving laws were easily implemented, but gun control is harder to impose? Drunk driving creates victims but does not control rulers. And while guns create victims, the right to bear arms is ultimately related to the effort to protect the populace against oppression (or attack). There is no balancing advantage to driving drunk, but there could be a balancing advantage to owning a gun. You want to switch the law to "go on red, stop on green"? Go ahead. Who cares? Of course that won't happen because it's pointless. You want to eliminate the permission to speak freely? That won't happen because it's serious. Why is it serious? Because it threatens the process of balancing to which Reciprocity necessarily leads. Of course these rights *can* be eliminated when systems change. Check the data available to us today from the patterns of oppression that emerge out of societies attempting to deny Reciprocity, and you will see that the agreements we have focused on here (people can own guns and speak freely) are among the first to go.

Repeating what I stated above, as a system matures, as it develops the ability to handle problems it has already faced, it recognizes those patterns and a new form of agreement emerges, an agreement that privileges certain prior resistances by "locking in" the resultant redefinition. This presumption of protection from redefinition is not attached to the average agreement. Thus, the insulation from redefinition by custodial arrangement is the "lock-in" and final quality that makes the underlying agreement a right, distinguishing it from other permission/prohibition and procedural agreements.

Ultimately, anything a government has to bestow upon its people comes from its people to begin with, and rights (which come from below) are held in custody by the subjects of the system that has produced them. What form does this custodial arrangement take? Sometimes, the custodial protection is made explicit: the First Amendment begins, "Congress shall make no law respecting"—and with those words, the rights regarding religion, speech, press, assembly, and petition are systematically insulated from legislative revision. And sometimes the custodial arrangement is put in place by other means. In the United States for instance, amendments to the Constitution are held to a higher standard for addition, revision, or repeal than are standard permission/prohibition statutes. Thus, this "higher bar" provides the insulation. Either way, this custodial arrangement—this (explicit or implicit) agreement to insulate a given agreement—creates power (the ability to influence other's actions) as do the agreements that it insulates (as do all agreements).

Here—toward the end of this section on system, with everything that has gone before in place and remaining under the subhead "Expansion of Agreements"—we come to an example of all of the above.

At the very start, I raised this problem: what power did the American Indians have? Apparently none—their lands were taken. So doesn't this disprove the rule at the outset? How can all people have power, and yet the Indians have none? This may be intriguing, but it is not a contradiction. There are specific reasons why the American Indians did not have power when Europeans invaded their lands, and there are specific reasons why they do today.

First, let me dispel any notion that I am about to embark on a complete history of the American-Indian experience. That is not my aim. Instead, I'm simply trying to present what Reciprocity can tell us about this phenomenon: there was a time when American Indians were utterly overrun, yet today, they participate fully in the American system even to the point that they are entitled to exercise privileges unavailable to non-Indians on the very lands that they had once lost. But how did this happen? Did the European invaders begin the relationship as heartless brutes and then mellow with age, becoming more open-minded as they slowly morphed into Americans? Or did the Indians improve their weaponry and reemerge as a more formidable force, thus taking back some of what had been taken from them?

If I started this study simply (with the exchange between the mother and driver on the bus), we have now officially arrived at complex. But again, there is nothing present in the interaction between the Indians and the settlers that wasn't right there in that opening example except one fact: the mother and the driver met within a system (accumulation of agreements) while the Indians and settlers first met in a state of force relations. What I want to narrate now (in summary fashion) is the overarching progress from force to power to the accumulation of agreements to the expansion of agreements because in the experience of the American Indians, we find an example of precisely this movement we've been tracing.

So the reason that the Indians did not have power when the Europeans invaded their lands is that neither side had power in that relationship. Saying that the Indians did not have power is telling only half the story. The colonists did not have power either. Instead, the parties were largely engaged in force relations.

Contact between invaders and indigenous peoples brought first conflict quickly, and conflict continued throughout (and after) the American Revolution, with Indians even fighting alongside the British as the American revolutionaries attempted to establish their new system. When Washington learned that the Six Nations (also known as the Iroquois Confederation) had joined forces with British troops, he ordered "the total destruction and devastation of their settlements and the capture of as many prisoners of every age and sex as possible."[57] In other words, Washington ordered retaliation. This is a state of force relations in which both sides are pursuing either unqualified acquiescence (complete surrender) or annihilation. The settlers attacked the Indians, and the Indians attacked the settlers. Did these attacks transfer power? No. They existed outside a system. Meeting in this wilderness, neither the settlers nor the Indians had any means of influencing the others' actions (power). Absent agreement, only force exists. So both parties were locked in the cycle of aggravation, aggression, recrimination, and retaliation, not exertion and transference. At the start, there were no agreements, no accumulation of agreements, no agreements that regulate the resolution of disagreements, no justice, no rights.*

---

*   I can hear objections rising. "What about the right to be left in peace and not driven from your land? Didn't the Indians have that right?" Rights and entitlement are different phenomena (in fact, rights only begin to emerge when those upon whom power is being exerted define those exertions as denying them something to which they feel entitled). But (despite the fact that we feel the Indians were treated unjustly) rights did not exist in the encounter between the colonists and the Indians. Here's where the retroactive application of justice (that tracing back) comes vividly into play: after rights are won, we are naturally inclined to trace exertions back to the point before power relations commenced and bestow the newly minted rights retroactively on those who acquiesced (and their ancestors)—often by invoking that sense of noumenal genesis that contradicts historical record. That tendency is exacerbated by this unavoidable irony: rights were won through the efforts of those who did not have the rights (why would they have fought in the first place—and then fought for rights—if they had them to begin with?). Based on the fact that it was the efforts (resistance) of those who did not have rights that brought the rights into existence, we feel like the rights were (or should have been) there all along. But they weren't (again, if they were, wouldn't the Indians—and the colonists in their own context—have invoked them and pursued balancing through nonviolent power relations as opposed to brutal force relations?). The colonists arrived on North American shores in large part because *they* did not have the rights they desired. So, obviously, the rights weren't there. But (following acquiescence) Reciprocity was. And the rights were created by the process Reciprocity describes: acquiescence, exertion, resistance, redefinition, subsequent agreement, and custodial designation. Every shred of historical data supports the conclusion that the rights we enjoy today are products of efforts made by our predecessors who did not have those rights but who pursued the pattern Reciprocity predicts in order to acquire them. Having said all of that, this important aside can also address a relevant question of our time: are there global human rights? The answer itself must start with a question: is there a global accumulation of agreements? Obviously not. But there is a common human condition. No one lives outside of acquiescence/agreement; therefore, *no one lives outside of Reciprocity*. Understanding the process by which rights are created can help those who are certainly entitled to, but have not yet secured, certain rights to establish them.

In the colonist/Indian dynamic we do not see merely the sort of *return* to force relations that we contemplated earlier. Instead, we find in reality the relation that was first presented in our most theoretical of theories: we find the clubber and the berry bringer brought forth in flesh and blood.

As Stephen Greenblatt recounts, "John Sparke, who sailed with Sir John Hawkins in 1564-65, noted that the French colonists in Florida 'would not take the pains so much as to fish in the river [gather berries] before their doors, but would have all things put in their mouths [gathered for them].' When the Indians [the intended berry bringers] wearied of this arrangement, the French [the aspiring clubbers] turned to extortion and robbery [clubbing] and before long [once the Indians—the ones upon whom power was being exerted—defined these exertions as beyond acceptable limits] there were bloody wars [force relations]. A similar situation seems to have arisen in the Virginia colony: despite land rich in game and ample fishing grounds, the English nearly starved to death when the exasperated Algonquins refused to build fishing weirs and plant corn."[58]

Why wouldn't the French fish? They fancied themselves clubbers, not berry bringers—literally. And we see here that the dynamic of the clubber-berry bringer relationship, first outlined in theory, was not so theoretical after all.

In review, the *potential* for power is found in the intention of the stronger party in a force relation—whether he is pursuing agreement or annihilation. But the power is actually *created* by the weaker party. The settlers in this instance were pursuing agreement (bring us fish and we won't rob/extort you). And as long as the Indians acquiesced, the two parties were engaged in power relations. But the people upon whom power is being exerted define its limits, and, as was stated above, success in force relations (the *we'll rob/extort you* part of "bring us fish or we'll rob/extort you") is contingent upon one calculation: as long as the one who is exerting force has made an accurate calculation of his own fitness versus his adversary's, he can club away all he wants. Early on, these settlers were making inaccurate calculations regarding their own fitness versus their adversary, and the shaky systems (agreements) they established quickly collapsed as the Indians refused to acquiesce at all, let alone pursue the ongoing cooperation that is necessary for power relations to continue.

Most importantly—with regard to the consequences of agreement and the fact that power is transferred through its own exertion—we now see this important prediction come true: following even the most elementary agreement as a consequence of the infusion of power throughout the system, the party who is initially less influential does use its influence (however slight) to begin to define limits on the future exertions of the more influential party. This is how agreements accumulate. At the point of each new exertion (e.g., the demand that fishing weirs be built), new agreements are reached, new limits are set, or the system disintegrates, and the parties return to (or initiate) force relations.

The British/French seriously misunderstood the dynamics of the remarkably tenuous power relation in which they were just barely engaged; they exerted as though they were rulers; the Indians defined their exertions as beyond acceptable limits, and the parties entered force relations. Even though the nascent system did disintegrate, we still find confirmation that balancing (however slight and short-lived) began immediately. In order for the French/English to continue in power relations with the Indians, they needed to make concessions (accept new limits on their exertions). In short, they needed to allow balancing to occur. It was their ignorance regarding this basic rule of human interaction (power is transferred through its own exertion) combined with their miscalculation regarding their own fitness for force relations that led them to failure. Stephen Greenblatt also points out the practical ramifications of the Europeans' refusal to engage in balancing and their concurrent inclination to keep clubbing: "'To live by the sweat of other men's brows' was the enviable lot of the gentleman . . . But the prospect could not be realized through violence alone, even if the Europeans had possessed a monopoly of it, because the relentless exercise of violence could actually reduce the food supply."[59] We can add to this accurate and pragmatic perspective a prediction from Reciprocity: To govern, which is precisely what the French/English were attempting to do in dictating the actions of the Indians, one must have some system (agreement) in place; therefore, force becomes power, and to govern purely by exertion is to constantly increase the potential for the transference of power from oneself. Following even the simplest agreement (that single cooperative link between Europeans and Indians), power was created. The Europeans refused to acknowledge that the Indians had influence over their actions, and thus, even these most basic systems faltered almost as soon as they formed. But neither the Europeans nor the Indians could escape this basic rule of human interaction, and unless one side was to be utterly annihilated, agreements had to form and hold.

In actuality, agreements were forming in many ways: most prominently between the settlers themselves (Articles of Confederation; Declaration of Independence; Constitution), but also between the Europeans and the Indians and between the independent Indian tribes (often in the form of confederations). And all of these agreements created power. Thus, slowly, the condition moved from those initial interactions in an uncharted wilderness to interactions under established systems—i.e., from force to power. And the inevitable balancing was not only reinitiated but sustained.

There is no question that the Indians lost their land as a result of the simple fact that the settlers increased their force-relation fitness (and sheer numbers) to a point that their abilities overtook the Indians. But again, it is not inherently logical that a defeated group would later be empowered to pursue restitution. How did the American Indians move from the state of being utterly overrun to their position today in which they are full citizens of the system established by those who overran them and, in addition, are even granted privileges denied to other citizens of that same system? The answer: a system that acknowledges the fact that power is transferred through its own exertion was formed around the Indians.

As Americans vested themselves with power (formed agreements), they also—albeit unwittingly—vested power in the Indians. Following integration (accomplished through agreements such as House Concurrent Resolution 108), the Indians were able to pursue the tracing back that justice requires, and ultimately, they were able to *expand* agreements. * Simply, the Indian experience can only be explained by the fact that system creates power, power is transferred through its own exertion, and the eventual exposure of exertions leads (backward) to justice (balancing) and finally expansion— that

---

* House Concurrent Resolution 108 shows us the official language by which agreements are expanded in the integrative sense. The resolution begins: "[I]t is the policy of Congress, as rapidly as possible, to make the Indians within the territorial limits of the United States subject to the same laws and entitled to the same privileges and responsibilities as are applicable to other citizens of the United States, to end their status as wards of the United States, and to grant them all of the rights and prerogatives pertaining to American citizenship." (HCR 108). Thus, we see in fact, what we have been discussing in theory: the HCR 108 agreement integrated the Indians and allowed them to acquire power under preexisting agreements (described as privileges, rights, and prerogatives). And this integration was one step along the continued expansion of agreements (ongoing acquisition of power) that the Indians would come to accomplish.

is, if two separate systems aren't to develop. While the general improvement in the settlers' force capacity explains their victory in war, the system those settlers set up (both created by and acknowledging Reciprocity) explains the subsequent Indian ascendance.

To begin to understand the process that led the parties out of force relations and toward expansion, we must look first for agreement. Agreements between the United States government and the Indian tribes were known as treaties—and there were many: "Between 1778, when the first treaty was signed with the Delawares, and 1868, when the final one was completed with the Nez Perces, there were 367 ratified Indian treaties."[60] In other words, agreements accumulated, and interactions moved from force relations to power relations.

Edward P. Smith, commissioner of Indian affairs, summed up the situation in 1873, five years after the final treaty was signed.

> We have in theory over sixty-five independent nations within
> our borders, with whom we have entered into treaty relations as
> being sovereign peoples; and at the same time the white agent
> is sent to control and supervise these foreign powers, and care
> for them as wards of the Government. This double condition
> of sovereignty and wardship involves increasing difficulties and
> absurdities.[61]

So, as was stated above, a system quite literally formed *around* the Indians. And while certain sovereign privileges were acknowledged, the treaties also included numerous and various instances of language such as: "The said Indian nations do acknowledge themselves and all their tribes to be under the protection of the United States and of no other sovereign whatsoever."[62] And: "The said bands also admit the right of the United States to regulate all trade and intercourse with them."[63] The Indians acquiesced. And what we witness here is the establishment of a strange sort of hybrid between separate systems and actual integration. Of course, in a system that recognizes and facilitates Reciprocity, the tracing back that justice requires will lead to the remedy of unjust laws and the expansion of agreements. The fact that this situation actually attempted to *establish* separate (sovereign) systems makes the predicted effects of balancing—the expansion of existing agreements to accommodate and empower more diverse/factions—even more obvious. Even under the circumstance in which two separate systems were being attempted,

Reciprocity's requisite tracing back led to the remedy of unjust laws under a single united system.

So agreements were formed, balancing emerged, and the tracing back began (and continues). But what about expansion (the acquisition of increasing amounts of power under existing agreements) as opposed to simple integration? Well, casino privileges are not an example of mere integration.* What we witness, in fact, following (and simultaneous with) the often problematic integration of the Indian nations, is a steady (though sometimes subject to reversals) expansion of agreements, enabling Indians to accumulate more and more power within the system. George Washington (who, as we have already seen, waged a brutal war with the Indians) and the other men who created the accumulation of agreements that constitutes the United States had no intention of empowering the Indians, yet such empowerment did commence and continue.

To insert another minor but apt example of Reciprocity's effect on Indian-American relations (and the consequent accumulation of power and expansion of agreements by Indians): the case of *Montana v. Blackfeet Tribe of Indians*, decided in 1985, held that "statutes [are to] be construed liberally in favor of the Indians."[64] Simply, this means that "ambiguities in treaties and statutes dealing with Indian rights are to be resolved in favor of the Indians."[65] But why? Isn't it supposed to be "to the victor go the spoils"? Why wouldn't ambiguities be resolved in favor of the United States government, the winner of the underlying conflict and the more influential (powerful) party in the system? The answer: because power is transferred through its own exertion, and the Indians hold the position of the party upon whom power was exerted. Thus, they hold the position of the party to whom power was transferred. This agreement to resolve ambiguities in the favor of Indians is

---

*   The Indian Gaming Regulatory Act of 1988 is just one high-profile act of balancing (on behalf of both the U.S. government and Indian tribes) instituted as the Indians acquired more power within the system and sought to redefine limits. "The major purpose of the Act, according to Congress, was 'to provide a statutory foundation for Indian gambling operations as a means of promoting economic development, self-sufficiency and strong tribal government'" (Indian Gaming: The National Information Site of the American Indian Gaming Industry). Additional examples of the redefinition of limits (and balancing) include: the Indian Civil Rights Act of 1968, the Indian Self-Determination and Education Act of 1975, the Indian Child Welfare Act of 1978, and the Indian Tribal Justice Act of 1993.

simply another example illustrating how the power that was transferred to the Indians is now allowed to be exercised. The treaties were the agreements that created power in the first place, and here we see Indians acquiring more power even under those agreements. *Montana v. Blackfeet Tribe of Indians* does not alter the original treaties but expands them in a way that further empowers the Indians.

Having recognized the Indians' systemic ascendance, the key question becomes how have the Indians accomplished this expansion of agreements? And the answer, of course, is resistance. Adam Fortunate Eagle Nordwall and his allies did not seize Alcatraz in 1969 because they actually wanted that rock; Indian activists did not barricade the Bureau of Indian Affairs in 1972 because they had a burning desire to inhabit that building. Those were acts of broadcast designed to expose exertions and facilitate the transfer of power. And they (among many others) worked—it was during this period that President Nixon led the revision (re-vision) of relations between the Indians and the U.S. government, saying, "The Indians of America need federal assistance—this much has long been clear. What has not always been clear, however, is that the federal government needs Indian energies and Indian leadership if its assistance is to be effective in improving the conditions of Indian life. It is a new and *balanced* relationship between the United States government and the first Americans that is at the heart of our approach to Indian problems [emphasis added]."[66] It should not surprise us that President Nixon would mention *balance* while being actively engaged in the process of balancing that Reciprocity predicts.

As promised, I'm not going to attempt to recount the entire American-Indian experience in a few pages. Hopefully, the facts I've presented are enough to illustrate with broad brushstrokes the process Reciprocity makes possible. By exposing exertions, the Indians also exposed the underlying transference of power, and therefore, (through this strategy of resistance) they were able to take that power and use it to redefine limits and expand agreements.

At the risk of overstating the case, I am comfortable saying that Reciprocity (the fact that power is transferred through its own exertion) and the consequent balancing that emerges is the only satisfactory explanation for the success (or even existence) of any restitution movement. A just system (one that is engaging in balancing) must redress past exertions, not merely as a matter of principle, but as the inevitable effect of the fact that power is transferred through its own exertion. Otherwise, it remains in violation of this basic rule of human interaction. And it remains unjust.*

Exertion, transference, redefinition/resistance, justice, tracing back, expansion: beginning from the point of force relations in the wilderness and moving forward, Reciprocity provides a concise explanation of the Indian experience (as well as the experience of any once-oppressed group).

Now, as an aside, I think it's worth asking: Who cares about that pre-system wilderness? Why should we be interested in such a wilderness today when no uncharted territory remains on earth? After all, the world is mapped and claimed. There is not a single square inch that has not already been subsumed under some system. So why worry about what went on in a pre-agreement wilderness? I say it is important precisely because—in point of fact—much (if not most) of the globe actually remains uncharted wilderness. Remember, the *wilderness* of which we speak is not a physical place, a forest, desert, or open sea; instead, it is the absence of agreement. Today's wilderness exists in the space *between* the systems. This is the space where wars are waged. This is where people are killed. That wilderness is the most important topic of our

---

* Today, Cambodia continues to grapple with this fact. In an editorial that appeared in the *Wall Street Journal* on August 1, 2006, the U.S. Ambassador to Cambodia, Joseph A. Mussomeli, described the dilemma this way: "One of the greatest crimes of the 20th century has gone unpunished for 30 years. Between 1975 and 1979, the Khmer Rouge systematically tortured, starved and 'smashed' approximately 2.2 million fellow Cambodians, or between one-fourth and one-third of the entire population" (Mussomeli, A12). After describing these atrocities in greater detail, the Ambassador then intuitively reaches the conclusion to which Reciprocity (the fact that power is transferred through its own exertion) leads: "Thirty years later, the country is still lost and broken, in more than just political and economic terms . . . All the country's flaws—from trafficking in persons to the rampant corruption that pervades every level of government—have been exacerbated by the failure to bring the leaders of the Khmer Rouge to justice [i.e., failure to engage in balancing] . . . A Khmer Rouge tribunal is a necessary first step to healing the three-decades-old wound that continues to fester. There will remain severe limitations on how far Cambodia can reform until some degree of justice [i.e., balancing] is rendered" (*Ibid.*). It is bold of the Ambassador to attribute "all of the country's flaws" to this single cause, but Reciprocity explains, supports (and predicts), everything the Ambassador wrote, including the fact that he wrote it to begin with. His editorial is, after all, an act of broadcast, which, as we will see, is the most common opening strategy for individuals seeking to pursue balancing.

time. And once we recognize the truth (and consequences) of Reciprocity, we begin to find answers as to how that void (absence of agreement) will be filled (or not).

Without delay, we must recognize that an astute review of all we have covered makes it clear that the answer to the absence of agreement is not simply agreement. (Wouldn't that be nice?) Instead, it is by looking not to the origin of power (agreement) but the ends to which Reciprocity ultimately leads (when systems do not fall back to force relations) that we will find our answers. Upon such an examination, it becomes quickly apparent that Reciprocity's answer for the eradication of the dangerous pre-system wilderness begins at the point where the rulers fall below the rules. Before that, we cannot have systems that acknowledge Reciprocity because we cannot have agreements that regulate the resolution of disagreements (why remain above the rules if not to retain ultimate authority over resolution? And why maintain authority over resolution if not to preempt/diminish the transfer of one's own power?). Thus, regimes that do not recognize Reciprocity cannot engage in justice/balancing (either internally or externally), and the world must ultimately rely on the return to force relations to redefine limits on the actions of such rulers. It is only after this point when rulers fall below the rules that systems do not dissolve to force relations and wars are avoided. (Please remember that "placing the ruler below the rules" is not precisely synonymous with the "rule of law" because under "rule of law" a ruler could attempt to rule via inherently unjust laws. Instead, explicitly placing the ruler below the rules is the starting point from which a system can come to comprise agreements that recognize and facilitate the fact that power is transferred through its own exertion).

Now, what I am about to write is so obvious that it probably doesn't need to be written, but here it is anyways: placing the rulers below the rules can only be done in two ways—internally or externally.

Internally: it is done through revolution. Be it violent or Velvet, every revolution centers around the effort to place the ruler below the rules. Externally: it is done by creating complete acquiescence (surrender) through force relations (as the North did to the South in the United States at the end of the Civil War and as the Allies did to Japan and Germany at the end of World War II); or by weakening the *regime* through competition (not empowering it through agreement) as was done during the cold war; or, and this can get extremely tricky, by strengthening the *people* through *direct* interaction (as might be happening in China), not indirectly or in such a way that the strengthening effort can be *re*directed (as, it turns out, was happening in the tragically ineffective UN Oil-for-Food Programme in Iraq).

Again, how this movement—the placing of rulers below the rules—will happen on a country-by-country basis cannot be predicted by Reciprocity (or anyone). The details of such victories must vary. But an understanding of the fact that power is transferred through its own exertion gives us two important pieces of knowledge. First, we have seen that such a movement toward balancing is unavoidable. It is inscribed in the very genetics of human interaction (since the ruler is in fact being influenced by the rules to begin with). Second, we know the equally unavoidable pattern (if not the precise details) by which each movement will proceed: exertion, transference, and redefinition. One way or another, the exertions of rulers do transfer power to those upon whom the exertions are made. As we will see in the "Broadcast" section, this knowledge has practical application because it is first through the exposure of those exertions that the transfer is facilitated. Broadcast reinforced by a refusal to acquiesce (a refusal founded on the irrefutable truth that rulers are ruled by the rules—whether they choose to admit it or not), those are the activities that must be initiated, encouraged, and unwaveringly supported if the dangerous pre-system wilderness is ever to be eradicated. The leader of a system that acknowledges Reciprocity must abide by the rules that govern that system (if the system is to survive). On the other hand, dictators cannot allow agreements to regulate the resolution of disagreements because they cannot accept their place below the rules (if *their* systems are to survive). It is only at that point—when agreements can regulate the resolution of disagreements—that power relations can take lasting effect, both internally and internationally.

When all rulers have taken their rightful place below the rules, then we will witness, in the words of Francis Fukuyama, "the end of history." All around the world, we see ascendance similar to that of the American Indians occurring in systems that acknowledge the fact that power is transferred through its own exertion. Indian ascendance occurred because the rule of Reciprocity dictates that the less influential individuals in a system can influence the actions of the more influential individuals, not because Indians improved their force capacity or because Europeans mellowed as they became Americans.

Francis Fukuyama uses Hegel's theory of the lord and bondsman as the starting point from which he interprets the direction of our current condition as follows: "The inherently unequal recognition of masters and slaves is replaced by universal and reciprocal recognition, where every citizen recognizes the dignity and humanity of every other citizen, and where that dignity is recognized in turn by the state through the granting of *rights* [emphasis in original]."[67] Fukuyama (via Hegel) is describing the exact same direction

I'm describing here; in fact, Fukuyama even uses the word *reciprocal*. But neither he nor Hegel precisely explain *how* we reach that state where human dignity is recognized (*human dignity* itself is a vague, indefinable term better substituted by Reciprocity: "The inherently unequal recognition is replaced by a recognition of the fact that power is transferred through its own exertion and that those upon whom power is being exerted define its limits"); nor do they explain how rights emerge (Reciprocity reveals that rights are not acquired through "granting"—a word that implies power flowing down from above—but won as the codification of resistance).

This is why I said at the outset that I've "dug this out" from between the cracks of the works of other thinkers. In their undeniably valuable studies, Hegel, Fukuyama, and many others approach the rule as I have written it, describing the effects of Reciprocity without describing Reciprocity. Hegel's proposition that human beings are driven forward by a need for recognition is a theory of human action (and possibly nature). I happen to agree that the desire for recognition is a significant driving force behind human behavior. However, based on the data we have today (which Hegel did not have), that theory cannot explain the balancing and ascendance we see around us. But the rule of Reciprocity can. As soon as an agreement is reached (even one as imbalanced as "you're a slave, and I'm your master"), power (the ability to influence the other's actions) is created and infused throughout the system. And balancing must occur if the system is to survive. Was it a desire for recognition that drove George Washington (and Candace Lightner) forward? Maybe. Maybe not. I don't know. But I can say for certain that in both instances there was a desire for justice (balancing), and that desire could not have been satisfied without the fact of Reciprocity. In the end, the desire for recognition doesn't lead to Reciprocity (or reciprocity); Reciprocity (the fact that the slave has influence over the master's actions) leads to recognition! Without this fact, the bondsmen would remain bondsmen (the berry bringers would remain berry bringers), and all the desire in the world would get them nowhere (unless they improved their fitness for force relations—or fled).

Taking this same topic (ascendance) from a different perspective, the desire for recognition may very well explain the emergence of tyrants, but the desire for berries—as synecdoche for material wealth and security—may also be an equally valid explanation. Tyrants do tend to collect a lot of stuff: there are no naked emperors in reality; they clothe themselves quite lavishly. In the end, it may very well be the desire for recognition that pushes lords up. But here are the truths that bring them down: Power is transferred through its own exertion; the point at which power is exerted is the point at which there exists the greatest potential for its transfer; the people upon whom power is being exerted define its limits; when the purpose of an exertion of power includes the maintenance of power, then power is maintained through calculated conservation, not unlimited exertion.

The historical evidence I cite (the events on the bus, the Declaration of Independence, American-Indian ascendance, and so on) not only comprises a series of separate events but also constitutes a collection of data that is explained and predicted by a single rule. It is the unavoidable oscillation of power created by Reciprocity that facilitates the ascendance of slaves and Indians and women and minorities of every sort who are at first held low. Why doesn't the clubber just continue to enforce the same limits that he established at the outset? It's not because he *wants* to raise up the berry bringer; it's because agreements must accumulate, and as they do, influence is dispersed.

Here now is the full process Reciprocity describes. And while reality may (will) reveal rapid advances, sudden reversals, simultaneous developments, and events "out of order," in the end, this is the aggregate, overarching direction:

> Force→Agreement→Accumulation of Agreements→External Authority→Agreements that Regulate the Resolution of Disagreements→Justice→Expansion/Rights→Oscillation

A system that acknowledges Reciprocity is a system that enters a state of oscillation, an animate yet stable state of exchange. As we will see immediately below, as well as in the "Power" section that follows, systems develop stability through oscillation while the rigidity that results from the attempted imposition of equilibrium (however well or long it may be maintained) always remains fragile.

Oscillation

Having traced the development of system from pre-system force relations to the final state of stable exchange, which is summarized by the word *oscillation*, we can now briefly consider the implications of oscillation for both the systems that institutionalize it and those that don't.

As I stated at the start, Foucault and others have tackled society's grand architecture, the development and consequences of our vast matrix of organizational machinery—the entire power grid, so to speak. I've simply gone inside to expose a single wire. Reciprocity is that wire, which eventually becomes evident in the system itself. Reciprocity leads to a state (*state* meaning *condition* but also *nation*) wherein the agreements themselves (once they come to embody the truth of Reciprocity) serve as the conduits through which the transfer of power occurs. A nation that codifies oscillation achieves a state of stable exchange.

Clearly, oscillation is not the condition of suppressed resistance that some often mistakenly refer to as the "stability" of oppressive regimes. Oscillation is true stability, achieved through perpetual adjustment. Without balancing, a body falls. And this metaphor is borne out as fact in systems as well: a state can achieve true stability only through the acknowledgement and facilitation of the exchange/transference of power that will inevitably happen within it. If a state does not allow for those inevitable exchanges, it is not stable—it is static. Such a state is paralyzed, brittle, and it will break. Václav Havel, writing of Communist Czechoslovakia in 1979 (a mere eleven years after Soviet tanks rolled in), confirms this fact, "The system has become so ossified politically that there is practically no way for . . . noncomformity to be implemented within its official structures."[68] So we see our choices: oscillation or ossification. The Soviet Union ossified. Cuba ossified. North Korea ossified. And so on.

Dictatorships cannot explicitly allow for oscillation. So *oscillation* is one word describing both what *is* going on in systems that acknowledge Reciprocity and what *isn't* going on (or isn't being acknowledged) in systems that don't.

The fact that power is transferred through its own exertion guarantees that transferences (however minor or suppressed) are happening as long as exertions are being made. Since exertions are constantly being made, transferences are constantly occurring. Oscillation describes that condition of constant exchange. Not surprisingly, we have already encountered this phenomenon in earlier examples. For instance, people were victimized by excessive exertions on the part of the police. These excessive exertions transferred power to those victims and their allies who redefined limits, and those limits were subsequently recorded as law/policy (the victim's doctrine). Police officers were victimized by excessive exertions on the part of civilians. These excessive exertions transferred power to those victims and their allies who redefined limits, and those limits were subsequently recorded as law/policy (the victim's doctrine). The ability to influence the others' actions *oscillates* between policemen and civilians in response/proportion to the exertions each group makes.

As I write this, General Motors (GM) is struggling to compete against foreign automakers who are operating under different systems (accumulations of agreements). As a result of agreements it entered into with the United

Auto Workers (UAW), GM is paying workers to sit in a "Job Bank" (a room monitored by supervisors) and do no work.[69] The UAW and GM are operating under a vast and complex accumulation of agreements, and I am not isolating this "Job Bank" agreement as the cause of GM's troubles. I'm simply highlighting it because it provides an excellent example of oscillation: the UAW was formed to remedy the imbalance of power that existed between owners and employees (who are generally dubbed "management" and "workers"). At the outset of the Second Industrial Revolution, of which the mass production of cars was but a part, owners had far more power than workers. The workers who formed the UAW were initially empowered by the (admittedly imbalanced) agreements they had with owners and then by the agreements they reached amongst themselves, particularly their coordinated refusal to continue to work, which is the capitalist equivalent of abandoning the system and falling back to force relations. In addition to forming agreements (creating power) amongst themselves, the workers used various forms of broadcast to expose the power that had been transferred to them by the exertions of management; they then took that power (ability to influence the other's actions) and used it to redefine the limits on management's power. In other words, the workers unionized. And over time, the union itself became more influential/powerful than management. How do we know that the union became more powerful than management? No owner would agree to the "Job Bank" concession—paying workers not to work—unless that were the case. Today, perhaps, the union has overexerted, transferred power (the ability to influence the union's actions) to management, and management will redefine new limits. This is oscillation.

Should workers be exploited by management? No. Should management pay workers to sit in a room and do nothing? No. Why? Because both of these extremes, if allowed to endure indefinitely, will lead to the demise of the entire enterprise and, thus, will harm both the workers and the management. Agreements that lead to such injury are, by definition, unjust. So balancing (and tracing back) must occur if injustice is to be avoided.

The rule of Reciprocity rests on the assumption that people will always exert and holds as one of its consequences the fact that those upon whom power is being exerted define its limits. This explains why we don't see a straight line from first agreement to stable oscillation, only a pattern of progress clumped around an axis. Different people define different limits in different ways under different circumstances. It also explains why limits vary from system to system. For instance, countries without a wide variety of races (today, most societies remain racially homogenous) will not experience the development of a victim's doctrine arising from exertions related to race. So if issues do arise, their systems will have less balancing with regard to race. Should there be racism on earth? No. Is there? Yes. How will it be eliminated? Through the process of exertion, transference, and redefinition that underlies oscillation.

The word *should* has now appeared a number of times in a short space, and it is appropriate to address this topic under oscillation because it is here where we see Reciprocity's relationship to *should*. The relationship is simple: Reciprocity does not dictate how a ruler should act toward the people or how the people should act toward the ruler. Instead, Reciprocity shows us how *shoulds* emerge.

Most earlier thinkers who took up the topic of the relationship between government and governed dealt frequently in *shoulds* because they were operating from the perspective of prescription; they were forced to make *should* statements to describe, in forward-looking fashion, the inevitable patterns that stem from Reciprocity and lead to systemic oscillation, patterns we have since experienced in fact. For instance, where Rousseau wrote, "A people, since it is subject to laws, *ought* to be the author of them [emphasis added],"[70] we can now take out *ought* and substitute *are* (in systems that acknowledge Reciprocity). Today, we have many systems in which the people *are* the authors of their own laws.

Returning once again to the idea that I "dug this out" from between the cracks of previous works, we can see that, in many ways, Rousseau—and the scholars who have studied him—are witnessing the effects of Reciprocity without having enough data to enable them to recognize Reciprocity itself. Though Rousseau never makes the statement in these precise terms, the idea that agreement creates power is inscribed between the lines of his *The Social Contract*. First, the very concept of "contract" implies that "[t]he state [i.e., the embodiment of power] [is] the outcome of a[n] . . . *agreement* among men [emphasis added]."[71] And, as has been previously observed, "Rousseau insists that if authority is to be legitimate the . . . acceptance must be both universal and unconstrained."[72] As Rousseau writes, "All legitimate authority among men must be based on *covenants* [emphasis added]."[73]

Rousseau is far from alone in his proximity to the truths that underlie Reciprocity. It has already been observed that both Hobbes and Locke agreed that "sovereignty derived its authority from the assent [acquiescence] of the people."[74] Even Hobbes, who placed little confidence in human progress (he famously described mankind's condition as "solitary, poor, nasty, brutish and short") saw that a first limit must be set—"Under [Hobbes'] account, the sovereign created by the original contract wields absolute untrammeled power . . . The *only* right individuals retain post-contract is to resist [set a limit against] the sovereign if they are threatened with death [emphasis in original]."[75] Today, the conclusions which those earlier thinkers reached now serve as the premises from which we begin. Once that first limit is set, once acquiescence occurs, both subject and ruler (albeit unwittingly) are placed beneath that original agreement, oscillation begins, and—here we reach our own, verifiable conclusion—the sovereign system that denies the existence of oscillation eventually topples (because it cannot make the adjustments requisite for balancing).

History (human interaction) has unfolded, and through its unfolding, it has revealed truths that were not available to our predecessors; Reciprocity and its effects consistently fill in the gaps that Rousseau and others left behind. For example, Rousseau's position on slavery has been summarized as "No agreement to enter into slavery could be a valid one because any agreement which is wholly to the advantage of one party and wholly to the disadvantage of the other is void in natural law."[76] Here, Reciprocity fills in the gap left behind by that vague placeholder—natural law. The slavery agreement is void (we would say destined for redefinition) because it violates not natural law (whatever that is) but because it attempts to oppose the fact that power is transferred through its own exertion—as well as *all* of Reciprocity's consequences. Slavery survives exclusively on the attempted denial of oscillation. It is for this reason (the fact that oscillation cannot be avoided) that we see, empirically, that wherever slavery appears the slaves are eventually freed.

Here is another of Rousseau's statements that can be profitably augmented by an understanding of Reciprocity: "Finally, any covenant which stipulated absolute dominion for one party and absolute obedience for the other would be illogical and nugatory. Is it not evident that he who is entitled to demand everything owes nothing? And does not the single fact of there being no reciprocity, no mutual obligation, nullify the act?"[77] From this study, we now know that there is *always* "reciprocity" *and* Reciprocity following any agreement. Thus, Rousseau is saying that it is "illogical and nugatory" to make an agreement that rejects the essence of agreement. It is, actually, impossible. But again we see Rousseau circling around Reciprocity as he invokes the word *reciprocity*.

Where Rousseau writes, "There is undoubtedly a universal justice which springs from reason alone, but if that justice is to be acknowledged as such it must be reciprocal,"[78] Reciprocity now enables us to define the concept of justice itself while also filling in the vague placeholder "reason" with Reciprocity. And we end up with, "There is undoubtedly a universal balancing which springs from the fact that power is transferred through its own exertion." That Rousseau then goes on to use the word *reciprocal* once again simply supports the assertion that he is writing about Reciprocity without the benefit of the data needed to identify the rule.

And one last example (just for fun): "Since the aim of war is to subdue a hostile state [that is, of course, based on the assumption that the stronger party in the force relation is pursuing acquiescence and not annihilation—otherwise the aim would be to destroy a hostile state], a combatant has the right to kill the defenders of that state while they are armed . . . war gives no right to inflict any more destruction than is necessary for victory. These principles . . . are derived from the nature of things; they are based on reason."[79] Now, once the combatant is unarmed (we are presuming he has laid down his arms/surrendered), then he has acquiesced. That act of acquiescence immediately transforms the relation from force to power, and the ongoing exertion on the part of the clubber (again, assuming he is seeking acquiescence) will only transfer power *away* from himself. Thus we could rewrite Rousseau's conclusion this way: "In war, it is not to the advantage of the stronger party to exert more force than is necessary to achieve surrender, and having achieved surrender, there is no advantage to continue forceful exertions. This principle is derived from Reciprocity; it is based on the fact that power is transferred through its own exertion." Again, "the nature of things" and "reason" are vague placeholders for the rule of Reciprocity. Power is transferred through its own exertion; the people upon whom the power is being exerted (in Rousseau's example, the vanquished soldiers) define its limits, and to exert is to transfer power away from oneself. Thus, once victory (acquiescence) has been achieved, the maintenance of power following acquiescence requires *calculated* conservation, not unlimited exertion. And in the long term, it requires acknowledgement of (and agreements that expressly facilitate) oscillation.

We encountered this same placeholder phenomenon earlier when we considered Bracton's perspective on monarchy: "[H]e is a king as long as he rules well but a tyrant when he oppresses [resists Reciprocity] by violent domination the people entrusted to his care. Let him, therefore, temper his power [ability to influence others' actions] by law [the victim's doctrine], which is the bridle of power [because it holds agreement], that he may live according to the laws, for the *law of mankind* has decreed that his own laws bind the lawgiver [emphasis added]."[80] That final phrase can be more accurately recast as: "Reciprocity demonstrates that agreements influence the actions of rulers."

Nietzsche, who disdainfully dismissed the social-contract perspective, wrote, "A pack of savages, a race of conquerors, themselves organized for war and able to organize others, fiercely dominating a population perhaps vastly superior in numbers yet amorphous and nomadic. Such was the beginning of the human polity; I take it we have got over that sentimentalism that would have it begin with a contract."[81] And though Nietzsche presents us with his own wonderfully vivid description of clubbers ("a pack of savages, a race of conquerors") in the wilderness, he cannot escape the fact that, at some point, agreements were reached (how else could those conquerors "organize others"?), and the genie of Reciprocity slipped like a wisp from the bottle, unseen by those savages as they numbed themselves on the intoxicating spirit of domination.

We began this "System" section with our cavemen, and we end here with Nietzsche's savages. But now we see that the point of the caveman discussion was not to speculate on what happened in prehistoric times but to map out, simply and clearly, what *will* happen within each and every system. Vicious clubbers do appear. Tilts do occur. Balancing can be (severely) disrupted on both the micro level (a terrible imbalance occurred in the bathroom of Brooklyn's Seventieth Precinct made worse by the wall of silence that surrounded it) and the macro level (at this writing, Castro's Cuba remains a prison). Yet every place we seem to see reversals, there is only progress; every effort to eradicate Reciprocity eventually erupts in even more balancing.

In this review of the causes and effects of system, we have seen Reciprocity's balancing effect emerge in many ways, from the interactions of children on a playground to the American Revolution. Reciprocity explains what happened between the mother and driver on the bus, the formation of MADD, the trial of Rodney King, the fall of kings, and the constitution of countries. We have moved from cavemen through King Hammurabi (and his present-day counterparts) to the resignation of the president of the United States. And one rule has bound these events together.

In the end, Reciprocity doesn't merely explain what has happened; it predicts what will happen. Whether it is acknowledged or not, power is transferred through its own exertion, and therefore, oscillation exists in every system. It cannot be avoided. Consequently, every system that is to survive must eventually acknowledge this fact. When that will happen is unpredictable. How it will happen is unknowable. But that it will happen is inevitable. Such a future sits at the foundation of human interaction and cannot be erased.

This is the topic we will now take up in the section on "Power": as human beings develop systems, some succeed while others fail. What can Reciprocity tell us about the efficacy (or lack thereof) of certain strategies of influence? And what new, hidden truths have we yet to uncover about the nature of power itself?

Power

Power is real. It is not an abstract concept but is, instead, a measurable phenomenon whose effects are (often) visible. I began this study with an unqualified endorsement of Michel Foucault's insight that "power comes from below." That statement was then proven through logical explication as well as empirical observation, with the exploration of the development and effects of system providing many examples that verify Foucault's assertion. But all of that was based on the particular definition of power adopted at the outset—power is the ability to influence another's actions.

Based on that definition, power is real, not abstract. The ability to influence another's actions actually exists; it can be observed and measured. In the bus example, the mother had the ability to influence the driver's actions (he did apologize), but he had the ability to make us all get off the bus (more power). Candace Lightner was able to influence the actions of the nation's lawmakers. Rodney King transferred power to the police by speeding, evading, and resisting arrest; then police exertions transferred power back to him, after which he influenced their actions by taking them to court. And Abner Louima influenced the actions of the officers who arrested him, using the power that their actions (and others' exertions against prior victims) transferred to him.

But is "the ability to influence another's actions" the definition of power that Foucault and others put forth? Well, not in so many words (or so few). In fact, most considerations of the topic of power have produced far more sinuous definitions. Here, for example, is how Foucault defines power in the same work in which he states so simply that it comes from below.

> It seems to me that power must be understood in the first instance
> as the multiplicity of force relations immanent in the sphere in
> which they operate and which constitute their own organization; as

the process which, through ceaseless struggles and confrontations, transforms, strengthens, or reverses them; as the support which these force relations find in one another, thus forming a chain or a system, or on the contrary, the disjunctions and contradictions which isolate them from one another; and lastly, as the strategies in which they take effect, whose general design or institutional crystallization is embodied in the state apparatus, in the formulation of the law, in the various social hegemonies.[82]

So M. Foucault was an undeniably brilliant man. Still, I contend that the definition of power we've been working with is much easier to understand and more useful than that sentence we just read.

At the outset, I stated that my objective is simple: "to expose and explain the rule of Reciprocity in a clear, concise, and vivid way." And I believe my definition of power remains consistent with that objective. I do not believe that, working from Foucault's definition above, we could make the assertion that power is not an abstract concept. Now, in fairness, Foucault also once characterized "a relationship of power" as "a mode of actions upon actions,"[83]* and this brings him much closer to us; but while undeniably concise, that definition is also relatively imprecise (relative to "the ability to influence another's actions"). Once we recognize that power is the ability to influence another's actions, we see that the exercise, act, mode (or method) of exerting that influence (taking "an action upon actions") is the *manifestation* of that power. An action upon actions may be a manifestation of power, but it is not power. Just as an object's falling to the ground is not gravity, but a manifestation of gravity.

In addition, it is important to make a distinction between the ability to influence another's actions and the ability to elicit a reaction. If the first caveman raised his club to strike the second caveman and scare him away, he would have taken an "action upon actions," but the second caveman would have reacted solely on instinct in the moment. The next time the two cavemen

---

*   The full quote is: "Let us come back to the definition of the exercise of power as a way in which certain actions may structure the field of other possible actions. What would be proper to a relationship of power, then, is that it be a mode of actions upon actions . . . To live in society [i.e., what we would call an accumulation of agreements, or system] is . . . to live in such a way that some can act on the actions of others [i.e., what we would call influence the actions of others]. A society without power relations can only be an abstraction" (Foucault, "The Subject and Power," 343).

met, the second caveman might raise *his* club and startle the first caveman away. Those are not examples of power relations; they are force relations in which actions are causing reactions. Now, the next time those two cavemen meet, if the second caveman runs away at the sight of the first caveman, then their ongoing interactions would have been altered by the first interaction, and one could conclude that the first caveman had established power over (ability to influence the actions of) the second caveman but only because the second caveman had acquiesced to the first caveman's desire for distance (and an agreement had been formed implicitly).

Why am I going into this? Two reasons: first, we've now entered a section entitled "Power," so it is simply sensible to reexamine our definition; second, and far more important, Foucault's statement above—"power must be understood . . . as . . . force relations"—stands in direct contradiction with the distinction between force and power that I proved in the previous section. (This is another reason why "a mode of actions upon actions" is relatively imprecise—absent that accurate distinction between force and power, two individuals in a wilderness hammering away at each other with clubs could be characterized as engaging in "a *mode* of actions upon actions," yet power would be utterly absent.)

Foucault is not alone in combining the phenomena of force and power. So it is probably worthwhile to reconsider my distinction between the two and ask this important question: can power be created without force? And if not, is there really a separation? Agreement creates power, but is force the only path to agreement? And if force *is* the only path to agreement, isn't it also the only path to power, and couldn't we then make the blanket statement "force creates power"? After all, force was the path to agreement (and power) for our cavemen.

Well, consider this: I'm married. My marriage is an agreement. The agreement created power: my wife has an ability to influence my actions in ways others do not—thus, she has power over me. For instance, she can call me up and ask me to pick up dinner on my way home with the reasonable expectation (actually, complete certainty) that I'll do it. She cannot however call a total stranger (or even a friend) with the same expectation. No agreement, no ability to influence the other's actions (power). Now, was our underlying agreement (marriage) forged through force? No. It was forged through love.

Force is not necessary to form sincere agreements (Gandhi led his country into new agreements precisely by *refusing* to engage in force; and Martin

Luther King, Jr. successfully employed a similar strategy in pursuit of new agreements). But agreements (implicit, explicit, lopsided, or harmonious) are necessary to create the ability to influence another's actions.

In pursuit of additional insights into power and how it's wielded, I'm going to use Reciprocity as a lens through which to view some of the institutional strategies human beings employ in the effort to influence each other's actions. And I'm going to consider what more Reciprocity can tell us about this phenomenon: some systems fail while others endure. In the process, we'll also look specifically at the strategies that are used to suspend, preempt, diminish, or deny Reciprocity (both its premises and effects).

The Denial/Diminishment of Reciprocity

Now, what does it mean to say that the ability to influence another's actions is transferred through its own exertion? Quite simply, it means the more I attempt to influence your actions, the more able I make you to influence mine. But certainly, we see many obvious instances in which this rule appears to have failed. Doesn't this immediately disqualify Reciprocity as a rule and perhaps even refute the whole idea outright?

No.

First, in order to understand Reciprocity's status as a rule, we must remain aware of where, when, and how this rule arises and applies.

An organism existing in an isolated state (free from interaction with any other beings) will still be affected by evolution—that is to say, even alone it will be affected by its genetic suitability, adaptability, fitness for the environment in which it exists. Similarly, that isolated organism will also be affected by gravity. Even alone, it will be held on earth by gravity's force. Such statements are not true for Reciprocity. An individual existing in an isolated condition will *not* be subject to Reciprocity. The fact that power is transferred through its own exertion is not a law of nature. It is a rule of human interaction.

Men are not molecules. We have consciousness and will. We can exert. We can resist. We can revolt. And we can acquiesce. But in order to engage in these acts, we must interact, and in the process of interacting, we do frequently form agreements. Those agreements create power, and the rule of Reciprocity emerges. OK, we already know all this. But why is it that the rule appears to fail in so many instances?

To answer this, let's look again at evolution and gravity. Would a seedless watermelon evolve in nature? It's less than likely. Since the abundance of seeds makes a watermelon more able to perpetuate its species, seedlessness runs counter to the survival of the fruit. There is little if any evolutionary advantage for a watermelon to develop the trait of seedlessness, so seedlessness would likely not evolve on its own. Yet seedless watermelons do exist. Does that mean that evolution is refuted? No. It means that an *effort* was made to manipulate the genes of those watermelons and suspend the natural direction of evolution. Now gravity: can a 150,000-pound machine float in the air? No. Yet such machines do take flight daily. Does that mean that the law of gravity failed? Again, no. It means that gravity is temporarily suspended by the *effort* of engines and pilots. To take another gravity example: If I were to toss a ball into the air, obviously, it would fly upward before it descended. If I concealed my toss and then only let you see that ball as it rose, you would say with certainty that the law of gravity is imprecise, that sometimes objects do fly upward. Around the world, at any given moment, human effort within systems is doing the equivalent of sending objects flying upward: propping up unjust regimes (regimes that deny balancing) by preempting, suspending and diminishing Reciprocity—with *effort*.

And here we find another interesting commonality that arises out of those gravity/evolution analogies: the efforts that scientists and farmers make to produce a seedless watermelon do not refute evolution; instead, the seedless watermelon emerges from an understanding of the phenomenon of evolution (more precisely, an understanding of the genetic variation among offspring that makes evolution possible), and it ultimately validates evolution's underlying truth. The same is true for airplanes and gravity; it is, in part, an understanding of gravity that allows pilots and planes to successfully resist it. And the same is true for authoritarian regimes and Reciprocity: as we will see, the efforts that dictators make to resist Reciprocity consistently reveal their understanding (and confirm the truth) of the rule.

We have already seen that systems attempting to deny Reciprocity exist in a condition that is always close to force relations (fight or flight are the only options for those entrapped in such systems). Now we can point out a shared characteristic that emerges from such close kinship: force relations must have a beginning and an end, and systems in which an effort is made to deny Reciprocity must also have a beginning and an end. On the other hand, power relations facilitated by systems that acknowledge Reciprocity and institutionalize oscillation, can continue indefinitely.

We are going to spend some time now looking at the exertion of power as it manifests itself in larger patterns. Along the way, we will necessarily consider the tools that are used to "suspend gravity" (strategies of both exertion and concealment). But abandoning the previous section's style of starting simply and then building, we're going to head straight to the complex.

Religion, that is to say the theocratic strategy that uses the claim and promise of a relationship with God (or some similar transcendent experience) to influence others' actions, provides a logical starting point in the examination of what Reciprocity reveals about power and how it's wielded.

Theocracy

In the beginning, the more powerful individuals in a system claim their power comes from above. Hammurabi defined it that way: he ruled "by the command of Shamash." King John did as well: British monarchs ruled by divine right. This common initial assertion comes as a natural consequence of the fact that most systems are at first forged through force, and the condition following acquiescence is a severely imbalanced one (although balancing begins immediately). Thus, at the outset, in this condition wherein it is not at all apparent that power comes from below, it benefits the ruler to emphasize the top-down model of power.

Now, if one wishes to perpetuate what we have already seen to be the false principle that power comes from above, there is no more powerful way to do that than to invoke God (the ultimate "above" entity) as your own authority. The advantages are obvious and immediate: as long as you are able to maintain the position of mediator between man and God, your pronouncements are both irrefutable and custom-made to provoke the influence you desire. And the theocratic strategy provides advantages to both ruler and ruled, simultaneously easing the establishment—and the pain—of oppression. As Nietzsche astutely points out, the theocratic system can help transform "submission before those one hates into obedience to One of whom they say he has commanded this submission."[84]

For the sake of clarity, and with the desire to avoid stimulating the sorts of prejudices that will block minds from honestly considering these ideas, it is essential to the validity of what follows that I make this simple point clear: I'm not discussing religious *beliefs*, but religious structure instead. It is religious structure employed strategically as a means of influence (not the details of specific faiths) with which we are concerned. But can the two be separated? Yes, they absolutely can. Catholicism is a religion. Buddhism is a religion. Islam is a religion. Judaism is a religion. Yet they all put forth different beliefs. Thus, the institution of religion and the terms of faith for any given religion are separate subjects.

So the question becomes—setting aside specific theologies, what is religious structure? There are, in fact, common qualities to the structure that supports each faith. And this generic structure can be examined on its own.

Here's how we'll start.

Picture an ordinary box. This unremarkable object will serve as our model for the generic structure of religion. Now, place three ordinary boxes in a row. For the sake of illustration, these will become the structures supporting the beliefs of the world's three dominant religions. But before we start adding details, let's begin by placing the exact same thing inside each box: the promise of a certain reward that is defined as superior to the common human condition. That is precisely what every religion holds within itself—the promise of a reward that transcends the common human condition. And most (though not all) religions put forth faith in God and abidance by God's wishes/instructions as the path along which one reaches that uncommon condition (i.e., how one enters the box).

Now, to move forward with this illustration employing the world's three main religions, take one of your blank boxes and begin decorating its exterior with these stories and images: the creation of heaven and earth by God in six days followed by a day of rest, the creation of man from clay (call him Adam), the creation of woman from Adam's rib (call her Eve), a garden, a snake, an apple, also add a man named Abraham, highlight his son Isaac and all of Isaac's descendants. Then attach a Star of David, a menorah, yarmulkes, and Passover to the outside of this box.

Now, turn to your second box. Take all the *same* images and stories from the box we just decorated and place them on this second box except do not transfer over the Star of David, the menorah, yarmulkes, and Passover. Instead, attach the image of a crucified man, his resurrection and other miracles, a virgin mother, twelve disciples, baptism and communion.

Now, take your third box. Put that same man named Abraham on it, highlight his first son Ishmael and all of his descendants, then add a man named Muhammad and his miracles, a place known as Mecca, mosques, prayer rugs, and the fasting month of Ramadan.

You now have before you three very sketchy representations (many more details could be added to each) of the world's most prominent religions: Judaism, Christianity, and Islam. And each one holds within itself the exact same thing: the promise of a relationship with God. But in these particular instances, the three religions hold within themselves not only the exact same promise (a relationship with God), they also hold within themselves *the exact same God*: the God of Abraham. Judaism, Christianity, and Islam all worship the God of Abraham, and since Abraham was a monotheist, they all worship the same God. This is not a trick of logic but a fact of history. Look again at all three boxes and you'll see that we placed Abraham on each. As Bruce Feiler has explained (and explored): "The great patriarch of the Hebrew Bible is also the spiritual forefather of the New Testament and the grand holy architect of the Koran. Abraham is the shared ancestor of Judaism, Christianity, and Islam."[85] So the insides of these boxes each hold a relationship with the God of Abraham. The *insides* are all the same.

Of course, where these three boxes differ is in the designs on their outsides, in the specific beliefs and practices that help adherents enter into a relationship with God. Many take the teachings of Islam (follow the Islamic faith) as their route into a relationship with God. Others follow Judaism, and still others choose Christianity.

What does this have to do with Reciprocity? Almost nothing except that it is essential to define what we're talking about when we talk about religion. We're talking about the box before it is decorated.

To be even more precise, all of this means:

One. We're not talking about the inside of the box. It is an empirically verifiable fact that many people have gained great benefit from establishing a relationship with the God (or promise) of their understanding, no matter how such a relationship was reached. One could only attribute a blanket rejection of this fact to the type of intellectual prejudice and contempt that prohibits open-minded investigation. Whether or not one believes in God (or any religious promise), one cannot deny that countless individuals have been aided by such a belief just as one cannot deny that God (and/or religious promise) has also been used as the justification for the infliction of countless injuries (a blanket rejection of that fact could only be attributed to the sort of blind faith that also prohibits open-minded investigation). That is not the debate in which we're interested here—although, as will soon become apparent, the particular model of religious structure we're considering helps us understand how such division (between aid and injury) does occur.

Two. In addition to being disinterested regarding anyone's relationship with God (or any particular promise), we're not concerned with any individual's relationship with the box (no matter how it may be decorated). For once we see religious structure in this way, we also come to recognize at least two obstacles that the decorated box presents to those pursuing its promise.

First, it is quite easy—and common—to become stuck on the outside of the box, to stop at those surface images and never make it inside at all. This explains how individuals commanded not to carve idols do in fact construct such idols (out of both statuary and people) and how others who profess the oneness of the universe then create a certain separation from their fellows by adorning themselves with new "spiritual" names and special garments. A list of such examples could be extended indefinitely, with each instance being explained by the same phenomenon: people becoming stuck on the outside of the box.

Second, in addition to becoming stuck on the outside of the box, it is also possible (perhaps even tempting) to open the box and pour one's own self inside—one's preexisting fears, hatred, prejudices, and overall preferences—then declare those to be the will of God. This can, of course, carry catastrophic consequences.

Three. Finally, we're not talking about the decorations themselves—the histories, stories, rituals, symbols, myths, metaphors, and metonymies that help define the beliefs of individual religions. Those details are irrelevant to the relationship between religious structure and Reciprocity. We're simply talking about the box. The box has qualities before anything is added to it. So it is the box itself, undecorated and independent—vulnerable to the whims of human ambition and able to be co-opted as a tool to influence others' actions—upon which we will apply Reciprocity's gaze.

So the first quality to note as we examine the unadorned box is that the box is finite; it has edges. It is an entity unto itself, and this is by design. Clearly, it does not have to be so—particularly since its insides are held to be universal. Thus, we must acknowledge that this is a choice. It happens on purpose and through some mechanism. So the question becomes, how are those borders defined? And the answer is clear: they are defined by agreement. Dispensing with simile (religious structure is like the unadorned box) and dealing now with reality, we see that religious structure is an accumulation of agreements. The borders are defined by the agreements reached among adherents. And here we run head-on into Reciprocity: agreement creates power. Thus religious structure is unavoidably a framework for influence, an instrument of power, and as such, it is subject to Reciprocity.

In taking up religious structure's relationship to Reciprocity, the box's second quality jumps out instantly. The box has an outside and an inside. Those borders (defined by agreement) that we noticed not only separate one box from another but also separate inside from out. And here we encounter our first strategy to counter Reciprocity: this outside-inside division becomes a mechanism for concealing exertions. If it is true that power is transferred through its own exertion, then anyone seeking to maintain a system (maintain agreement and thus power) that does not acknowledge this fact must develop a strategy to deny or diminish the potential for transference. Concealment is such a strategy. God as guise explains both why theocracy emerges as a primary governmental system—it enables rulers to exert without acknowledging the transference of power their exertions potentially open up—as well as why it fails to endure—religious structure denies balancing.

Theocracy's simple strategy (and institutional effort) for denying Reciprocity can be most clearly expressed as: "I can see inside the box, and you can't." "I can tell you what God wants (or what it takes to reach the promise)." Thus, divine, clerical, monastic, or spiritual authority, no matter how well intentioned, can become a mask behind which exertion is concealed: My exertion didn't transfer power to you because it wasn't my exertion; it was God's. And God's exertions don't transfer power to you because God is an entity against which you cannot, in turn, exert influence.

A system that declares that the ability to influence another's actions comes from above and that the power transferred by the higher entity's exertions (as carried out through the exertions of that higher entity's agents) cannot in turn be exercised by those upon whom the power was initially exerted is not only an unjust system (one that denies balancing) but is also a system that violates three irrefutable truths of power that have already been proven: agreement creates power; power comes from below; and power is transferred through its own exertion.

Within the context of a governmental system, the invocation of God, no matter how sincere, attempts to divorce authority from agreement. But in order to have a system that states authority comes from God, one must have the agreement that authority comes from God. An agreement that states "authority comes from a source other than this agreement" is obviously paradoxical and ultimately self-canceling. In order for a system to assert that God bestows the ability to influence another's actions, we must *agree* that God bestows that power; thus, the agreement is still creating the power. So we need not look at the details of religious laws to see why theocracies fail. The concept of God emerges naturally from humanity's interactions with its surroundings. Theocracies emerge (at an initial state of extreme imbalance) because they provide a number of advantages to rulers: they pull power away from agreement; they contend power comes from above (not from the rulers, but from the "One of whom they say he has commanded this submission"); and they deny the fact that power is transferred through its own exertion. But once we recognize the truth of Reciprocity, we see that theocracy's perceived advantages are also the reasons for its downfall. Theocracy fails because it is a power structure (accumulation of agreements) that defies the essence of power. If not for those truths of power with which theocracy unavoidably conflicts, the system would reign worldwide to this day.*

Again, just as force relations must have a beginning and an end, systems in which an effort is made to resist Reciprocity (and deny oscillation) must also have a beginning and an end. As human interaction proceeds and the rule of Reciprocity (along with its consequences) becomes more and more apparent, religion assumes its new role as a system within a system. Religion's realm of influence (power) is redefined not as the ultimate authority over man's interactions with man (secular laws—arising out of exertion, transference, and redefinition—take on that role) but as the arbiter of man's relationship to God.

None of this has any bearing whatsoever on whether or not God itself exists (or whether any of the assorted religious promises are true). Again, the failure of religious rule is not explained by a failure of faith, but by a fallacy of power, the false principle that power comes from above. The freeing of religion from the responsibility of governing society actually strengthens the power (influence) of its agreements. The "separation of church and state," as it is referred to under the United States' accumulation of agreements, frees religion from its structural contradiction with the basic rule of human interaction (since it no longer acts as the systemic authority) and thus absolves it from the need to engage in fear-inducing exertions and coercion.

As we'll see when we examine Reciprocity's relation to authoritarianism, coercion (i.e., any threat—including eternal damnation—intended to influence others' actions and preempt balancing) is corrosive. It weakens the

---

* To those who would assert that it is science, not Reciprocity, that has undermined the theocratic system, I say this: for better or for worse, science cannot undermine faith because religion can always pursue a retreat into causation. Science has revealed remarkable truths at the inconceivably tiny subatomic level as well as the inconceivably large realm of galaxies. But religion can always retreat to causation and ask, "What caused those atoms, protons, electrons, and those nebulae?" "What caused the Big Bang?" If string theory ends up untying the conflict between general relativity and quantum mechanics, religion can then ask, "Well, where did those 'strings' come from?" Scientific discovery cannot adequately explain theocracy's failure (or the failure of any dictatorial system for that matter); it is theocracy's inherent conflict with Reciprocity, the fact that, ultimately, it cannot acknowledge oscillation, which explains the system's inability to govern human interaction (and thus its recurrent demise).

foundation of any system as it wrenches power from its source then attempts to hammer it back downward. But for now, having used Reciprocity to expose the inherent weakness in generic religious structure (irregardless of faith), we can briefly explore an interesting aspect of faith itself.

In many of the world's major religions, there exists a fascinating belief-based relationship with Reciprocity. At the same time that religious structure denies Reciprocity, religious faith often supports it:

> Do unto others as you would have them do unto you, for this is the law and the prophets. (Christianity)

> What is hurtful to yourself do not do to your fellow man. That is the whole of the Torah and the remainder is but commentary. (Judaism)

> Do unto all men as you would wish to have done unto you; and reject for others what you would reject for yourselves. (Islam)

> Hurt not others with that which pains yourself. (Buddhism)

> Tzu-Kung asked: "Is there one principle upon which one's whole life may proceed?" The Master replied, "Is not Reciprocity such a principle?—what you do not yourself desire, do not put before others." (Confucianism)

> This is the sum of all true righteousness—Treat others, as thou wouldst thyself be treated. Do nothing to thy neighbor, which hereafter Thou wouldst not have thy neighbor do to thee. (Hinduism)[86]

This concept, referred to by Christians as the golden rule, stands consistent with the rule of Reciprocity, and it is not surprising that religious institutions, dedicated as they are to exploring human experience in their own fashion, would share similar insights into a rule that sits at the foundation of human interaction. Reciprocity confirms that you are well advised to "do unto others as you would have them do unto you" not because it's holy, but because it's human.

Now, if the concept of Karma is more to your liking, consider this additional belief-based consistency:

It is nature's rule, that as we sow, we shall reap. (Buddhism)

Whatever a man sows, that he will also reap. (Christianity)

A liberal man will be enriched, and one who waters will himself be watered. (Judaism)

What proceeds from you will return to you. (Confucianism)

Thou canst not gather what thou dost not sow; as thou dost plant the tree so it will grow. (Hinduism)

Whatever man soweth, that he shall reap. If he soweth trouble, trouble shall be his harvest. If a man sow poison, he cannot expect ambrosia. (Sikhism)[87]

"As you sow, so shall you reap" is revealed by Reciprocity as well: Officer Volpe sowed trouble and reaped trouble; kings who created victims became victims themselves; the dictator who rules by fear (denies oscillation) lives in fear. And the list goes on. Religion dictates guidelines on our behavior. But those guidelines themselves (particularly the ones that endure) sometimes arise from the very same pattern of exertion, transference, and redefinition that Reciprocity predicts. Within the metaphor of "as you sow, so shall you reap," *sowing* equals exerting, which equals transferring power. Systems that acknowledge Reciprocity and allow for oscillation (systems that facilitate balancing) are, in effect, reinforcing and even codifying "as you sow, so shall you reap." Murder transfers power. Adultery transfers power. Theft transfers power. The laws of the church, which we call morality, are merely the victim's doctrine under a different label. This is why I went to such pains to separate structure from belief above—it is religious structure (and its ultimate opposition to oscillation), not necessarily the details of specific beliefs, that opposes Reciprocity. Any given theocratic system might put forth beliefs consistent with Reciprocity, but religious structure will always contradict it.

Also, in considering the unsustainable nature of the theocratic system, one must acknowledge that God (as authority) can be as useful to those who wish to place rulers below the rules as it is to rulers attempting to remain above them. In short, invoking the will of a deity can be a strategy of the clubber who wishes to maintain power, but it can also be a strategy of the berry bringer seeking to redefine limits. Individuals pursuing redefinition often invoke God as a motivating force. As we have already seen, the Declaration of Independence is a document written in pursuit of Reciprocity, arising from Reciprocity; it is a redefinition of limits by those upon whom power was being exerted, but it is also an exertion itself, one that engages in its own strategies of diminishment by drawing legitimacy from the invocation of a higher source. America's revolutionaries rested their own cause in part upon "the Laws of Nature and of Nature's God."[88] Of course, we have already encountered this with Rousseau: Reciprocity fills in the gap left behind by such vague placeholders as "the nature of things." Here, Reciprocity is precisely the rule to which the drafters of the declaration are referring with their imprecise term, *the laws of nature*. But the fact that this additional term—*Nature's God*—was employed by these men as the justification for the pursuit of justice and a just system shows us that God (and a system that credits God as the source of power within human interaction) can be as dangerous to the king as it is to his subjects. That is precisely why many of today's authoritarian states outlaw religion. Just as agreement puts the ruler below the rules (whether he admits it or not), faith puts God above the dictator.

In the modern authoritarian system, the common God is dispensed with and replaced by the common good. Exertions are then concealed, and the denial of Reciprocity is justified under this new guise. It is that strategy, its consequences, and its problems that we will now take up.

Authoritarianism

This could easily be the shortest subsection of this book. Authoritarianism, by definition and explicit intention, exerts effort against balancing and attempts to outlaw oscillation through the centralization of power. And that's why it fails.

To support this simple truth, I would then present the Soviet Union's 1936 Constitution (Stalin's Constitution), which attempted to outlaw oscillation by placing total control of the country's lands and laws in the hands of a single body, the Supreme Soviet of the USSR. According to that constitution, the jurisdiction of the Supreme Soviet—the "highest organ" of the state—encompassed these areas among others: decisions regarding war and peace; foreign trade; establishment of the national economic plans of the USSR; approval of the single state budget; administration of the banks, industrial and agricultural establishments; administration of transport and communications; organization of state insurance; raising and granting of loans; establishment of the basic principles for the use of the land; establishment of the basic principles in the spheres of education and public health; legislation on the judicial system and judicial procedure, criminal, and civil codes; laws on citizenship of the Union; and, of course, control over the observance of the constitution itself.[89]

And with that, this subsection would be done.

The elimination of Reciprocity is the raison d'etre of the authoritarian system. The entire point of the authoritarian state (whatever form it takes) is to impose "stability" (which, as we have already seen, is actually stasis) by concentrating power in a central authority. So the point of this subsection is not to prove that the authoritarian system attempts this but to examine the strategies it uses, and in the process to show that rather than refuting Reciprocity, the authoritarian regime's efforts in fact prove the truth of the rule.

Now, Reciprocity has already helped us understand the process by which dictators often seize power, that is, seize—for personal use—the power that is transferred to them (as members of an oppressed populace) by the exertions of the previous ruler: Utilizing broadcast, the aspiring dictator exposes the exertions of the outgoing regime then takes the power transferred by those exertions and uses it against that regime and/or the revolution's opponents. He then co-opts the people into new agreements that diminish/deny Reciprocity under the pretense that these agreements are necessitated by the current, unsettled circumstances (i.e., that the exertions of his enemies—or whoever is "unsettling" the circumstances—are actually transferring power *to* him).

But that is just the beginning. In examining the common strategies of influence employed among these systems, the most interesting question is not "how do tyrannies rise?" but "why do they fall?" To answer this question, I am going to look first at what Reciprocity can tell us about how those dictators who do seize power manage to *maintain* it. Having rejected God as their guise, how do they perpetuate systems without acknowledging that their own exertions transfer power away from themselves (that is to say, without acknowledging oscillation)? And to start, I am going to raise one of those "hidden truths" about power, an implication embedded in the rule of Reciprocity itself, which we can now make explicit: power can be lost.

Ask the Romans, the Nazis, American slaveholders, Republicans, Democrats, and the chairwoman of your local PTA. Ask anyone. Ask yourself. To say that "power is transferred" is to say that it can be lost—by degrees—through its own exertion. The rule of Reciprocity underlies all systems whether the system's leaders embrace or deny this fact, and exertion-transference creates that pulsing heart of oscillation beating (however faintly) at the center of every system. Because exertion and transference can never be completely eliminated if a system is to survive, the dictator who attempts to exert without loss (that is, attempts to deny oscillation) must mitigate or mask his exertions in some way in order to minimize transfer.

The common-good concept that prompted the transition to this subsection is such a mitigating mask. And it is a mask we have already encountered.

Lenin: "It's *better* [in the common good] for dozens and hundreds of intellectuals to serve days and weeks in prison than that 10,000 should take a beating [emphasis added]."[90]

Minh: "To-day we need to *consolidate* this freedom and independence . . . [which] requires the sacrifice [for the common good] . . . of our compatriots all over the country [emphasis added]."[91]

Mao: "The present Chinese People's Political Consultative Conference is convened on an entirely new foundation. It is representative of the people of the *whole country* [representative of the common good] and enjoys their confidence and support [emphasis added]."[92]

Castro: "This is the party of the country . . . [I]t is the duty of all of us to see that the congress is an example of revolutionary *unity* [embodiment of the common good] [emphasis added]."[93]

Pursuit of the common good excuses the diminishment of Reciprocity; it justifies the notion of exertion without transference; it justifies the inhibition of balancing; it justifies the denial of justice, all on the grounds that the weight of this common good tips the scales in favor of the ruler's exertions, particularly those efforts being made to centralize power. Early on in the bus observation, I stated that the concept of concealed exertion becomes profoundly important later. This is where it becomes important. This common-good mask is designed to create the illusion that the efforts to concentrate power (deny oscillation) are not for the benefit of the dictator but for the good of the people; in other words, the notion of the common good implies that the regime's exertions are not being made against the people but on their behalf and, therefore, don't transfer power away from the dictator.

In reality, this notion of the common good is made manifest (and reinforced) in many ways both small and large, including mandatory participation in events such as May Day, "Working Saturday," and "Gold Week," as well as the requirement to display the slogan "Workers of the World, Unite!" in the windows of shops,[94] not to mention the nationalization of private property, and so on. And manifestation of the mask-like nature of the common good can even be found in the name of the nation itself. North Korea's official name is the Democratic People's Republic of North Korea. Why this redundancy? Isn't every democracy by definition the people's? Isn't *Democratic People's* a bit of overkill? Obviously, one wouldn't need to label the country with this double-mask pseudonym and synonym for the common good if the country were actually the people's. And more important to the topic at hand, one wouldn't need this obfuscation at all if not for the truth of Reciprocity. If Kim Jong Il could hold power more securely by calling his country "The Kim Jong Il Nation of Terror," he undoubtedly would. Why conceal *any* exertion, why engage in *any* minimizing strategies if not for the fact that power is transferred through its own exertion? Reciprocity provides the only explanation for this strategy of concealment: power is transferred through its own exertion, so the dictator's exertions must be (strategically) concealed. In the instance of North Korea, the very name of the country serves as merely one of the many masks behind which the ongoing effort against balancing is being (poorly) concealed.

"Tyranny, as Tocqueville warned, need not announce itself with guns and trumpets. It may come softly."[95] That's true. And when it takes that route, it invariably tiptoes in behind the elimination of those laws (victim's doctrines) that facilitate balancing—free speech, free press, etc.—replacing them with new laws that protect the *ruler* from victimization. But tyranny may also arrive with trumpets performing the march of the common good, announcing a revolution that is, in fact, not a revolution (the placing of the ruler below the rules) but merely the procession of dictators through a revolving door—one tyrant taking over where the last left off. Here, the common good acts as guardian, giving the new dictator enough time to get through that door then standing outside once he's in, serving as sentry and providing security against attack. Absent the willingness to establish laws that recognize Reciprocity, such a sentry, accomplice, or mask (whatever metaphor you prefer to illustrate the strategy of concealment) is always necessary.

Much of what we've talked about with regard to the common good as justification for the elimination of justice (balancing) has focused on the word *good*—the strategy of masking exertions behind the assertion they are good for the people, not the dictator. But the concept of *common* brings its own advantage as well. If there is a common good, then there is one good. Therefore, the power to administer that good can (and, perhaps, must) be centralized. It follows naturally that the consolidation of power will be justified by this purported unity (Minh: "Today we need to consolidate this freedom and independence"; Castro: "congress is an example of revolutionary unity").

There are so many illustrations of this (the entire communist system is built upon this ideal of the common good) that it hardly seems necessary to highlight one. But I will because the particular instance I have in mind not only illustrates the invocation of the common good as rationale for the consolidation of power but also provides a real-life example of precisely the sort of masking that Reciprocity predicts: due to the fact that power is transferred through its own exertion, dictators must attempt to conceal the true nature of their regimes; thus, they will often *feign* balancing at the same time they make efforts to suppress it.

In October 2002 as the United States and its allies were preparing to go to war against Iraq, Saddam Hussein held an election. At that election, 11,445,638 ballots were reportedly cast—and 11,445,638 people voted for Saddam Hussein.[96] That purported, one-hundred-percent victory demonstrates a number of points, but we'll look only at two (for the moment):

First, it shows us that Saddam Hussein felt compelled to pretend that balancing existed in his country—and not just any kind of balancing, but the sort of balancing that arises after the "club" has moved from persuasion to punishment, when violence (or its threat) has been abandoned as the primary means of influence. Saddam attempted to accomplish this by putting on that ridiculous charade of free elections. Following the election, Izzat Ibrahim, vice chairman of Saddam's Revolutionary Command Council* stated that this election (in which Saddam stood as the sole candidate) was "a unique manifestation of democracy which is superior to all other forms of democracies even in these countries which are besieging Iraq . . . Someone who does not know the Iraqi people, he will not believe this percentage, but it is real . . . We don't have opposition in Iraq."[97] So this election makes visible the strategy we've been discussing—there was a "common good" embodied by Saddam Hussein—while also presenting another effort at concealment: the (remarkably poor) illusion of balancing (or more precisely, a poor attempt to mask its absence) through the mechanism of the vote.

But this particular example also demonstrates beyond a shadow of a doubt that extraordinary efforts had been made to centralize power. "We don't have

---

* Note that twenty-three years after Saddam seized power, governmental bodies were still labeled "revolutionary." Why? Revolution in perpetuity is just another mask and effort to oppose Reciprocity: as long as the "revolution" continues, those new rulers never have to fall below the rules. In this way, "vive la revolución!" becomes not a clarion call for the recognition of Reciprocity, but a calculated cover for ongoing oppression.

opposition in Iraq" says it all. Saddam had the ability to influence the actions of a remarkable number of people—"Some voters stuffed bunches of ballots into boxes, saying they represented the votes of their entire families."[98] Yet the centralization of power, in the end, is also just an illusion; albeit one that is performed far more convincingly.

Here is another one of those important "hidden truths" that's not so hidden: the statement that power is transferred through its own exertion says that power in action is power transferred, and therefore, it *cannot* be centralized. If power comes from below, it cannot be centralized. If power is created by agreement, it cannot be centralized because agreement, by definition, requires at least two parties vested with the ability to influence each other's actions. Thus, Reciprocity reveals the fatal flaw hidden in the authoritarian regime's strategy of power: power is never centralized.

Within the authoritarian state, those upon whom power is being exerted are denied the opportunity to exercise the power they receive through those exertions (denied justice), but the power is there just the same, and it builds until that moment (the "door-closing" event, the "reactive agent") arises when those to whom power has been transferred take it and wield it to define new limits. Reciprocity's second consequence comes into play here: the people upon whom power is being exerted define its limits,—not the people who are exerting. And as long as those upon whom power is being exerted continue to cooperate, the system will survive. Delving deeper into power as we've defined it, we begin to uncover new layers: agreement creates power, and acquiescence creates agreement. But acquiescence (the acceptance of power) is not an isolated act—it is an ongoing behavior. So what is acquiescence in action? Acquiescence in action is cooperation.

This word, *cooperation*, becomes vitally important here. As we've already established, power is the ability to influence another's actions, and it is drawn from agreement. But if cooperation sustains agreement and agreement establishes power, then cooperation sits as the foundation of power. This is a simple truth, with profound consequences. Cooperation—not naked exertion—is the essence of power. Every agreement (however imbalanced) is sustained by cooperation. In sum, the parties to any agreement must operate together (co-operate) if that agreement (and thus, the system) is to endure. This is true for any situation in which power exists—from rulers and ruled to parents and children. Authentic power is created by co-operation. The more co-operation exists, the more true power exists; the less co-operation exists (i.e., the more any system relies on the authoritarian, because-I-said-so approach) the less true authority exists. Here, Reciprocity's third consequence becomes apparent: power comes from agreement; agreement requires co-operation; therefore, the ability to influence another's actions is maintained through co-operation (calculated conservation) not unlimited exertion.

A system that acknowledges Reciprocity recognizes the necessity of co-operation. Authoritarian states do not.* While the dictators emphasize the consolidation of power (which creates monolithic immobility), the liberators, as we have already seen, emphasize power's unavoidable dispersion and the ongoing motion—oscillation—that co-operation requires:

Washington: "This government . . . *containing within itself a provision for its own amendment* [emphasis added]."[99]

Gandhi: "The real power is in your hands."[100] [As clear a statement of governmental co-operation as there has ever been].

Mandela: "Ours has been a quest for . . . a democracy in which the government . . . will not be able to govern the country as it pleases [but will co-operate instead]."[101]

Havel: "There must be structures that in principle place no limits on *the genesis of different structures* . . . These structures should naturally rise from *below* [first emphasis added]."[102]

The logic behind this necessity for revision is not complicated. To say that the system will fail if the agreements that constitute the system can't be revised is the same as saying that the agreements will fail when they are no longer agreed to, that is, when co-operation disintegrates. Thus, systems that acknowledge Reciprocity are amenable to amendment, providing for co-operation even in the revision of the system itself. Authoritarian regimes, on the other hand, attempt to create authority by eliminating co-operation. As Fukuyama observed, "the

---

* This is why agreements with dictators prove futile so frequently—the leaders of those authoritarian regimes cannot completely co-operate, cannot allow themselves to fall fully below the rules (if they wish to sustain their authoritarian reign). Such co-operation can only prove to be: 1. a mask behind which they conceal abrogation of the agreement(s) and/or pursue a separate, perhaps more dangerous agenda or 2. the beginning of the end of the authoritarian regime. Unfortunately, the counter-party or -parties to the agreement(s) cannot control which of these outcomes will materialize.

Soviet state systematically attacked all potential competing sources of authority in Russian society, including opposition political parties, the press, trade unions, private enterprises, and the Church."[103] What does it mean to say that the "Soviet state . . . attacked all potential competing sources of authority"? It means that the leaders of that authoritarian regime refused to co-operate with those institutions. This did not strengthen the system; it weakened it. Reciprocity reveals that such authoritarian actions do not foster authority, but merely sustain naked acquiescence (and produce stagnation).

Oscillation guarantees motion; agreements accumulate (and expand) through resistance. By combining those two facts, we see that if the system doesn't allow for that inevitable resistance, then it retards expansion; and the unavoidable friction caused by the attempt to suppress oscillation creates cracks in the system's structure. In other words, the attempt to dismantle this fundamental rule of human interaction—power is transferred through its own exertion—creates a fatal flaw in the foundation of any system. But we don't have to rely on the metaphor of the cracked foundation to make this point. The logic itself is simple. You can't have an agreement that destroys the essence of agreement: all parties are vested with the ability to influence each other's actions. Once you have an agreement, you have that fact. Thus, you can't have an enduring system that attempts to deny the fact that power is vested throughout.

This section is called "Power," but it could just as easily have been titled "Exertion." Here, as we review (re-view) the various exertions of authoritarian regimes through the lens of Reciprocity, we see that those regimes attempt to manufacture top-down authority through the establishment of laws that remain under the ruler's sole control. This is an effort against Reciprocity. But even though this particular effort to create centralization is visible, it's also an act of concealment. The misdirection works like this: the United States of America has laws; the Democratic People's Republic of North Korea has laws; See, we're the same! France has a constitution; the USSR has a constitution; See, we're the same! That's why the distinction between rule by law, rule of law and the rule of Reciprocity is so important. Rule by law is (and the rule of law can sometimes be) both an effort against Reciprocity and a strategy of concealment.*

Once we understand the truths of Reciprocity, we also begin to understand why human history—those grand exertions, transferences, and redefinitions that become inscribed in common memory—has proceeded as it has. For here is another hidden truth: the fact that power is transferred through its own

---

* We saw this clearly in Stalin's Constitution, a document in which the rule of law attempts to outlaw the rule of Reciprocity.

exertion means that power is nowhere permanent. The system that acknowledges Reciprocity reflects this fact and achieves longevity through the recognition that power resides in the agreements, not the leaders, instilling influence in offices not officeholders, empowering principles not personalities, and establishing processes that make the transfer of power not only predictable but required.

On the other hand, succession is a problem in systems that don't acknowledge Reciprocity and don't allow for oscillation. Given that individuals—no matter how remarkable—are always temporary, the conundrum is obvious: if we all agree that George Washington has final autonomous authority (the final say), what are we left with when George Washington dies? A lack of agreement—an absence of system. Why can't the authoritarian ruler's power simply be passed along like an object from successor to successor to successor without disruption or interruption?* The answer is found in the same truth we've been looking at all along: power cannot be centralized. Recognizing this, we now see that a deeper question underlies the entire discussion; the real question becomes: if power cannot be centralized, if it is instead in constant motion, how is it grasped? And we see that it is grasped in the same way that it is created: through acquiescence (i.e., fidelity to the agreement). The more sincere the fidelity is, the greater the power; the more harmonious the agreement, the more stable the system; the more acknowledging of Reciprocity the system, the longer it endures. Every system that is maintained through exertion encounters difficulties upon the death of its rulers—and eventually fails. But a system based on fidelity to agreement (the acceptance of the fact that both parties—leaders and people—have the ability to influence each other's actions) can continue indefinitely. The point is simple: without agreement, there is no power; without power, there is no ability to influence another's actions; thus, to maintain the ability to influence another's actions (power), one must maintain agreement.

Again, any system that is not destined to fall back to force relations must become capable of balancing (not simply containing) the power held by all factions operating within it. Saddam's system, incapable as it was of balancing, was destined—one way or another—to fall back into that state force relations near which it always (and in which it often) existed. We have proven this in numerous ways already, and we will find new proof soon. Saddam Hussein (like every other authoritarian ruler) did not maintain power through

---

* Even under the most successful, long-standing monarchical systems, major disruptions, interruptions, sudden twists, and unexpected turns have characterized the transfer of power from monarch to monarch, family to family, dynasty to dynasty.

balancing (regardless of what his sham election was intended to convey). But here is an important fact we simply cannot ignore: Saddam Hussein's "election" was not held in the weeks or months following his seizing power. It was held twenty-three years after he took over. In truth, Saddam sustained his efforts against Reciprocity and held power for more than two decades.

So how did Saddam manage this? So far, we've seen that dictators make an effort to deny Reciprocity by attempting to centralize power. But at the same time, we've also seen that power cannot be centralized. Then how is the "tipped scale" actually held in that apparently non-balancing condition for so long? Given Reciprocity's second consequence—those upon whom power is being exerted define its limits—we have already concluded that as long as those upon whom power is being exerted continue to co-operate, the system will survive. Therefore, the trick is to persuade the oppressed populace to set lower limits (or higher, depending on how you look at it); in other words, encourage those upon whom power is being exerted to define even extreme exertions as being within acceptable limits. Marching in under the banner of the common good may work at the outset, but it can't explain such systems' endurance beyond the point when the common good is clearly discredited. The common good is never the source of power. The true source of power is always agreement (even if it comes in the form of naked acquiescence). So the question becomes, absent the willingness to recognize Reciprocity and maintain fidelity to the just system it produces, how is ongoing acquiescence achieved?

Of course, the first answer is fear.

In reviewing the efforts (those exertions that exist behind the masks) by which dictators maintain imbalanced systems, the evocation of fear stands out as the initial (and universal) strategy. We've seen this already in a number of places, including Natan Sharansky's penetrating and uncompromising distinction between a fear society and a free society as well as theocracy's evocation of the fear of God as the ultimate influence. But we've also seen that God can undermine the theocratic ruler. Therefore, it is not surprising that the dictator replaces mediated fear of God with direct fear of himself.*

We can easily identify many of the techniques by which dictators instill fear in the populace, including: mass arrests, secret arrests, public executions,

---

* This strategy of swapping deity for dictator is often overt: "[T]he personality cults around Lenin and Stalin were explicitly blasphemous, with the dictators elevated into all-seeing, all-providing gods . . . Hitler, too, was cast as a replacement for God, sometimes explicitly, as in a 1937 painting of a haranguing Führer titled 'In the beginning was the Word'" (Kirsch, "Twilight of the Ideologies," 15).

covert murders, secret police, not-so-secret (and visibly brutal) police—to name but a few. And what we find in even this most superficial survey of fear-inducing techniques is that opposite acts (mass arrests/secret arrests) are producing an identical effect—keeping the system from balancing. If opposite efforts can produce the same effect (holding the tipped scale in place) then we need not dwell on the details of those efforts but should search instead for some unifying phenomenon that can explain their success. If public executions and covert murders can both inhibit balancing, then it's not simply those acts that are maintaining the imbalance, but the fear those acts produce and—even more specifically—something about the nature of fear itself that makes these opposite strategies effective for the dictator attempting to resist oscillation.

Here we can apply Reciprocity to this examination of the evocation of fear to see if one of the rule's key predictions is borne out yet again. If power is transferred through its own exertion, and if rulers who attempt to deny oscillation must also minimize/mask their exertions in order to inhibit transference, then, according to Reciprocity, the evocation of fear must be a technique by which exertion can be minimized/masked.

That is, in fact, the case.

Even if the fear-inducing exertion is visible and extreme (a public execution for example), it is still a technique intended to minimize exertion. Why? Because this temporary exertion produces long-term effect. Instilling fear requires effort, but it is an effort that reduces its own need. The evocation of fear is a technique that diminishes (but does not eliminate) the need for exertion over time because once in place, the fear arises on its own—from within the populace. Knowing that jackboot thugs have beaten citizens in the streets before will likely inspire naked acquiescence among those who later encounter such thugs. In fact, in the final analysis, what does the term *naked acquiescence* mean if not "fear"? Thus, a series of well-orchestrated exertions can produce the desired effect (ongoing acquiescence)—without the need for ongoing exertion, that is to say, without heightening the potential for some sudden, uncontrollable transference coming as the consequence of a "door-closing" event. Following the initial evocation, fear emerges on its own steam, absent (or simply under threat of) the continuation of those initial visible fear-inducing exertions. Of course we've seen this truth illustrated already: Iraqis weren't driven to the polls at gunpoint; they were driven there by the fear produced by Saddam's previous exertions.

This strategy of early, fear-evoking exertion is common. Lenin did it. Minh did it. Mao did it. Castro did it. Straight off, each of those dictators engaged in open and often extreme exertions against select members of the populace in order to impose the sort of equilibrium (state of rest) such regimes require (Lenin: "It's better for dozens and hundreds of intellectuals to serve days and weeks in prison").* Of course, while the fear-inducing exertions subside, they do not cease completely. So the question arises, why doesn't the first "crackdown" simply keep the people down? Reciprocity explains why such overt oppressive onslaughts come in waves: the fear-inducing exertions inspire acquiescence, but the power that continues to be transferred from ruler to ruled subsequently builds again until visible signs of resistance emerge, at which point another calculated wave of (visible) fear-inducing exertions persuades the populace to forego exercising the power it has accumulated and so on. As each wave carries away its own Philosophy Steamer, it leaves renewed fear in its wake.

To illustrate the dictator's understanding of fear, in July 1982, in the Iraqi village of Dujail, "Saddam Hussein was nearly killed . . . when gunmen opened fire on his motorcade. The dictator's reprisal came swiftly: That night, security forces arrested 350 villagers, including 15-year-old Ahmad Hassan Mohammad . . . He described seeing 'a machine that looked like a grinder and had some blood and hair [on it and said he] saw bodies of people from Dujail.' Of Mr. Mohammad's 10 brothers, seven were murdered by Saddam's henchmen, along with 141 others from Dujail . . . [T]he purpose of the massacre was not to dispense justice [i.e., engage in balancing] but to make an example of the villagers. 'You people of Dujail, we have disciplined Iraq through you,' Mr. Mohammad recalled one of the torturers saying."[104] Thus, their explicit intention was not just to "discipline" Dujail but the entire country—the murder of approximately 150 Iraqis was intended to keep the remaining twenty-six million or so in line, which it did.

---

*   Interestingly, Lenin's infamous Philosophy Steamer upon which he summarily deported sixty-seven Russian intellectuals is a clear example of open, fear-inducing exertion. Even though "Lenin's decision to banish these potential threats to the state, rather than torture, imprison, or kill them, was unusually mild . . . By eliminating them, Lenin cannily eliminated an intellectual threat to the Bolshevik regime" (Kirsch, "Lenin's First Purge," 15). "What made the men of the Philosophy Steamer objects of suspicion to Lenin . . . was that they represented a 'third way' for Russia, between the obstinate old regime and the ruthless new one." (*Ibid.*) The men who were deported "were not all philosophers—they included historians, economists, literary critics, journalists, and mathematicians—and they were not all deported on a single ship; it took two tourist steamers, sailing six weeks apart to deposit them and their families at the Baltic Port of Stettin" (*Ibid.*).

If a system does not recognize Reciprocity and does not allow for the necessary balancing, then the system must (there is logically no other option) attempt to impose a manner of equilibrium—that state of rest—in which the power of the ruler is offset not by the power of the people but by the fear that the ruler's exertions instill. Fear quiets things down fast. And fear of the regime inevitably serves as the foundation of the authoritarian system's false stability. Reciprocity explains why there is simply no exception to this anywhere and why there never will be: unless the dictator injects some mechanism of self-restraint among the people, some phenomenon discouraging them from pursuing the balancing that naturally emerges as a result of Reciprocity, the tyrant will be forced to continue the sort of nonstop exertions that either are (or lead to) force relations. In other words, oscillation cannot be avoided; therefore, the people must be persuaded to abandon its advantages themselves. Reciprocity (and the consequent inevitability of oscillation) shows us that the supposed self-sustaining stability of the authoritarian regime is always an illusion; underneath the various masks and acts of misdirection, there are real men exerting real effort, pushing, pushing to prop up the regime and keep the imbalanced immobile system from toppling. And in the end, Reciprocity reveals the paradox of authoritarian stability: at the same time that dictators work to impose their state of rest ("equilibrium"), they must also maintain a severe disequilibrium. Such a perverse system can be sustained temporarily through effort, but it most certainly cannot proceed indefinitely on its own.

Once we recognize the efficacy (and inevitability) of fear as a strategy to "stabilize" the state, we begin to improve our understanding of the *foreign* policies of authoritarian regimes as well. One way or another, any given nation must interact with others even if such interaction comes in the form of flat-out refusal (through explicit or *de facto* agreement) not to interact. Thus, the authoritarian leader must make efforts to resist oscillation internationally as well as internally. And everything we have reviewed regarding the internal paradox of authoritarian regimes also applies to such regimes' relations to the outside world. Just as fear creates the illusion of stability at home, the fear that fear societies export abroad creates illusory stability in the international arena.

Ironically, diplomatic efforts to foster that false state of rest that foregoes balancing with authoritarian regimes tend to sustain or even increase the instability those diplomats are attempting to eliminate. To cite (for brevity's sake) an oft-cited example, Neville Chamberlain learned this lesson firsthand from Adolf Hitler: Hitler's apparent co-operation at Munich was merely a mask under whose guise he took not only the Sudetenland but also the power created by the appeasing agreement. Having no intention and—due to the nature of the authoritarian regime—being incapable of maintaining co-operation, Hitler then continued to use the influence he had gained, combined with the fear he was creating abroad, in order to pursue further concessions until the international system (accumulation of agreements) collapsed and the world entered into force relations. This strategy also provided the blueprint for Yasir Arafat's career—leverage the power created by agreements while continuing to foster the fear created by action in abrogation of those same agreements. There are, of course, others whom we could add to the list of those who have pursued (or are pursuing) such a strategy.

Just as fear provides the universal foundation of the authoritarian regime's longevity at home, it is also an ever-present ingredient in the foreign policies of those regimes. To wit: Benito Mussolini kept both his adversaries and allies in states of fear-inducing uncertainty with contradictory rejections and celebrations of war, assurances of peaceful intentions and blunt dismissals of the notion of "perpetual peace"; Nikita Khrushchev excoriated the United States while pounding his shoe upon a UN podium and, on another occasion, coupled his threats with a vivid illustration of the dictator's elimination of the deity by announcing, "History is on our side. We will bury you . . . If God existed, we would thank him for this"[105]; Saddam Hussein led the world to believe (and perhaps believed himself) that he had weapons of mass destruction;* and Kim Jong Il rattles his nuclear saber louder and louder as his country grows weaker and weaker under the starving stagnation his system has imposed. This list could also be extended with each example illustrating the same point: the threats that accompany (and facilitate) the exportation of fear are but one more mask designed to distract from (conceal) the underlying instability of the authoritarian system; in other words, such aggressive posturing is intended to hide inherent weakness behind apparent strength.

An obvious question now comes naturally to mind: if the authoritarian regime's exportation of fear and its antagonism of enemies raise the possibility of resistance and a return to force relations entering from *outside*, then why do such regimes engage in these activities at all? A benefit must exist to counterweigh the potential cost. Reciprocity assists us in recognizing that there are, actually, two explanations (one logical and one practical) for why dictators take this calculated (and sometimes miscalculated) risk.

---

* United Nations Security Council Resolutions 661, 678, 686, 687, 688, 707, 715, 986, 1284, 1382, and 1441 provide a remarkable record and detailed inventory of Saddam's exportation of fear over the course of more than a decade.

First, Reciprocity has already demonstrated that authoritarian regimes cannot co-operate without forfeiting the fear that perpetuates their false authority. Logically, this inability to co-operate would apply to foreign relations as well as internal interactions. The authoritarian regime cannot refuse to co-operate nationally while sincerely engaging in international co-operation unless it is somehow able to run these two systems simultaneously yet separately or unless it is willing to risk the chance that such co-operation abroad will seep in and undermine its ersatz authority with true authority (co-operation) at home.*

The second reason to risk external attack is purely practical. The exportation of fear and antagonism of nations actually serves a separate purpose for the authoritarian ruler, one that is yet another example of both effort against balancing and concealment of exertions combined. The leaders who refuse to acknowledge Reciprocity must find justifications for such refusal. This means that dictators need enemies. Defining one's own exertions as necessitated by the exertions of one's enemy is not only a strategy of concealment (concealing the true purpose of those exertions) but also an effort against balancing, one that makes possible this simple act of misdirection: the exertions against you (our people) aren't originating from this regime; they're necessitated by the actions of our enemy, so it is actually our enemy who is transferring its power to you.

The creation or elevation of enemies is another effort at misdirection, a strategy of diversion that masks the real purpose of authoritarian exertions, which is always the diminishment of oscillation.

But the authoritarian regime gains one more advantage from the perpetuation of fear at home and abroad. For there is yet another dimension to fear—fear of the consequences if the dictator were to be overthrown. Both internally and internationally, there often exists not only a fear of the dictator but also a fear of losing the dictator. This can be called the devil-we-know

---

*   In this context, Reciprocity predicts that China will either take a great leap backward in international co-operation or move forward with internal co-operation to a point where the system acknowledges Reciprocity. As we will see in the coming subsections, a capitalist dictatorship such as China's cannot be sustained indefinitely. Thus: "China's leadership is stepping up its efforts to build a legal system that can handle the demands of a complex, market-driven economy, as managing the fast-growing nation becomes increasingly challenging" (Batson, A4). Such developments can, of course, reverse; but the point is, for reasons that will become even clearer momentarily, China's status quo cannot be sustained. Political cooperation must accompany the capitalist economic cooperation that the country is so actively pursuing.

dilemma: is it better to deal with the devil we know, or risk the possibility that a worse one will enter following an overthrow? Such a fear is often most obvious in the appeasing actions of other nations, but it exists among the citizens of authoritarian regimes as well. After all, agreements (however imbalanced) have been reached, and stasis can have its appeal. Confined within the boundaries of the authoritarian regime, those who have avoided or survived extreme exertions can still say, "Well, at least I live." As the people's standards and levels of expectation drop precipitously, the authoritarian ruler finds his sustenance in the perpetuation of competing fears: fear of the dictator and fear of losing him to something worse.

At this point, having used Reciprocity as the tool with which to expose and dissect the many reasons for the authoritarian regime's reliance on fear, it is time to redirect our attention to the issue that hides at the heart of this topic. All of these strategies—masking, minimizing, misdirection—belie a separate, simultaneous truth about fear in the authoritarian regime. The fact is, as a result of Reciprocity, authoritarian rulers live in the same state of fear they create for those they rule. Aware as they are that they hold no real authority, that their systems must be propped up or fall, these rulers live uneasily under the threat of such a collapse. And just as the stability of the authoritarian regime belies instability, the authoritarian regime's security measures belie insecurity. In fact, it is the fear the dictator feels himself that prompts him to instill fear in his people.

This example from Zimbabwe's authoritarian regime clearly illustrates the concept: "A tsunami has rolled through Zimbabwe [remember: Reciprocity explains why overt oppressive crackdowns come in waves], different from the tidal waves that hit Asia in 2004. Ours came last year, in the form of bulldozers and soldiers. Vibrant towns were reduced to flat and desolate grounds. More than 700,000 people lost their homes and livelihood. Why? President Robert Mugabe thought that the poor people [power comes from below] who lived in these urban areas represented a political threat. He *feared* that the citizens might mobilize [create agreements] against him. So he launched a pre-emptive strike [pre-emption is always easier in systems that do not acknowledge Reciprocity] against those already suffering under his policies. He called it 'Operation Murambatsvina,' literally 'Operation Clear the Filth'—the 'filth' being hundreds of thousands of Zimbabwean men, women and children [emphasis added]."[106]

In short, the fear that infects the nation affects the dictator, and we see this all around us. You can start a newspaper in New York City tomorrow if you wish. But ask Mr. Mugabe why you can't do the same in Zimbabwe. Ask Fidel Castro why you can't do the same in Cuba. Ask Kim Jong Il why you can't do the same in North Korea. Ask Moammar Gadhafi. Ask the Saudis and so on. It's the dictator's fear of balancing—the dictator's own insecurity—that prohibits free broadcast and other such actions conducive to balancing.

Consider this example from Iraq: On April 11, 2003, following the fall of Saddam Hussein's authoritarian regime, Eason Jordan, chief news executive at CNN published an op-ed piece in the *New York Times* in which he personally disclosed the fact that for over a decade CNN had acquiesced to Saddam's requirements by refusing to report numerous atrocities perpetrated by that regime against the Iraqi people. In Mr. Eason's own words, "Over the last dozen years I made 13 trips to Baghdad to lobby the government to keep CNN's Baghdad bureau open and to arrange interviews with Iraqi leaders. Each time I visited, I became more distressed by what I saw and heard—awful things that could not be reported because doing so would have jeopardized the lives of Iraqis, particularly those on our Baghdad staff."[107] This is a remarkable example of precisely how fear works to forestall oscillation. The single theme running throughout the newsman's unintended mea culpa is this: fear over the severe consequences that would befall his staff and others persuaded Mr. Jordan to refrain from complete disclosure. Thus it was fear that drove CNN to collude with the dictator and transform itself into one more mechanism of concealment, helping to perpetuate the regime's exertions (by hiding those "awful truths") rather than exposing (broadcasting) them and working to facilitate their end. By his own admission, Mr. Jordan was frightened into acquiescence.

But this example comes here at the transition from fear *of* the dictator to the dictator's own fear because it demonstrates this point as well: Saddam Hussein's own insecurity (based on an inherent understanding that he lacked true authority) could not allow for free broadcast. Saddam Hussein knew full well that exposure of his exertions would weaken, not strengthen, his hold on power—why?—because power is transferred through its own exertion. In short, Saddam Hussein could not allow free broadcast in his country because he also lived in fear.*

The evocation of fear is a double-edged sword, which if wielded recklessly, can prove as dangerous to the dictator as it does to those he rules. Here it

---

* Now consider this astonishing postscript, proof positive that the dictator's anxiety is actually well-advised: When Iraq was attacked on March 19, 2003, the naked acquiescence that previously bound the country instantly evaporated; the regime's instability was exposed; the system collapsed; and the dictator's precarious position was placed on stunning display—the ruler of the country, the purported unanimous choice of over eleven million voters, Saddam Hussein himself, literally crawled down into a dirty hole, alone.

is clear that Reciprocity's third consequence—power is maintained through calculated conservation, not unlimited exertion—is as important to the ruler making efforts to deny Reciprocity as it is to the elected official whose system recognizes the rule. At the same time that Reciprocity explains why authoritarian regimes lean on fear as their stabilizing mechanism, the rule also explains why those who refuse to acknowledge Reciprocity (explicitly) inevitably acknowledge it (implicitly) by masking, moderating, and even minimizing their exertions.

The unstable nature of fear—and the consequent fact that long-standing systems move toward moderation—has been observed under a variety of historical circumstances.

In Renaissance England: "[I]f some anxiety is salutary, it may also go too far [transfer too much power] and evoke not obedience but a sullen withdrawal into discontented silence or even an outburst of rash rebellion [falling back to force relations] . . . These scenarios are at most only partially and superficially in the control of the authorities; if at such times the prince seems to manipulate the anxieties of others, he inevitably discloses *his own half-buried fears* . . . Public maimings and executions were designed to arouse fear and to set the stage for the royal pardons that would demonstrate that the prince's justice was tempered [his exertions were moderated] with mercy [emphasis added]."[108]

In pre-revolutionary France: "[The] practice of torture was . . . a policy of terror: to make everyone aware, through the body of the criminal, of the unrestrained presence of the sovereign."[109] "He alone must remain master."[110] "[But] [i]f the crowd gathered round the scaffold, it was not simply to witness the sufferings of the condemned man or to excite the anger of the executioner: it was also to hear an individual who had nothing more to lose curse the judges, the laws, the government and religion [expose the exertions made against him] . . . Under the protection of imminent death, the criminal could say everything [because he could not transfer any more power away from himself] and the crowd cheered."[111]

In post-Stalinist Russia: "The transition away from pure terror was in some sense inevitable, because under the Stalinist system, no one in the leadership itself could ever feel secure."[112]

Reciprocity explains why such observations are universally applicable to authoritarian systems: the moderation of exertions—that reluctance to "go too far" and "transition away from pure terror"—can only be explained by the fact that power is transferred through its own exertion and that those upon whom power is being exerted define its limits. Thus, dictators have long understood that power is maintained through calculated conservation, not unlimited exertion. Once one understands Reciprocity's effect on systems, one recognizes not only what happens under authoritarian regimes but also *why* it happens and why it *must* happen as it does. Specifically, tyrants must temper their exertions in order to avoid the sort of overexertion that will transfer so much power away that the imbalanced system falls back into force relations, enters revolution, and finally crosses that threshold beyond which lies the redefinition of limits that places the ruler below rules that recognize Reciprocity.

Posit again the per contra proposition that power is not transferred through its own exertion: power is maintained through its own exertion. In that instance, dictators would continuously exert, maintain, and consolidate power as their territories expanded to encompass the earth. But as we have already seen, that is not a description of reality. Instead, the reality is that authoritarian systems must temper their exertions, and that even under such conditions of moderation, those rulers continue to *lose* power over time; this systemic erosion is clearly explained by Reciprocity and its consequences.

Interestingly, the phenomenon underlying the tempering of exertions (which seems so complex when considered in terms of national and international histories) was already illustrated and explained quite simply: as a result of the fact that power is infused throughout the system and transferred through its own exertion, the cause and effect surrounding the very act of clubbing will eventually reverse. Clubbing will no longer be accepted as a technique for encouraging acquiescence but only as the (generally extreme) consequence of a breach of the accumulation of agreements. Clubbing becomes punishment, not persuasion—i.e., exertions are tempered.

Having established the fact that fear affects the dictator and then having connected that fact to Reciprocity's third consequence—power is maintained through calculated conservation, not unlimited exertion—the understanding that emerges can be applied in order to explain another common phenomenon regarding the authoritarian regime's exertion of power. Consider this: three of the four men on our short list of liberators—Mohandas Gandhi, Nelson Mandela, and Václav Havel—were all jailed, but not killed, by their governments.

That cannot be a coincidence.

Why didn't any of those separate and distinct authoritarian regimes kill their high-profile dissidents? Did each of those regimes, operating at times and places far removed from one another, have its own independent reason for foregoing assassination, three separate explanations based solely on the circumstances of each instance? Or is there one underlying explanation uniting all three examples? The answer, of course, is that there is one explanation: to kill those rebels would be to transfer power away from the regime to the rebel's allies and thus increase the potential for a significant redefinition of limits. Killing those dissidents would have effectuated a high-profile abrogation of agreements—in short, by that single, visible act of violence, the state itself would have fallen back to force relations with its people and created an even more prominent emblem of transference. Early on when force relations are ongoing or the transition to power relations remains recent, the prospective (or reigning) authoritarian regime can (and will) openly kill its opponents. But as the imbalanced system begins to ossify (all three men were imprisoned under ossified authoritarian systems), the tyrant becomes less able to risk the transfer of power that such executions create. Where does that leave the imprisoned dissidents? They exist in a sort of limbo, locked up in a condition that characterizes in microcosm the plight of all the people: they become prisoners held in the state of suspended animation that is created by the restraint of oscillation, that is to say, created by exertion without the acknowledgement of transference.

As stated very early on in this study, individuals who hold more influence within a system and who understand Reciprocity will restrain (though not necessarily refrain from) certain exertions and thus maintain more power longer just as less influential individuals who understand the rule will pursue certain strategies that tend to draw power to them as opposed to transferring it away. Here it is worthwhile to consider briefly Gandhi's transcendent response to the restraint of oscillation. Gandhi's overarching philosophy of nonviolence combined with the specific strategy of hunger strikes served to jump-start oscillation in a number of ways simultaneously. By refusing to co-operate (without falling back to force relations or exerting in a force-like manner), Gandhi not only drew to himself the power transferred by his adversaries' exertions (without transferring any back) but also (through hunger strikes) effectively *increased* his enemy's transfer of power to him while attracting broadcast to his plight, further exposing the exertions of his oppressors. Ultimately, he forced his opponents toward precisely that event of which they were most afraid—his death. Absent the rule of Reciprocity, there is no systemic rationale for the success of Satyagraha. In sum, Reciprocity provides the most precise explanation for the efficacy of Gandhi's strategies of nonviolence and self-starvation: by refusing to exert against his enemies (transfer power to them) while simultaneously increasing the effects of their exertions (drawing power from them) and engaging in a strategy designed to broadcast those exertions (expose the power that had been transferred to him and his allies), Gandhi was able to lead his people toward a system that recognizes the truth of the rule upon which he was relying all along.

Expanding this topic beyond the imprisonment of individuals, a broader, underlying question arises: why don't dictators simply destroy all opposition? Stephen Greenblatt presents this same query more eloquently: "But why, we must ask ourselves, should power record other voices, permit subversive inquiries, register at its very center the transgressions that will ultimately violate it?"[113] And Mr. Greenblatt also supplies the answer (albeit a bit more tentatively): "The answer may be in part that power, even in a colonial situation, is not monolithic."[114] The rule of Reciprocity demonstrates that Mr. Greenblatt is completely correct: power is not monolithic, but is infused throughout the system even at that initial stage ("even in a colonial situation") between the clubber and the berry bringer. Remember, in the interactions between invaders and American Indians, we found this truth immediately extant: following even the most elementary agreement, as a consequence of the infusion of power throughout the system, the party who is initially less influential does use its influence—however slight—to begin to define limits on the future exertions of the more influential party. In other words, an understanding of Reciprocity reveals that those who wield the most power in a system inevitably "permit subversive inquiries" because power is infused throughout all systems and that such permission increases over time (if the system does not fall back to force relations) because power is transferred through its own exertion.

By once again combining two facts—power is infused throughout the system, and power is maintained through calculated conservation, not unlimited exertion—we come to recognize that tolerance of some resistance, unavoidable as it may be, actually delivers a number of advantages to the ruler who is fearful of that very resistance, that is, the ruler seeking to maintain power without acknowledging Reciprocity. Such advantages include:

1. Tolerance of some resistance equals diminished exertion by the ruler, which transfers less power to those who are resisting. Of course, followed to its inevitable end, this leads to the explicit recognition of oscillation and the institution of systemic balancing.

2. Because power is transferred through its own exertion, it can be transferred "up" as well as "down," thus the tolerance of resistance allows for the possibility that dissidents might transfer some power back to rulers. An overexertion on the part of dissidents (if properly

exposed, controlled and skillfully defined through state-sponsored broadcast) can potentially become a transfer of power to the powerful.

3. Tolerance of some resistance allows rulers to take the pulse of their opponents' power.

4. Tolerance of some resistance encourages those who are resisting to reveal themselves.

5. Tolerance of some resistance supplies rulers with that invaluable enemy upon whom they can place the blame for their own ongoing exertions.

In the end, Reciprocity explains the movement toward tolerance within tyrannies by providing an underlying theorem to support the observations and conclusions reached by prior writers. For example, what Francis Fukuyama described as that "transition away from pure terror," Václav Havel also captured in his concept of the "post-totalitarian state." In his essay *The Power of the Powerless*, Havel examines this movement toward moderation and emphasis on concealment, stating, "[There is] a profound difference between our system—in terms of the nature of power—and what we traditionally understand by dictatorship."[115] So what is the defining characteristic of that "profound difference," the quality that distinguished the Soviet Union at full maturity from itself at earlier stages? Havel's answer: "[T]his system, *for a thousand reasons*, can no longer base itself on the unadulterated, brutal, and arbitrary application of power, eliminating all expressions of noncomformity [emphasis added]."[116] Instead, Havel observes, the rulers must limit and conceal their exertions behind the mask of ideology.

As Havel explains, "The smaller a dictatorship and the less stratified by modernization the society under it, the more directly the will of the dictator can be exercised. In other words, the dictator can employ more or less naked discipline . . . But the more complex the mechanisms of power become, the larger and more stratified the society they embrace, and the longer they have operated historically . . . the greater the importance attached to the ideological excuse [which is itself a mask designed to help rulers resist Reciprocity]."[117] In addition to confirming the general direction that Reciprocity predicts, Václav Havel, the future prisoner and president states explicitly that this condition "has not appeared out of thin air."[118] Instead, he characterizes the reliance on ideology as "a natural and inevitable consequence of the present historical phase of the system."[119] Clearly, Havel is describing the effects of the accumulation of agreements while also observing the same direction

Reciprocity predicts. But immersed as he is in the details of his country's oppression, he naturally sees "a thousand reasons" for the developments he describes (that is, a thousand reasons for the regime's moderation of exertion) whereas Reciprocity reveals one reason (power is transferred through its own exertion) played out in a thousand ways. In short, Reciprocity explains the pattern that Havel observed.

The point here is not simply to show (again) that Reciprocity has been inscribed between the lines of others' observations. Instead, I am using Havel's insights as a lever to push forward, away from the topic of the open terror created by the "unadulterated, brutal, and arbitrary application of power," and toward direct consideration of a different phenomenon—the phenomenon of coercion. It is here, at the transition from the application of "naked discipline" to the invocation of that "ideological excuse" where we see coercion seize the reins, unseating fear-inducing exertions as the primary tool for perpetuating the authoritarian system.

Let's begin this consideration of coercion with Havel's own beguilingly simple example: "The manager of a fruit and vegetable shop places in his window, among the onions and carrots, the slogan: 'Workers of the World, Unite!' Why does he do it? What is he trying to communicate to the world?"[120] Those are the kinds of simple queries—applied to an apparently everyday act—that tend to elicit clear and original insights. Not surprisingly, Havel's answers are as straightforward as his questions.

First, why does he do it? The answer: "He does it because these things must be done if one is to get along in life."[121] And what is he trying to communicate? The answer: "I am obedient and therefore I have the right to be left in peace."[122]

In the vocabulary of Reciprocity, the greengrocer's sign is saying, "I am not exerting; therefore, I am not transferring power away from myself or giving you an increased ability to influence my actions." But—and here is the sign's relevance to the topic of coercion—was the greengrocer beaten into acquiescence? No. Was he even overtly threatened? Unlikely. The greengrocer was coerced into placing the sign in his window through a complex collection of pressures, what Havel describes as "well-developed mechanisms for the direct and indirect manipulation of the entire population."[123] And all of these coercive tactics boil down into the single threat that the greengrocer won't be "left in peace," won't be able "to get along in life" if he refuses to acquiesce.

Although the distinction between fear and coercion may seem minor when one considers solely the ends to which each leads (either way, the greengrocer is putting that sign in his window), the difference between the means—"brutal application of power" versus "well-developed mechanisms for the manipulation of the population"—is immeasurably important. At this stage in the development of the authoritarian system, not only are the exertions concealed but their effects are allowed to be hidden as well. Here, even fear itself is masked. As Havel himself points out: "[I]f the greengrocer had been instructed to display the slogan, 'I am afraid and therefore unquestionably obedient,' he would not be nearly as indifferent to its semantics, even though the statement would reflect the truth."[124] Havel, of course, understands that fear still forms the foundation of the authoritarian regime, but at this point where the authoritarian system has assembled its own accumulation of agreements (the point at which, in Havel's words, those "more complex . . . mechanisms of power" have "operated historically" and are encompassing a "larger and more stratified . . . society"), the greengrocer's power combines with the dictator's own fear to produce a system perpetuated by coercion as opposed to overt, explicit exertion.

So what is *coercion*?

As stated in passing earlier, coercion is the threat issued with the intent to preempt balancing and sustain imbalance.

To the question, how is the tipped scale held in the tipped position? The first answer was fear. The second answer is the coercion that is made possible by the presence of that fear.

Moving beyond the state of domination that characterizes force relations and (often) the initial stages of power relations (particularly in nascent authoritarian regimes), as we look at the techniques by which dictators survive, we see that at this stage coercion emerges as the method of choice for resisting Reciprocity. Once agreements have been reached, any threat intended to influence actions and prevent balancing is coercion whether such a threat is explicit, implicit, violent, economic, social, or other. This is true for interactions between the state and its own people as well as the state and foreign states. It is also true of interactions between the private citizens of any given state. The cliché mafia soldier out collecting "protection" money around the neighborhood is obviously engaged in an act of coercion. Even if the transaction is allowed to appear completely cordial, gentlemanly, and voluntary, the fact is that sometime, somewhere, someone established the fear that is a prerequisite to the coercive threat. Coercion, when backed by physical exertion, can create what appear to be pockets of force relations within (or beneath the surface of) a system—the sort of subsystem that is often referred to as the underworld. But it is essential to recognize that even those "underworld" interactions are power relations, not force relations. They are not only power relations (interactions based on agreements) within the context of the underworld pockets they do create, but they are also power relations within the systems that encompass them, a fact that becomes most clear in the balancing that follows the exposure of such coercion: mafia dons do go to prison after their exertions are exposed.

Here, toward the middle of this section called "Power," it is important to go back to basics in order to avoid any confusion that might arise regarding power's own origins.

Clearly, the dictator's single greatest fear is that the people will overcome their own fear. Why? Because when dictators lose their control over fear, they lose their power. But doesn't that mean that fear creates power? Or consider this: in the acts of coercion we're now considering, the evocation of fear is influencing others' actions. So again, isn't fear creating power (the ability to influence another's actions)? No. Fear does not create power. You can have fear without power. You can have power without fear. But you cannot have power without agreement. Sometimes agreement follows from fear; sometimes it doesn't (sometimes it follows from love). So the dictator's single greatest fear is not simply that the people will overcome their own fear but that they will stop *acquiescing* as a result. Thus, we have simply reached the same conclusion—acquiescence creates power—along a different path.

Authoritarian systems, like all systems, are dependant upon acquiescence, so they cannot help but enter into power relations (with all that entails); but whereas imbalance is the essence of force, balancing is the essence of power. Thus, as Reciprocity becomes more apparent within the system—as exertion, transference, and redefinition moves the unjust system closer and closer to the acknowledgment of oscillation—dictators must shift their strategies of control. Progressing from the condition predominated by fear-inducing exertions, through the state perpetuated by coercion, we enter yet another stage in which a new phenomenon rises to prominence: corruption.

How is the tipped scale held in the tipped position (how is Reciprocity resisted) for extended periods? The first answer was fear. The second answer was the coercion made possible by the presence of that fear. The third answer is corruption (another technique to inhibit oscillation and forego justice), which is sometimes made possible through coercion and sometimes, simply, a concealment of exertions that emerges as systems mature.

In order to understand what Reciprocity can tell us about corruption, we must first acknowledge this hidden fact about agreement—every explicit agreement carries with it a second implicit agreement established concurrently. The implicit agreement is simple: to abide by the agreement. And it is the presence of that concurrent implicit agreement—the agreement to abide by an agreement—that makes corruption possible.

So what is *corruption*?

Corruption is simply the secret sub-agreement not to abide by an agreement. And corruption is but another mechanism of concealment and an effort to preempt balancing.

Corruption can occur within systems that acknowledge Reciprocity as well as those that do not, and it can exist at every level throughout a system (it can exist anywhere agreements are reached). But no matter where it occurs, corruption always entails the abrogation of an agreement and the prevention of balancing to some degree. This is true whether one considers the elaborate manipulation of an election by a ruler or the simple instance of a policeman accepting payments from individuals looking to dodge traffic tickets. In every instance, corruption is the concealed agreement to breach an agreement and avoid balancing (justice). The classic implement of corruption—the bribe—is simply the incentive to engage in that breach.

At the outset, corruption is not the predominant phenomenon in the authoritarian regime because the agreements (be they explicit or implicit) and balancing that make corruption possible have not yet accumulated. Early on (both within their own regimes as well as in their interactions with other nations), dictators can break agreements and *gain* power if they capitalize on the fear created by their violations in order to lure their counterparties into new agreements (thus creating new power). But elected officials lose power if they break agreements (since their systems have recognized that agreement creates power in the first place). Therefore, as the authoritarian system endures and matures, as it stands between those two poles—the initial stage of force relations and the moment when free elections emerge—that is to say, as Reciprocity moves the regime (however slowly) to moderate its exertions, authoritarian officials seize upon corruption (hidden breach) as their method for masking (and perpetuating) the ongoing denial of oscillation. To wit: In a country where the consumption of alcohol is forbidden and media is strictly controlled, "the well-to-do Iranian drinks and reads and watches what he wishes. He does as he pleases behind the walls of his private mansions and villas. In return for his private comforts, the affluent Iranian . . . sacrifice[s] freedom of speech, most of his civil rights, and his freedom of association. The upper-middle class has been bought off by this pact [the secret sub-agreement not to abide by the agreements restricting what Iranians are allowed to drink, read, and watch] . . . These are the kind of people who can afford mansions in Shahrak-e-Qarb or in Lavasan, up in the desirable hills."[125] This is not only an example of corruption in a mature state; it is also an example of mature corruption—the bribes are flowing both ways. The regime is bribing the rich (with drinks and televisions), and the people are bribing the regime: "[When] the enforcers of Islamist law appeared on the roof[s] . . . in . . . Sharak-e-Qarb to seize all satellite dishes . . . Every household received an order to attend a hearing of the revolutionary court [the court is a mask to disguise extortive exertions], where the magistrate—typically a mullah—will levy [extort] fines. The fines help the friends of the courts, while for [the wealthy] . . . erecting another satellite dish is . . . easy."[126]

As with every concept presented in this subsection, there are innumerable illustrations of the fact that as Reciprocity moves a regime to moderate its exertions, corruption (hidden breach) emerges as the strategy of choice for masking (and perpetuating) the ongoing efforts to resist oscillation. Consider these headlines that appeared in the *Wall Street Journal* just during the time I've been writing this book: "As Vietnam Grows, So Does Graft: Communist Party Congress Sets Sights on Corruption"[127] and "In Chinese Province, Bling from Bribes Goes Up for Bid: Corrupt Officials' Graft Included Rolexes, Minks; Auction's Mixed Message."[128] One would not likely have seen such headlines under the nascent Minh or Mao regimes. As the authoritarian system matures, Reciprocity and its consequences cause corruption (as opposed to fear-inducing exertions) to become both more common and more prominent. So given the abundance of available illustrations, I'm really drawing the following example of corruption almost at random not only because it has happened to come into my hands just as I am writing this but because it adds a few interesting twists.

Here's the example: on September 13, 2006, Chinese attorneys Li Jinsong, Zhang Lihui, Li Fangping, Teng Biao and Xu Zhiyong published an editorial (note: this is an act of broadcast), which appeared under the headline "Blind Injustice" (also note: in addition to confirming that the authoritarian regime will move toward corruption as the preferred means for denying oscillation, the piece also demonstrates that Reciprocity's definition of "injustice"—the denial of balancing—is accurate, useful and often understood instinctively). In their piece, these Beijing attorneys state that as the chosen lawyers of a gentleman named Chen Guangcheng, an advocate for the rights of Chinese villagers, "We were prevented from presenting a fair defense by obstacles erected by Chinese authorities. A local court imposed unacceptable terms on us defending our client . . . Before the trial, we had been detained by police, intimidated [coerced], and one lawyer was not freed until the trial was over . . . That's why we are using these columns to outline [broadcast] the defense that was never presented in court . . . The real criminal suspects in this case are the officials responsible for obstructing justice [inhibiting balancing] and undermining the country's legal reform. These local officials could hardly have acted with such contempt and disregard for the law unless they had been given the green light by authorities higher up [unless there had been a secret subagreement to abrogate the legal system's explicit agreements]."[129]

This is a classic example of corruption, which, as I said, adds a few interesting twists. The first twist is this: in this particular example of corruption, the agreements the parties are secretly agreeing not to abide by are actually agreements that regulate the resolution of disagreements. It is at this stage of the authoritarian system's progress toward the acknowledgement of Reciprocity where we find this earlier point most clearly illustrated: even if agreements that regulate the resolution of disagreements are in place (and sometimes followed) as long as the ruler remains above the rules, those agreements can, and will be, broken. Here, the agreements to regulate the resolution of disagreements act as a mask behind which the authoritarian regime conceals its exertions in an effort to minimize transference.

The second twist: although the authoritarian regime has developed corruption as a mechanism for maintaining imbalance, it still continues to coerce through intimidation and even engages in fear-inducing exertions, in this instance by means of incarceration; but it does not rely on such exertions or coercion as its final solution. Instead, the authorities prefer to rely on the secret sub-agreement—between local officials and those higher up—to violate the Chinese legal system's controlling agreements. And in that preference, we clearly see the progress from fear-inducing exertions through coercion to corruption. As a consequence of Reciprocity, the regime that has reached this state of corruption no longer relies fully on fear-inducing exertions or coercion (though those actions do continue to a certain extent) in order to deny oscillation; instead, the authoritarian regime acts as if it's abiding by agreements when in fact it is forming hidden agreements to violate them. At this stage, the show trial must go on because it is an important mask behind which authoritarian rulers conceal their denial of oscillation.

Here is the final twist provided by this example: in essence, corruption is the act of pretending that something isn't happening when it actually is (or pretending something is happening when it actually isn't); therefore, exposure (broadcast) is the enemy of corruption. The exertions that corruption conceals can continue indefinitely without the loss of power as long as those exertions remain secret—as long as they stay within their pocket of corruption—but as they begin to be broadcast, the power exerted through those corrupt acts is lost (sometimes slowly, sometimes immediately) to whomever was being damaged by the secret sub-agreement(s).* Thus, separate from the contents of the Chinese attorneys' article, the very act of writing such an editorial (authoritarian regimes fear free broadcast) will enliven oscillation even if it triggers increased exertion by the regime, because increased exertion ultimately equals increased transfer of power to those upon whom the exertions are being made (and their allies).

In the end, any system (be it national or international) that is going to sustain itself indefinitely must create a state in which the incentive (reward) for abiding by the laws is greater than the incentive for breaking them. The recognition of Reciprocity is the required means to this end as it facilitates the balancing process, instituting victim's doctrines and redefining limits until both the clubber and the berry bringer stand to gain more from honoring agreements than from (secretly) breaching them. Abiding by agreements is known as integrity, and the absence of integrity leads, by degrees, to disintegration.

At the outset, the efforts to centralize power allow authoritarian rulers to contain oscillation (but never eliminate it). Having placed their stranglehold upon oscillation, they then continue to contain it through fear. As agreements inevitably accumulate and power becomes (more obviously) dispersed throughout the system, fear-inducing exertions give way to coercion, and coercion slowly morphs into corruption until corruption is exposed, after which the system eventually disintegrates into force relations, or the regime is finally forced to recognize Reciprocity.

Near the end of the "System" section, I outlined the general pattern of movement from force relations to open oscillation. Here we encounter the dark side of that pattern. This is what plays out under the authoritarian regime when the transition from force relations to power relations is not recognized and the accumulation of agreements is not initially acknowledged as external authority:

---

* In short, corruption abhors broadcast. Recognition of the importance of broadcast as a tool for the eradication of corruption reveals another reason why CNN's secret, implicit arrangement with Saddam's regime was doubly damaging to both the Iraqi and American publics. It was damaging because it was itself a corrupt act (inhibiting balancing by pretending that something wasn't going on when it actually was), but it was also a corrupt act that assisted the regime in continuing its more widespread corruption, coercion, and fear-inducing exertions.

Force→ Fear→ Coercion→ Corruption→ Exposure→ Acknowledgement of External Authority→ Institution or Enforcement of Agreements that Regulate the Resolution of Dis-
agreements→Justice→Expansion/Rights→Oscillation

Now, as we have already seen, at any given time, fear-inducing exertions,
coercion, and corruption can (and do) exist simultaneously; and within the
above pattern (as it was with that earlier force-to-oscillation outline), reality
will reveal rapid advances, sudden reversals, simultaneous developments, and
events "out of order."

Of course, following the exposure of fear-inducing exertions, coercion, and
corruption,* the authoritarian system can simply fall back to force relations.
If the system does suffer such a setback, then the abbreviated pattern simply
repeats, a visual representation of the revolving door through which one
dictatorial regime replaces another:

Fear→ Coercion→ Corruption→ Exposure→ Fear→ Coercion→
Corruption→Exposure

A system—or systems—can also enter into the painfully prolonged cycle
of violence that sometimes sets in upon the interactions of specific groups
in conflict (e.g., Israelis and Palestinians). This pattern describes a history of
hostility (feud) in which beginning and end is lost to the confusing jumble
of exertion, aggravation, recrimination, and revenge:

→ Force→ Fear→ Force→ Fear→ Force→ Fear→ Force→ Fear→
Force→Fear→

I began this consideration of Reciprocity's relationship to authoritarianism
by taking up the topic of the centralization of power under the rubric of
the common good and showing that power, in fact, cannot be centralized. I
then traced the consequences of this fact throughout the many stages of the
authoritarian regime's governmental system from fear-inducing exertions

---

* Note: Exposure does not have to wait for the presence of corruption. It can
occur at any time following the formation of agreements even at the point when
fear-inducing exertions remain the authoritarian regime's primary mechanism for
denying oscillation. Obviously, that sort of early exposure (broadcast) is made more
likely through the aid and efforts of allies operating beyond the regime's borders.

to corruption. We can now take the lessons brought forth through this examination and apply them to the authoritarian regime's manifestation of power within another arena of human interaction—economic systems.

To start, let's consider this connection: the redistribution of wealth, a significant component of the corruption that occurs under authoritarian regimes (and often explicitly constitutes the basis of such regimes' economic systems) flows from the same notion of the common good that helps those regimes throttle oscillation at the outset. Minh: "To-day we need to consolidate this freedom and independence . . . [which] requires the sacrifice [for the common good] . . . of our compatriots all over the country . . . This is the meaning of 'Gold Week.' 'Gold Week' will collect the gold given . . . mainly by the well-off families to devote it to our most pressing and important task [i.e., redistribute it]."[130] The redistribution of wealth is also indicative of the basic paternalism that underlies (and undermines) the authoritarian state: "'We' [the rulers] know better than 'they' [the people] [what] is in their own good."[131]

In any paternalistic system, the father figure defines the common good for the family, and under the inevitable corruption (secret agreements to abrogate agreements) of the authoritarian regime, being familiar with the paterfamilias will bring wealth one's way.

Inevitably, a system that attempts to centralize political power also makes efforts to create and sustain a centralized economy. Why is this inevitable? Reciprocity has already given us the answer: because to do otherwise would be to maintain two separate systems simultaneously—one system that contends power is concentrated and one that acknowledges power is dispersed. But we have already seen, both logically and empirically, that two such conflicting systems cannot be maintained together indefinitely. So given what Reciprocity has shown regarding the centralization of power (power cannot be centralized), wouldn't we expect to find the same problems with centralization in the economic arena as we have in the governmental/political sphere? In other words, just as Reciprocity leads political systems from authoritarianism to open oscillation, wouldn't the fact that power is transferred through its own exertion (and the consequences of that fact) move economic systems from controlled economies to free markets?

That is the question we will now address: given the truths that Reciprocity reveals, is economic centralization any more viable than governmental centralization? Here, communism—employed as an extreme example of a centralized economic system—becomes the first framework of economic influence upon which Reciprocity's truths and consequences will be applied.

But before that, we will look (briefly) at Reciprocity's basic relationship and relevance to matters of economics.

Reciprocity and Economy

I am not an economist, so my approach (by necessity) is to take up this topic in a way that dispenses with almost every element of complexity that makes economics both challenging and enjoyable to those who are. There are no graphs or (formal) formulas in the following pages. My goals here are easily defined: first, to make explicit two fairly obvious premises regarding Reciprocity's relevance to economic systems; then, in the coming subsections (communism and capitalism), to apply some of the conclusions we've already reached in order to provide Reciprocity's explanation for certain patterns, particularly the recurrent rise and failure of communist/centralized economic systems and the simultaneous success (defined by the ability to sustain itself) of free-market capitalism.

With regard to Reciprocity's relevance to economics, here is the first premise I wish to make explicit: economies only emerge as a product of human interaction. No human interaction, no economies. Reciprocity is therefore relevant as a rule of human interaction applicable wherever agreements are reached.

Here is the second premise: economic systems are just that—systems. They *are* accumulations of agreements; agreements create power; power produces Reciprocity; therefore, economic systems are subject to Reciprocity and all of its consequences.

And here is one final observation: just as you can find Reciprocity woven between the seams of the works of certain earlier philosophers and political scientists, so too can the truths that Reciprocity reveals be seen written between the lines of the works of many economists who previously took up the topic of centralized vs. decentralized economies. Just as we found evidence of Reciprocity in the works of Foucault, Rousseau, Fukuyama, Havel, and others, so we will find the same in the thoughts of Friedman, Hayek, Smith, and more. In fact, just as Reciprocity provided the theorem underlying Havel's observations on the development of a post-totalitarian state, Reciprocity—as we will soon see—simply helps make Smith's "invisible hand" a bit more visible.

Communism

Let's begin with the basic fact that the establishment of a communist system is itself an exertion. It is an exertion made possible by the prior exertions of (and resultant transfer of power by) individuals and/or groups that previously acquired more power within the predecessor system. I will call those individuals capitalists though it does not have to be so. The communist redefinition could come in response to exertions by pure-bred, play-by-the-rules capitalists, a corrupt authoritarian regime, or some hybrid of the two. Regardless of what sort of exertions the ascendant communists have defined as beyond acceptable limits, the truth is that those communists are doing nothing more and nothing less than forming agreements among themselves and using the power transferred to them in order to redefine limits on the actions of their oppressors (just as the founders of the United States of America did nothing more and nothing less than form agreements among themselves and use the power transferred to them in order to redefine limits on the actions of *their* oppressors).

Such a simple truth is universally applicable and accurate with regard to every situation in which communism has been established. And this irrefutable fact—communism is an exertion (and redefinition of limits) in a pattern of exertion, transference, and redefinition—explains communism's recurrent rise. Communism emerges as a result of the transfer of power made possible by the exertions of prior rulers. But that understanding also becomes critical to the effort of discerning if or where communism goes awry relative to Reciprocity. Why? Because communists—viewing all of history through the tight focus of the materialist's lens—have never understood that simple truth themselves; and it is that lack of perspective, the inability to see the broader pattern of human interaction (exertion, transference, redefinition—and the history it creates), from which the seeds of communism's conflict with Reciprocity begin to sprout.

In short, Marx's materialist history is simply a tracing of exertions and transferences viewed from within the narrowed scope of economic determinism; to wit, the communists declare, "The history of all hitherto existing society is the history of class struggles."[132] Reciprocity reveals that that statement, as bold and broad as it may seem, is actually incomplete. Where Marx sees solely "class struggles," there is actually interaction, acquiescence/agreement, exertion, transference, and redefinition on a far broader scale. Clearly, individuals situated within the same class do struggle with each other—are those struggles and the events they produce somehow outside the scope of "the history of all hitherto existing society?" Handicapped by his nearsightedness, Marx cannot see the forest of exertions and transferences through the trees of factories, farms, imports, exports, etc.—all of which are simply *some* of the products of acquiescence/agreement, exertion, transference, and redefinition. The dynamics that developed to create the general boundaries Marx defined as bourgeois and proletariat came only from acquiescence/agreement. And Marx's call to revolution was simply a rallying cry against proletarian acquiescence, a call for a redefinition of limits made necessary (and possible) by so-called bourgeois exertions and transferences.

Now, that's all well and good, and we could simply write off Marx as one more among many who did not or could not recognize Reciprocity in part because he did not have the data we have today (much of which come from communism's own exertions and transferences). But communism's relationship to Reciprocity does not end with Marx's myopia. Instead, here's where things get tricky. Marx's (limited) vision dooms his intellectual descendants to a destiny in which the systems they assemble are required not simply to address/redress capitalist excesses, but are forced, instead, to attempt to eliminate Reciprocity altogether.

Why?

Reciprocity shows us that communism's inevitable conflict with the foundational rule of human interaction is written in those very two words that sit at the heart of the Marxist perspective: class struggles. Here's the problem Reciprocity helps us see: to eliminate class struggles—the goal of the communist accumulation of agreements—is to eliminate both class and struggle, which, in turn, requires the (impossible) elimination of Reciprocity. To understand why this is so, let's take those two concepts one at a time.

First, class: how do classes form? Classes form only and always as the consequence of some combinations of (and ongoing engagements in) exertion, acquiescence, further exertion, transference, resistance, redefinition, and expansion. That is to say, they emerge naturally out of and continue to grow and change through Reciprocity. To eliminate class, one would need to impose the sort of system that not only inhibits exertions and transferences but also holds down oscillation when the phenomenon of exertion/transference does inevitably occur. Coincidentally, that describes not only the impossible world without Reciprocity but also the state that communism approximates wherever it takes hold. In reality, to actively institute its classless economy, communism does always resist Reciprocity through the inhibition of exertion and transference and the attempted elimination of oscillation.

Now, struggles: what are struggles except exertion, transference, and redefinition? Can there be a better word for this pattern than *struggles*? Is this not what we've been talking about all along? If you accepted the insights gained from the examples of the driver and the mother on the bus, Rodney King, King Hammurabi, President Nixon, and so on, did you not also accept the fact that such struggles are an element of human interaction? To eliminate class struggles is not only to attempt to eliminate class but to eliminate the underlying struggles through which those classes formed. Let's consider again the image of a world without Reciprocity. What would such a society look like? Without the facts that agreements create power, power is infused throughout, and power is transferred through its own exertion, human society would come to constitute an ossified hierarchy frozen forever and absorbing all future generations into its monolithic, stagnant structure. Of course, that is not a description of reality. However, it is, again, a description of both the impossible world without Reciprocity as well as the state that communism approximates wherever it takes hold.*

In looking at communism's most basic intention (noble as it may be) we immediately see that: 1. To achieve it, you would need to eliminate Reciprocity, which means you would need to eliminate agreement (since Reciprocity emerges wherever agreement is reached); 2. Reciprocity predicts what such a society would need to look like, and 3. The state Reciprocity predicts is, approximately, how communist societies do end up taking shape—monolithic and stagnant with a systemic stranglehold on oscillation. So Reciprocity shows us right from the outset that the communist call to action is actually a call to conflict with the most fundamental rule of human interaction.†

---

* To those who would now shout, "China, China, look at China's growth! Its economy is not stagnant!" The answer is obvious: China's is not a communist system. It is a capitalist dictatorship; and one of its systems (centralized political/decentralizing economic) will have to give way to the other. The two cannot be sustained side by side indefinitely. As an aside to this aside: China did stagnate into a monolith under Mao only to reanimate after Deng introduced capitalist reforms. As a result of China's entering into an increasing number of capitalist agreements, Reciprocity is now pushing the system toward the recognition of Reciprocity.

† Ironically, but not surprisingly, the recognition and pursuit of Reciprocity (rather than its elimination) is *more* likely to lead toward the economic justice that communism promises. This point can be proven in short form: as we have already seen, you can't have *any sort* of justice (including economic) without recognition of Reciprocity. The more recognition of Reciprocity—the more justice/balancing; the less recognition—the less justice. And the same point (Reciprocity leads to economic justice) can be proven in long form as well: Imagine a world in which all governmental systems (e.g., political, economic, legal) recognize and facilitate Reciprocity, both its causes and its consequences. In that world, those upon whom power was being exerted would continually redefine limits (over time) until the balancing that Reciprocity demands would lead those systems into economic justice. Remember, the fact that power is transferred through its own exertion means it is always in motion, and some form of oscillation will always be occurring, both politically and economically. In the systems that approximate such a state—that is to say, today's systems that do facilitate Reciprocity—this is in fact a description of reality: over time, the less powerful gain power, redefine limits, and remove the artificial obstacles to their upward mobility. So here's the irony: the system that attempts to eliminate such struggles cannot possibly reach the end toward which those struggles will ultimately lead. By attempting to impose balance, communists eliminate the balancing that is necessary to reach the ends they desire.

This, in a nutshell, is communism's basic and inevitable conflict with Reciprocity: in order to eliminate class struggle, you would need to eliminate (in descending order from surface to source)—class, struggle, Reciprocity, power, and agreement. Taking this in ascending order (from cause to effect), obviously no society can exist without agreement; therefore, it can't exist without power, Reciprocity, struggle (oscillation), or the fluid degrees of disparity (e.g., class) that oscillation requires. All agreements create the potential for oscillation (the ebb and flow of power). So unless someone can invent an economic system that eliminates agreement (some have certainly tried), then every economy that comprises agreements yet attempts to prohibit balancing will self-destruct under this self-contradiction. Ultimately, the actions needed to end class struggles are exertions. They are also agreements that create power, Reciprocity, and oscillation. And in the process, they perpetuate the very struggles they seek to cease.

Now, in addition to communism's basic conflict (and ironic relationship) with Reciprocity, there is also an underlying paradox that emerges as communists act to establish their economic system: as communist revolutionaries move to create their classless society (that is, as they unwittingly make efforts to *eliminate* Reciprocity) they rely unavoidably *on* Reciprocity.

Marx, Engels, and their allies were doing nothing more than utilizing broadcast to expose the exertions of early capitalists, take the power transferred by those exertions, and use that power to define new limits. Consider this quote from the *Communist Manifesto*: "Modern bourgeois society . . . has conjured up such gigantic means of production and of exchange [that it] is like the sorcerer, who is no longer able to control the powers of the nether world which he has called up by his spells."[133] Now, what new light can Reciprocity shed on such an assertion? First, if you peel away the rhetoric of "nether world," "sorcerers," and "spells," you see that Marx and Engels are describing the effects of Reciprocity: the bourgeoisie are no longer able to control the power they created in the first place when they entered into various arrangements of agreement with, and acquiescence by, the proletariat. Why? Because the exertions of "modern bourgeois society" have transferred power to the proletariat.

But Marx and Engels do not peel away the rhetoric. This may be due, first and foremost, to the fact that they don't understand the cause and effect I just outlined. Thus they are relying on emotional appeal to make up for (and cover up) their lack of insight. The capitalist's power is not derived from the "nether world" by way of "spells." (While it has already been proven that power does come from below, it doesn't come from *that far* below.) In reality, capitalist power is derived from agreement by way of acquiescence. In looking at how these men choose to express themselves, it becomes apparent that this sort of discourse has its own purpose. The authors of such a sentence are attempting to establish consensus via a form of exertion designed to look like exposure (a concept we will consider later in "Broadcast"). Reciprocity shows us what these revolutionaries are actually doing. They are using broadcast as a means both to expose the exertions of their enemies and *increase* those exertions by equating capitalists with satanic sorcerers. This is a strategy straight out of Reciprocity's playbook: expose the exertions in order to facilitate the transfer then exercise the power that has been transferred. And it is a strategy that could not be possible without the fact that power is transferred through its own exertion.

Ultimately, Marx and his allies were merely exercising the power that had been transferred to them as members/allies/representatives of a group (the proletariat) against whom exertions were being made. Hence, as stated at the outset, the institution of communism is nothing more or less than another redefinition of limits made possible by the preceding exertions and transferences. But with their tendency to elevate (or lower) capitalists into sinister status (rather than recognizing them, and themselves, as individuals interacting within a system that emerges from the pattern of exertion, transference, and redefinition), communists attempt to leapfrog Reciprocity to an end that they have predefined as just. In short, eliminate the bogeyman of capitalism and you eliminate class struggle; eliminate class struggle and you end humanity's painful history; end that history and you move humanity forward to a new golden age, or "higher phase" so to speak. But that tunnel vision—viewing the whole of human history as one of "class struggles," rather than recognizing class struggles as merely one facet, among many, of the overall pattern of acquiescence, exertion, redefinition, etc.—makes it impossible for the communist to see this truth: it is not capitalism per se that causes the injustices they set out to remedy, but the encumbrance of oscillation within early capitalist systems that caused those very injustices.

If we want to place the same communist blinders on ourselves, we will then "see" that we actually entered Marxist materialist history at the outset when we considered the case of the clubber (bourgeoisie) and the berry bringer (proletariat). The berry bringer produces berries, but the clubber controls the means of production (he controls the berry bringer). And there you have the very class struggle communism attempts to eliminate. This example, by virtue of its simplicity, reveals two insights:

First, it shows us how unrealistic it would be to attempt to eliminate those classes, in effect make them both berry bringers (if they were both clubbers, they would starve), without either: 1. instituting agreements that recognize and facilitate Reciprocity and, thus, oscillation or 2. bringing in another clubber (e.g., Stalin, Minh, Mao, Castro, Chávez,* etc.). And so we see how communism itself, in its (genuine or disingenuous) rush toward a justice it cannot reach, becomes but another mask behind which a new clubber hides his club. Communism is simply the economic form of the same "common good" concealment that is utilized to invoke and perpetuate political centralization.

Second, this brief return to the clubber-berry bringer example shows that agreements (even if they take the form of naked acquiescence) must be reached before production can begin: no acquiescence, no berry deliveries. Once agreements are reached, power is infused throughout, and every exertion becomes subject to Reciprocity. You cannot have production without agreement; you cannot have agreement without power; you cannot have power without Reciprocity. And all of that means: communists cannot avoid oscillation any more than capitalists.

So precisely what Reciprocity predicts will happen, did happen. The champions of Marxism took the power transferred to them as representatives of the proletariat and used that power to define new limits. In so doing, they also exerted and transferred power away from themselves. Incapable of acknowledging Reciprocity within their new system, the communists created a new set of oppressed people to whom they also, unwittingly, transferred power. Thus, the iron curtain rose and fell with the pendulum-swing of oscillation.

---

* Latin America's currently (albeit temporarily) ascendant communist-in-chief is once again demonstrating that the imposition of the communist system remains the strategy of choice for clubbers seeking to establish dictatorship. "On June 14, 2006, President Chávez—dressed in military fatigues—gave a speech on the occasion of the delivery of a batch of Kalashnikov AK-103s to an army battalion. He brandished a weapon [club], then pointed it at a cameraman and said: 'With this rifle . . . I could take out that wee red light on your camera.' Moments later, he declared: 'We have to review the licenses of the TV companies'" (Granier, A12). Five months later, he said: "I'm reminding certain media, above all in television, that they mustn't be surprised if I say, 'There are no more licenses for certain TV channels . . . I'm the head of state'" (*Ibid.*). Remarkably, President Chávez shows us not only that the imposition of communism requires a (new) clubber, but that the clubber will (as predicted) instinctively attack the mechanisms of balancing (free speech, free press) in his effort to deny Reciprocity.

That pendulum-swing of oscillation, which finally caused the eastern bloc to crumble, can be seen in many places, including in the context of two documents already cited. By juxtaposing the opening lines of the *Communist Manifesto* against the opening lines of Havel's *The Power of the Powerless*, written approximately 130 years later, we see the oscillation that lifted and then felled the communists in eastern Europe:

Marx: "A spectre is haunting Europe—the spectre of Communism."[134]

Havel: "A spectre is haunting Eastern Europe: the spectre of what in the West is called 'dissent.'"[135]

Of course, that is no coincidence—Havel is intentionally echoing Marx to make a point. And the point he is making is precisely the pattern that Reciprocity predicts: the exertions of communists (dissenters in their own day) transferred power away from them and to the new dissidents. In the end, the communists' own exertions became the ones against which the later dissident dissented. And from that century-spanning correspondence between Marx and Havel we gain a vivid illustration of oscillation.

The question is—did it have to be so?

And Reciprocity's answer is unequivocally yes.

Once we recognize that the creation and maintenance of a communist system requires the formation of agreements and that the interactions under those agreements will entail exertions, transferences, redefinitions, and further accumulation of agreements, we also see that communism cannot somehow transcend Reciprocity. This is, of course, true of any system. So we come quickly to the key question that can be applied to any such framework of power: can the accumulation of agreements take into account and acknowledge the fact that power comes from below, is infused throughout the system, and transferred through its own exertion? Applying this query to the power structure at hand, we must ask, can the communist economic system recognize and institutionalize Reciprocity, or are there characteristics inherent in its form (apart from its goals) that put it into conflict with Reciprocity, making that requisite recognition difficult, if not impossible?

Again, unless someone can concoct a way to operate indefinitely under two conflicting systems, any system that attempts to centralize political power must also make efforts to create and sustain a centralized economy. The reverse is true as well: any system that attempts to establish a centralized economy must also attempt to centralize political power, which is to say, it must—to greater or lesser degrees—set itself upon the path to authoritarianism (what Hayek termed "the road to serfdom"). And every system that attempts to centralize power eventually runs up against this same problem: power cannot be centralized.

After all the analyses of authoritarianism and communism are said and done, the problem is actually quite simple, and we have already penetrated to its core. The entire conflict (the impossibility of centralization in any sphere of power) is found at the genesis of power itself. Agreement creates power. Therefore, to have centralized power, one must have centralized agreement; but that is a nonsensical notion. Agreement, by definition, must include multiple parties infused with the ability to influence each other's actions. There can be no such thing as "centralized agreement;" therefore, neither political nor economic systems can be centralized. Communism requires a centralized economy (this is true at the outset both in theory and practice, and it remains always true in practice); therefore, communism is doomed to conflict with the fact that power is disbursed throughout and transferred through its own exertion.

Now consider this: how, exactly, does the economy become centralized under the communist economic system? Answer: the state seizes control of the means of production. In other words, a new clubber comes in and takes over the berry bringer. This is not a controversial perspective, Marx and Engels admitted as much themselves: "Of course, in the beginning this [the establishment of the communist system] cannot be effected except by means of despotic inroads."[136] So here's a riddle: which comes first, the chicken (the despot) or the egg (a centralized economy)? The solution: it doesn't matter. Whichever emerges first, the other will surely follow. Again, Reciprocity shows us that two incompatible accumulations of agreements—one that says power is disbursed throughout the system and one that says power is centralized—cannot be sustained simultaneously.

Of course, I have employed communism simply as an extreme example of government intervention and economic centralization. By analyzing this far end of the spectrum, we can see most clearly the problems that Reciprocity reveals. As economic systems become more or less centralized, the problems identified here will become more or less present.

Now, it is empirically verifiable that communist systems can endure for a period of time (just as a ball tossed into the air will rise for an amount of time determined by the effort with which it is thrust upward), but they cannot sustain themselves indefinitely; this is true whether one considers the case of an isolated commune in Humboldt County, California, or a collection of nations cordoned off behind an iron curtain; and Reciprocity has just revealed a number of reasons why the communist economic system is, inevitably, unsustainable. At the same time, it is also empirically verifiable that free-market capitalism can and does endure.

So now the question is—why?

Capitalism

The preceding subsection focused primarily on the fact that the very goals of communism (even in their conceptual form) conflict with the reality of how power is created and maintained. But it touched only lightly on the difficulties associated with implementation of a communist system. Once you see the impossibility of the system's endurance even in theory, then those thousand reasons (by Havel's count) for communism's non-theoretical failure become secondary. In reality, there are many difficulties entwined with the implementation and perpetuation of a centralized economic system, the most glaring of which is the problem of distribution.

When communists seek to end class struggles, what end are they really seeking? They are seeking a certain equalization that can best be described as "just distribution." Thus, the communist slogan, general formula, and highest principle for distribution is: "From each according to his ability, to each according to his needs!"[137]

In the communist economic formulary, ability drives production, and need guides distribution. That is a seemingly logical (and even admirable) ambition. But in reality, the materials that come *from* those who are producing according to their own abilities still must be distributed *to* those who are consuming according to their own needs (such distribution will, of course, include need-based distribution back to everyone who is producing). The point is, for production to be distributed justly (from ability to need), it still must be distributed. Therefore, judgments must be made regarding that distribution. And the only question is, how will those judgments be reached? Those judgments can only be rendered in one of two ways: through the process of exertion, transference, and redefinition that follows even the most basic agreement(s), or by dictate from a central authority. As Milton Friedman observed: "If prices [set by free markets] are not allowed to ration goods and workers, there must be some other means to do so."[138] In short, distribution will be guided by the invisible hand of free markets or the hidden hand of the dictator.

I have gone to great lengths throughout this book to define common terms such as *power, system, law, justice, rights, religious structure, coercion* and *corruption* (even *maturity*) in order to eliminate uncertainty as to what I mean when I use those broad concepts; and I have—wherever possible—incorporated the knowledge that power is transferred through its own exertion into my definitions. So what do I mean when I use the term *free markets*?

Thomas C. Schelling provides the sort of lively depiction that is hard to improve upon as the starting point for finding Reciprocity's definition of free markets: "Tens of millions of people making billions of decisions every week about what to buy and what to sell and where to work and how much to save and how much to borrow and what orders to fill and what stocks to accumulate and where to move and what schools to go to and what jobs to take and where to build the supermarkets and movie theatres and electric power stations, when to invest in buildings above ground and mine shafts underground and fleets of trucks and ships and aircraft."[139]

Now, that is a wonderfully vivid depiction, but it's not a definition (nor was it meant to be). Still, we can use that colorful collection of activities as a starting point from which to find the commonalities that will lead toward definition. In the end, all of these behaviors share a few basic elements: they are interactions; they are interactions requiring agreements; *and* they are interactions involving the exchange of natural resources and/or knowledge.

Taking these one at a time:

Every action Mr. Schelling describes requires human interaction. That's simple.

Next, every one of those interactions also requires the participants' involvement in agreements on a variety of levels. For instance, when you decide "what stocks to accumulate" (and then actually accumulate them), you enter into a variety of agreements that define your power as a shareholder. But in addition to the agreements defining your influence as a part-owner of the enterprise, your purchase of stock connects you directly or indirectly to so many agreements it would be impossible to enumerate them all. To illustrate this point, let's say that you decide to accumulate the stock of the Coca-Cola Company. The purchase of even a single share of Coca-Cola will connect you to agreements ranging from your agreement to pay taxes on the dividends you collect, to the agreement that Coca-Cola delivery trucks will stop on red and go on green, to the company's agreement to comply with the Sarbanes-Oxley Act. Of course, you could only be held personally responsible for the payment of your own taxes. However, your indirect connection to those other agreements still carries potential liability for you. Coca-Cola's widespread, continued breach of the agreement to stop on red and go on green would lead not only to an immediate avalanche of lawsuits but also to the eventual dissolution of the company, the total devaluation of its stock, and the loss of your money; refusal to comply with Sarbanes-Oxley would do the same. Every interaction enumerated above engulfs the participants in a veritable sea of agreements.

Finally, every interaction enumerated also involves the exchange of natural resources and/or knowledge. Obviously, the decision to purchase a mine shaft would involve natural resources. So let's stick with the example that is less obviously connected to resources: "what stocks to accumulate." Going online or calling a broker and shifting around a few digits in databases may feel far removed from the grit and grime called to mind by the term *natural resources*, but such transactions must inevitably trace back to that base. If you accumulate the stock of the Coca-Cola Company, you are buying shares in the production of a group of people who have reached agreement about what to do with water, sugar, a proprietary concoction of flavorings, and the aluminum, glass, or plastic within which they package their product (of course, that is a gross oversimplification—the natural resources would extend to include the petroleum that powers the trucks, the steel that supports buildings, the cotton from which uniforms are made, the neon in neon signs, the grass and soil that surrounds the corporate campus, and much, much more); obviously, all capital ultimately traces back to natural resources and/or knowledge.

So what are *free markets*?

First, markets are power relations involving the exchange of natural resources and/or knowledge. Even the first exchange, before laws and possibly even before language, was an economic interaction with agreement. You don't need a sea of agreements, only one (be it implicit or explicit), to constitute an economic system. In the case of bartering foodstuffs, the agreement would be that the goods being exchanged are edible. Were you to trade inedible eggs for edible vegetables, you would transfer power to those who traded the vegetables to you, and they could then influence your actions by, at a minimum, refusing to do business with you again and forcing you to find a new trade partner or only agreeing to enter back into the system if you offered certain concessions such as extra eggs to make up for the breach. Of course, they could also club you, which would either stabilize power relations (by reinforcing your acquiescence) or prompt a falling back to force relations. Any way you look at it, that exertion on your part would transfer power and most likely lead to the redefinition of limits and the creation of new agreements affecting future exchanges.

So if markets are power relations involving the exchange of natural resources and/or knowledge, then what makes markets free? The recognition of Reciprocity (of course). To the extent that a system recognizes the fact that power is transferred through its own exertion and facilitates oscillation, it is free. To the extent a system inhibits oscillation, it is controlled. The participants in free markets are able to find their own way, define their own limits, form their own victim's doctrines free from the control of some central command whose own exertions are artificially shielded from Reciprocity (by effort).

So free markets are power relations involving the exchange of natural resources and/or knowledge under agreements that recognize Reciprocity.

Given this understanding, and based on what we have already seen regarding Reciprocity's effect on systems, we can now also reach this conclusion: markets will always move in the direction of freedom. Markets are accumulations of agreements; agreements create power; power manifests Reciprocity; therefore, markets will always move themselves (that is to say the human beings interacting to create the market will always—despite temporary reversals—move the market) toward the recognition and facilitation of oscillation (freedom) and away from control (denial of oscillation). This will always occur by virtue of the fact that Reciprocity directs every system toward the recognition of Reciprocity.

Now consider this: Mr. Schelling follows his wonderful depiction of free markets with an analogy, "Whether this system works well or ill, in most countries and especially the countries with comparatively undirected economic systems, the system works the way ant colonies work."[140]

Well, not really.

Once one understands the role of Reciprocity in free markets, one sees that such a comparison is inaccurate. In fact, that comparison with ant colonies *proves* the role of Reciprocity in free markets.

I know next to nothing about ant colonies, and I'm not going to research them to make my point because my point is simple, and I do know this: ants are not forming agreements (systems) in the way humans form agreements. Ants are driven into action by a complex set of instincts that have developed over time and have been shaped by a variety of factors including their various environments. Now this might open up a can of worms (or ants) among various biologists, behaviorists, anthropologists, entomologists, etc., so I want to stick very close to the only point about which I am absolutely confident: though ants can act in coordinated fashion, there is no evidence whatsoever that ants are forming agreements in the sense we have defined agreement. And here, in this section dedicated to the forms and effects of power exertions, it makes perfect sense to look a little closer at agreement, the action that creates power in the first place.

For the sake of moving forward, we have to this point operated with the definition of agreement as acquiescence—spanning a spectrum from naked acquiescence to more consensual, harmonious accords. And that took us a long way into new understandings of the creation, maintenance, and loss of power in human interaction. But now it is time to make another implicit point explicit: in the sense in which it is relevant to Reciprocity, agreement defines *future* behavior. Agreement as we've been handling it, is not "we agree that the sky is blue," or "we agree our neighbor is weird." The agreement that creates power always has a future component to it. In other words, we have been treating agreement as "an arrangement between two or more persons as to a course of action."[141] The berry bringer agreed to bring berries (in the future) if the clubber agreed not to club him (in the future). Ants are acting and interacting on instinct only in the present. Ants are not forming agreements regarding future behavior. Therefore they are not creating power, and their actions are not subject to Reciprocity. The participants in free markets are operating under numerous agreements with future components; those agreements are creating power and the actions of the participants in those systems are subject to Reciprocity; thus, free markets do not work in "the way ant colonies work." They work in the way all accumulations of agreements work—through the process of exertion, transference, and redefinition made possible by the rule of Reciprocity.

OK, so now we have a definition of free market activity that distinguishes it from other coordinated human (and ant!) activity. But what can Reciprocity tell us about distribution within those free markets? If distribution is not to be dictated, then how is it to be determined? In the free-market system, production according to one's ability is followed by distribution according to one's production. That is to say, distribution (how much you get) is determined by the value of what you produce, and that value is not calculated independently (by edict of some governing body) but through the *interactive* law of supply and demand.

So if only a few people can hit a baseball over a fence and a lot of people are eager to pay to watch someone hit a baseball over a fence, then that baseball player (limited supply) will earn a remarkable amount of money *only* as a result of the relationship between his supply and fans' demand. Now, the demand for garbage collectors is much greater than the demand for baseball players; but so is the supply. This combination of supply and demand conspires to place a lower price on the services of a garbage collector than on those of the baseball player even though you and I might hold the opinion that the garbage collector's services are far more important to society. You can carry out this same analysis with regard to a variety of not-so-socially-valuable vs. socially-valuable pairings: bond traders vs. social workers, actors vs. teachers, rock stars vs. doctors, and so on. But here's the solution free markets provide: if you don't like those distributions, then don't participate in the bond market, don't spend your money at ballparks, movies, or rock concerts; if you do, do. The money that those ballplayers, bond traders, actors, and rock stars are receiving does not materialize out of thin air. Contrary to the conspiracy theorists (and communists), in a free-market economy, there is no sinister, satanic lord holding sway over the masses and controlling the flow of vast rivers of revenue with dramatic waves of his wand and secret spells. There are only those "[t]ens of millions of people making billions of decisions every week about what to buy and what to sell and where to work," and so on. Does wealth accrue to the one who owns significant amounts of stock in the Coca-Cola Company? Of course. But only because people buy Coke.

In this way, the free market allows every participant to influence distribution and move the system through the balancing act that is justice. It does not let you set "just distribution" via the issuance of dictates from on high. But it does allow you to exert influence in a variety of ways, including through your own individual purchase power. A command economy, on the other hand, does not. To further illustrate the justice (balancing) of the free market economy in action, let's return to the example of the Coca-Cola Company's use of natural resources.

Many people may feel the company's use of those resources is fine. Many others might not; and if they don't, then they don't buy Coca-Cola. If enough people agree with the first group, then the company thrives. If enough people agree with the second group, then the company closes. Could somebody else do something better with those natural resources? Possibly. The question is, how are you going to reach that "something better?" If you do it through a centralized decision maker, then you will oppose Reciprocity and set yourself upon the path that leads either to force relations or (hopefully in your lifetime) back to the point where the ruler re-acknowledges oscillation; in which case, you will end up right back where you started: in a free market where somebody can manufacture Coca-Cola.

While it is true that free markets will never empower you as czar, they do empower you. The free market empowers participants in precisely the way any system that acknowledges Reciprocity empowers its participants. The facts that free markets operate under agreements, agreements create power, and power is transferred through its own exertion mean that—as long as the system recognizes Reciprocity—even as a single customer, you can potentially exert influence over the Coca-Cola Company's actions, and the Coca-Cola Company's exertions will transfer power to you. Given that, in the end, every society's economic, political, and legal systems must eventually conform with each other (they all must either acknowledge or oppose the fact that power is transferred through its own exertion), we see that in societies with free markets, every participant's influence extends beyond purchase power—that is to say, every participant in the free-market economy has influence beyond the "to buy or not to buy" choice I just outlined.

Let me give a simple example. I happen to be allergic to processed sugar. Over the course of many years, it became clear to me that processed sugar (particularly high-fructose corn syrup) reacts in my body almost exactly as alcohol reacts in the body of an alcoholic. So I personally don't consume any foods with added sugar, including Coca-Cola. Someone else, however, might find that he thrives on drinking Cherry Coke morning, noon, and night. Still another individual might discover that she enjoys a cold Coke on a hot day every once in a while. Drinking Coca-Cola hurts me but helps others. What to do?

Reciprocity takes care of it.

In a system that acknowledges Reciprocity, if Coke creates victims, then those victims and their allies will take the power transferred to them by the exertions of the company and use it to influence the company's ongoing actions. I choose to exert my influence over junk-food manufacturers through purchase power alone (I just don't buy the stuff). But in systems that recognize Reciprocity, others can pursue different options. For instance, the mother of an obese child who feels that food manufacturers are responsible for her child's condition could ally herself with like-minded moms and found a group, Mothers Against Selling Sugar (MASS), dedicated to reducing the amounts of sugar sold to children and, thus, to reducing childhood obesity. That group could follow exactly the same strategy that MADD did: expose exertions, take the power transferred by those exertions, and use it to redefine limits. Of course, the people who enjoy Coca-Cola will resist such redefinitions of limits, and through the process of balancing, both parties will eventually reach some form of agreement/redefinition of limits (perhaps removal of soda vending machines from school cafeterias). That is how the free market handles likes and wishes and shoulds—through the process of exertion, transference, and redefinition that guides and connects the political, legal, and economic systems. Such a scenario cannot occur in a centralized economy. But, once again, it would be pointless to appoint a sugar czar because that strategy will lead in a circle. After tilting at windmills in the futile fight to sustain a command economy, Reciprocity will steer the system back to an acknowledgment of Reciprocity. In contrast to the imposition of resolutions by dictate, systemic acknowledgment of Reciprocity enables agreements to be defined by a million little dictators, each exposing, exerting, resisting, competing, and cooperating in their own way.

Obviously, we've seen this all before; I'm simply taking the same truths we found in legal/political systems and applying them to economic systems. This idea—that the same phenomenon can guide both legal and economic systems—is not original. "Hayek applied the 'invisible hand' idea of the market to the common law, elaborating the view that the law is a self-correcting spontaneously grown order that inures to the benefit of all while not being the intentional product of anyone."[142] What Reciprocity brings to the table is that it specifies the underlying phenomenon (the phenomenon underlying the creation of the common law). The law *does* grow "spontaneously" (without a master plan) out of exertions, transferences, and redefinitions; and the law (victim's doctrine) *is* "self-correcting" given that it is amended and revised not by a mastermind, but by new victims.

Similarly, Milton Friedman has already illustrated the inevitable development of overall dictatorship as the result of centralized distribution:

> In a free market society, it is enough to have the funds. The suppliers of paper are as willing to sell it to the *Daily Worker* as to the *Wall Street Journal*. In a socialist society, it would not be enough to have the funds. The hypothetical supporter of capitalism would have to persuade a government factory making paper to sell to him, the government printing press to print his pamphlets, a government post office to distribute them among the people, a government agency to agree to rent him a hall in which to talk.[143]

Again, you can start a newspaper in New York City tomorrow if you like, and you'll succeed or fail based only on your ability to bring in more subscription and advertising revenue than it costs you to write, print, and distribute the publication. But in a centralized economy, someone will need to make judgments regarding the distribution of the paper. And if the ruler does not judge the free press to be a high priority, then you will not be able to start that newspaper. Given what we now know about Reciprocity, its effects, and the efforts needed to suppress it, it is not surprising that you can't start a paper in countries like Cuba regardless of whether or not the raw materials are available. It is the dictator's own hidden hand, his own exertions concealed behind the various masks we have already exposed, that is permitting, prohibiting, and generally guiding the distribution of goods.*

Reciprocity has proven that we can no longer theorize about a society in which the dictator of a centralized system manifests benevolence to the degree that allows for oscillation since such allowance would necessarily lead to the recognition that power is transferred through its own exertion, is therefore disbursed, and *cannot* be centralized. Thus, the dictator would go from benevolent to irrelevant as external authority was inevitably acknowledged. But just for the sake of exploring Reciprocity's relation to the distribution of goods in a free-market system (while further illustrating the real difficulties associated with the implementation of communism/socialism or any other form of economic centralization and centralized distribution), let's now indulge our imaginations with the vision of a centralized economy in which enough paper can be produced for everyone's use and in which the benevolent dictator will allow everyone to use it for whatever purpose they see fit (even active opposition to his regime).

Here's the problem that would still arise: paper is not the only product in an economy, and not all products can be manufactured as readily as paper. While you might be able to increase the production of paper to the point where everyone who wants it has it, you cannot markedly increase the number of houses with views of the San Francisco Bay, apartments along the Ostozhenka district's Golden Mile in Moscow, cuts of filet mignon that can be taken from a cow, or the products of master craftsman: the watch whose mechanisms are finely tuned, the car whose interior is lush, the violin that produces the most stirring sounds because its dimensions, its every curve and hollow have all been crafted with a level of care and excellence approaching perfection. How can a system possibly distribute any of those goods according to need? Who gets the Stradivarius, and who gets the commonplace fiddle? Who *needs* filet mignon or the house on the hill above the fog as opposed to ground round and a Spartan apartment? In the end, no system can possibly distribute any of those goods without relying on some other mechanism of

---

* It would be unconscionable to let this statement stop with the topic of paper. The fact that the dictator's hand must guide distribution has deadly consequences in that it extends to influence the distribution of food, shelter, medicine, education, and a variety of other resources that are vital to the well-being of the people.

influence besides "need" to guide their distribution.* As a result of the fact that another mechanism of influence is necessary, we see that the centralized economic system does develop such methods of influence and that (just as with political centralization) those methods do evolve—from fear-inducing exertions through coercion to corruption.

We have already seen Reciprocity's effect on the resolution of disagreements in political and legal systems: systems that acknowledge Reciprocity discourage violence as the means by which disagreements are resolved. We can now extend this truth into the economic arena to recognize that just as the vote replaces violence as the mechanism of resolution in the political system, money reduces mayhem in the economic system. Just as Reciprocity develops free elections as the means of exchange for political power (ballots replace bullets), it develops cash to replace clubs as the means of economic exchange. Over time, violence is diminished as more and more disputes are resolved through the new tactics of exertion, transference, and redefinition that capitalism creates—pricing, bidding, bargaining, etc. Capitalism develops money (the symbolic representation of the underlying concentration of capital) as its instrument of influence, mediating mechanism, and measure that determines what goes to whom, and here is money's basic relationship to Reciprocity: money rests on and manifests agreement; it is just one among many financial instruments arising from the accumulation of agreements.

Ask yourself this: before money emerged as the means to purchase property, who would have occupied that house on the hill? It won't take you long to find your answer: the person who was strong enough to seize and defend that property through physical force. As Reciprocity moves victims to define new limits, free markets, like free elections, turn conflict into competition and allow contests to be resolved nonviolently. Let's consider the problem

---

* This tells us at least three things about distribution in a centralized system:

1. No matter how benevolent the dictator may be, eventually some distributions must be dictated.

2. Centralization discourages mastery because mastery complicates distribution; thus, under a centralized system, goods and services will suffer a certain reversion to the mean (a movement toward uniform mediocrity): e.g., generic apartments, functional (as opposed to comfortable) clothes and adequate (though hardly efficient) automobiles, etc.

3. That reversion to the mean inspires the formation of gray/black markets.

further: there's a parcel of land up on a hill; many people desire to occupy it; some of them may even believe they *need* it. But that land upon the hill is a perfectly inelastic supply: its production cannot be increased (stretched) in response to demand. So how will that parcel be distributed? Its distribution can be decided through physical conflict: the person who kills the most wins. It can be settled through coercion: the person who threatens the most wins. It can be settled through corruption: the person who bribes the most wins. Or it can be settled at open auction: the person who bids the most wins. As systems move toward the recognition of Reciprocity, the mechanisms that influence distribution do also evolve. In contemplating the development of systems from clubbers and berry bringers to employers and employees, we see that free-market capitalism doesn't create economic inequality (the unequal distribution of natural resources/knowledge); instead, economic inequality creates free-market capitalism (an accumulation of agreements capable of facilitating balancing)—via the rule of Reciprocity and its effects.

As societies are shaped by Reciprocity, power relations replace force relations as the interactive manner of exchange. Thus, money (just one among many manifestations of the underlying agreements) replaces the club as the primary instrument facilitating economic exchange. All forms of economic agreement establish Reciprocity (though not all acknowledge it); Reciprocity requires oscillation, and oscillation requires disparity. Recognition of Reciprocity engenders *fluid* degrees of disparity while suppression of oscillation necessarily ossifies into more static division.

Under systems that promise not merely to treat individuals equally but actually to create equality, the party leaders, the commandantes, the priests, the mullahs, inevitably form the upper classes. It always comes back to the house on the hill. Someone is going to get it.* Under such circumstances, the leaders assume the position of a privileged class; they take the mansion, the compound, the palace. They take it for themselves under the guise of the common good. Then as Reciprocity moves those systems back toward revolution, the deception, double-talk, and convoluted logic designed to conceal the rulers' exertions and justify their hypocrisy is exposed and expelled.

---

*   Recall this example from Iran: "These [the people who can afford to bribe officials through the concealing mechanism of revolutionary-court fines] are the kind of people who can afford mansions in Sharak-e-Qarb or in Lavasan, *up in the desirable hills*, where former President Akbar Hashemi Rafsanjani and his ilk live [emphasis added]" (Farzami, A18). In Iran, coercion and corruption still play a major role in distributing that "house on the hill."

172 | Stephen Michael Strager

Those lies always perish under the pressure of Reciprocity—and with them the liars. These statements regarding the rise and fall of such systems are neither predictions nor opinions; they are empirical facts. Today, we have information that was not available to many of our predecessors: we have the historical data to support such assertions as well as the theorem to explain why it must always be so—power comes from below, is dispersed throughout the system, and transferred through its own exertion.

To sum up in a single sentence: economic disparity preexists free-market capitalism,* and the accumulation of capitalist agreements develops from Reciprocity as a system that facilitates distribution while discouraging violence.

Now, unquestionably, the military-industrial complex is a capitalist entity that requires war (or the threat of war) for its own survival. No war, no military-industrial complex—that's true. But the military-industrial complex is not created by capitalism. As we have seen, it is created by the lack of agreement; that is the wilderness within which wars are waged. The fact that systems that resist Reciprocity cannot enter into and abide by agreements raises the likelihood of force relations. Thus, it is not capitalism (a system that must recognize Reciprocity if it is to survive) but the existence of systems that oppose Reciprocity that makes force relations (and the military-industrial complex) necessary.

Consider this random headline that popped up online literally as I was writing those last few paragraphs: "An Amsterdam Court froze the sale of ABN Amro's LaSalle unit to Bank of America, dealing a blow to ABN's planned merger with Barclays. The decision boosts the chances of a rival bid for all of ABN and will likely spark a legal war."[144] A legal war is not a war. The "blow" that was dealt was not physical. Capitalism's accumulation of agreements acknowledges Reciprocity, and Reciprocity guides systems away from violence. Rather than resorting to physical conflict in order to resolve disputes over distribution, the capitalist accumulation of agreements substitutes the exchange of currency for the exchange of blows. This random example also confirms a conclusion reached much earlier. ABN Amro is a bank based in the Netherlands. Barclays is British. And Bank of America is American. This is nothing if not an international dispute. Yet we can be absolutely certain that a world war will not erupt over the Amsterdam Court's actions. Why? Is it because the Dutch, British, and Americans have reached a higher plane of consciousness? No. It's because their systems have developed under Reciprocity to acknowledge Reciprocity. The Dutch, British, and Americans are operating within a shared economic system (capitalism) and governmental systems in

---

* Economic disparity starts at the move from hunters and gatherers to first farmers.

which agreements that regulate the resolution of disagreements are in place (and followed); thus, they will not fight each other (except in court) to resolve this complex dispute involving billions of dollars.

Not surprisingly, we have already seen Reciprocity's effect on markets: the peaceful exchange of eggs for vegetables that we posited earlier is obviously a movement away from force (simply snatching those goods) and toward an accumulation of agreements that facilitates the exchange of natural resources/knowledge. As economic systems advance to encompass more and more complex goods and services (you could not possibly accumulate the number of eggs you would need to trade for the Empire State Building), cash eventually replaces the club as the instrument of exchange.*

Having explored Reciprocity's explanations for why the centralized economic system (e.g., communism) cannot survive, we are now seeing why capitalism can sustain itself. The economic form most likely to sustain itself will be the one that best acknowledges Reciprocity. The mechanism of distribution that is most consistent with the basic rule of human interaction will be the one most likely to endure.

Every economic system needs a mechanism of distribution. By definition, the dictator dictates. He dictates who takes the house on the hill and the prime cut of beef. That is the theocratic solution. It is the authoritarian solution. It is the communist solution. But Reciprocity undermines those systems and leads to a new solution—the free-market solution—that recognizes oscillation and the truths upon which oscillation rests. The fact that agreements must occur, that agreements create power, that power is transferred through its own exertion, and that all of this is the unavoidable consequence of human interaction also explains why systems that acknowledge Reciprocity engage in capitalism. You can't have production without agreement. And once agreement is formed, the entire system is charged through with power and the phenomenon of Reciprocity. Ultimately, the economic system that recognizes Reciprocity will be best able to sustain itself because, as a result of the fact that production requires agreement, every system must reach a recognition of Reciprocity or fall back to force relations at some point anyway.

---

* And even if you did manage to accumulate some number of eggs equivalent in value to the Empire State Building, an egg's value is based on its edibility, which is perishable. The time span of its utility is finite. Money's value, however, is maintained through agreement. As long as the agreement remains, the money holds its value. Thus, capitalism projects a foundation upon which human beings can interact indefinitely.

Now, the fact that money emerges from agreement and acts as one instrument in Reciprocity's discouragement of violence can be proven in the inverse as well: "Lenin's famous dictum [is] that the most effective way to destroy a society is to destroy its money."[145] To "destroy a society" is to eradicate its agreements and return it to force relations—thus, create money: discourage violence; destroy money: create violence.*

Capitalism, obviously, is not a panacea. It clearly discourages but cannot eliminate violence. And its extraordinary efficacy and efficiency often reveal themselves in dangerous ways: the rapid extrication of natural resources that exacts a high toll on the environment and executes a certain violence against nature, the remarkable ability to reach into even remote areas to access/exploit inexpensive labor. No one could argue that the urge for profit never supersedes humanitarian concerns within a capitalist system. In fact, that is the sole argument against capitalism. People will destroy nature, produce dangerous products (and by-products), privilege the profit-motive, and harm/exploit others in the process of transforming natural resources into wealth. But as we have already seen, societies must (one way or another) utilize natural resources (somebody somewhere is going to pick and eat the berries—multiply that by billions of berry eaters and you're certain to run into some overexertions along the way). And when these same problems—pollution, destruction, poisonous by-products—occur under centralized economies, the injured have no recourse against the offending entities except (ultimately) revolution.

On the other hand, the capitalist economic system, acknowledging and facilitating the fact that power is transferred through its own exertion and acting in conjunction with legal and political systems, does provide a check against such abuses. First, the accumulation (and dispersion) of power provides an alternative means of influence. In the free market, innocent parties—insurers, property owners, stockholders for instance—will lose their own wealth if such abuses persist. Many parties have a vested interest in seeing that such abuses cease. So they will resist harmful behavior; they

---

* When mobs smashed the windows of Starbucks stores in economic protest on the streets of Seattle in 1999, who was it that was engaging in this violence? *Anti*-capitalists. And what were they seeking? Anarchy. And what is *anarchy*? Absence of government. Since government emerges from agreement, the world's anarchists are seeking a state without agreement (for as soon as they form even a single agreement, they have created a governing system). Since money is agreement, they seek to destroy money. And by their efforts, they show us precisely how disputes would need to be (and once were) resolved in their world.

will expose overexertions and use their own power to define new limits. Such actions would not be possible without Reciprocity, and they are not possible in societies that deny Reciprocity. Then there are those who actually earn their living by exposing such abuse and seeking remedy. In a system whose agreements recognize Reciprocity and facilitate oscillation, victims turn to the law. And all of that goes a long way toward explaining this common phenomenon: in societies that acknowledge Reciprocity, you find more lawyers on the streets; in societies that don't, you find more soldiers.

As Milton Friedman stated with characteristically sound and lucid logic: "[T]here are only two ways of coordinating the economic activities of millions. One is central direction involving the use of coercion—the technique of the army and of the modern totalitarian state. The other is voluntary co-operation of individuals—the technique of the market place."[146] Clearly, the concept of Reciprocity is woven throughout Mr. Friedman's account, and Reciprocity provides the theorem underlying his empirical observations. One system (involving the use of coercion) denies Reciprocity; the other (involving voluntary co-operation) is built upon it. As we have seen, coercion is the dictator's technique, born from and based on fear. On the other hand, co-operation is born of agreement; it is the essence of authority and the steward of every system.

In the end, those who despise the competitive marketplace miss this important point (the secret to capitalism's success): capitalism replaces conflict with competition—and competition is cooperation.

Yes, competition is cooperation.

Capitalism is competition. But competition is cooperation. This is not a contradiction. Simply, you cannot have competition without agreement. Every form of competition is based on multiple agreements. The contestants in a race all agree to begin behind the same line and run within their own lane, and they agree to start at once, and the finish line is also predetermined and agreed upon; so the first one there wins. Tennis players, football, basketball, baseball, hockey, cricket, chess players—they all compete under complex accumulations of agreements. So do candidates in an election, and so do companies in the marketplace. Ultimately, agreement forms the basis of all competition: athletic, political, economic, etc. Without rules, you don't have competition. You have conflict. And this brings us right back to the point where Reciprocity always leads: if the ruler refuses to recognize the truths about power (including the fact that he is operating under rules), then the system is driven by conflict, not competition, and is therefore doomed to collapse rather than advance.

Obviously, any system riddled with conflict (as opposed to buoyed by competition/cooperation) can't survive. Capitalism is competition;

competition requires cooperation (Friedman: "the central principle of a market economy is co-operation."[147]); cooperation requires agreement; agreement creates power; power is transferred through its own exertion. Therefore, the competitive system must recognize Reciprocity, and it does so through the development of, abidance by, and enforcement of rules.

No matter how acquiescence may be reached (by club or by love), agreement ends conflict, and the end of conflict is the start of cooperation. As interactions move from force to power and as ongoing interactions stimulate the accumulation of agreements and redefinition of limits, competition emerges as one form of cooperation, permeating society's three main systems: free markets, free elections, and just court systems (just court systems engage in balancing through competition—prosecution vs. defense, plaintiff vs. defendant). * As stated above, capitalist interaction immediately engulfs participants in a veritable sea of agreements, which, as we now know, means they also become engulfed in co-operation.

Remaining loyal to the spirit of demystifying complex concepts, let's look at the relationship of competition/cooperation to an economic example touched on earlier: wealth accrues to the one who invests in Coca-Cola. That's obvious, but to understand its implications in relation to competition/cooperation, we must ask: what is *investing*? Investing is buying something today that you believe someone else will pay more for in the future. That is the universal definition of investing. It doesn't matter whether

---

* Again and again, throughout this analysis, we're encountering the stubborn truth that a society's systems will coincide and, thus, cannot be separated. You cannot maintain indefinitely an economic system that recognizes Reciprocity alongside legal or political systems that do not because the legal, economic, and political systems will all inevitably intersect. Considering that lawmakers (and in some systems, even judges) are also politicians, you can see that separating the political and legal systems is really a nonstarter. And since the laws often affect economic interaction, all three arenas are inextricably intertwined. This also underscores the inadequacy of the communist emphasis on economic interactions and helps explain a fact we have already encountered: "China's leadership is stepping up its efforts to build a *legal system* that can handle the demands of a complex, *market-driven economy*, as managing the fast-growing nation becomes increasingly challenging [emphasis added]" (Batson, A4). Economic interactions are interactions, and they cannot be isolated from other interactions either in practice or analysis.

you're investing in shares of stock, parcels of property, works of fine art or comic books; in each and every instance, you're buying something today that you believe someone else will pay more for in the future. Now, how you *form* that belief will tend to have a significant impact on your success or failure. In fact, that is truly the crux of the investor's entire endeavor: forming reasonable expectations about future value based, in part, on reliable calculations of current value in tandem with a sound perspective on the factors that will influence demand and supply in the future. Given the fact that the formation of belief is the crux of investing, it is not surprising that the oscillation that molds the markets for investment also produces rules defining the proper and improper formation of such beliefs. Let's say you independently assess the value of a company, compare your valuation to the market's valuation (as reflected in the company's current stock price), then purchase the stock because you believe it's undervalued;[148] that's one example of proper formation of belief. Let's say you receive a call from a company's CEO tipping you off to a pending event and purchase or sell stock based on that information: that's one example of improper formation of belief. Why? The ongoing act of balancing also leads to the ongoing discouragement of unfair/imbalanced advantage.

The point here is not to examine the philosophy underlying the victim's doctrine defining limits on insider trading; the point is that such limits would not exist were it not for Reciprocity's effect on systems. Where did those rules defining proper and improper formation of belief come from? Restrictions against insider trading, price manipulation, improper disclosure, etc., all developed out of the process of exertion, transference, and redefinition made possible by Reciprocity. The New York Stock Exchange was founded in 1792. The SEC was established in 1934. What happened in the interim 142 years? Exertion, transference, and redefinition—that's what happened. The SEC was not created on the whim of a capitalist sorcerer. It was created as the result of the efforts of victims to expose and resist exertions and redefine limits. Because the marketplace is cooperative, investors form common rules in order to compete. At times when capitalism strays from co-operation, Reciprocity institutes corrective measures (i.e., leads to the redefinition of limits), sometimes even inspiring the formation of institutions (e.g., the SEC) to referee the competition and enforce the rules. Recently, "activist investors" have hoisted the banner of resistance, exposing inadequate corporate governance, taking the power transferred by the overexertions of certain directors and CEOs and using that power to redefine limits. In the future, as new events occur, new rules will form through the process of interaction.

Competition is not a panacea. But the advantages of competition over conflict are obvious and numerous.*

Again, Milton Friedman has already observed the multidimensional advantages of competition: "The consumer is protected from coercion by the seller because of the presence of other sellers with whom he can deal. The seller is protected from coercion by the consumer because of other consumers to whom he can sell. The employee is protected from coercion by the employer because of other employers for whom he can work, and so on."[149] That's true. But all the employers (or employers in a certain sector) could theoretically collude and create agreements among themselves to influence their employees through coercion. Then what? Then nothing—they would do it, and that would be that except for the fact that their exertion would transfer power to employees who would then redefine limits. In power relations, one can always penetrate below effect (free-market competition diminishes coercion) to cause: Reciprocity and its consequences.

Now, here's a whopper of a conundrum that could have been raised earlier but was better left until we touched on the competition/cooperation nexus. As was proven above, employing "need" as the mechanism of distribution is impossible, particularly with regard to products that are not easily manufactured (who *needs* a Rolls Royce?). But what about medicine? Drugs require centuries of accumulated understanding and sometimes decades of research and development (R&D) to produce. Medicines are not easily created but can *only* be distributed according to need. No one who doesn't need the drug would even want it (generally speaking). So what can the fact that power is transferred through its own exertion tell us about this case?

In order to answer that question fully, we must break down the transaction into its two most significant components: discovery and distribution.

First, discovery.

R&D is nothing more than institutional nomenclature for "the attempt at discovery." And there is only one way to encourage discovery: expand possibility.

---

* Considering again those systems that promise to *create* equality, what is the common denominator in their strategies for achieving that goal? Eliminate competition. Ironically, that is the fastest way to ossify disparity. Eliminating competition means reducing cooperation and raising the potential for conflict. On the other hand, competition arises from and furthers the balancing necessary to shape a just society, and it does so because it requires that participants abide by agreements. This primacy of the agreement leads the system into a state of oscillation that allows for the individual/group advancements (and declines) necessary to achieve systemic equality.

"[O]ne can compel individuals to be at certain places at certain times; but one can hardly compel individuals to put forward their best efforts . . . the substitution of compulsion for co-operation [the steward of every system] changes the amount of resources available."[150] So what *does* inspire individuals to put forth their best efforts and increase the system's resources? The promise of possibility. Compulsion restricts possibility. Co-operation expands it. Different people are inspired by different possibilities, so the more possibilities a system allows for, the more discoveries its people will produce. This truth is easy to illustrate. For example, had the British government restricted the movement of its citizens (e.g., compelled them to remain within the country's borders and made it impossible to travel abroad), Charles Darwin could not have set sail aboard HMS *Beagle*, and it would not have been possible for him to gather the data he used to describe evolution. Similarly, if the Moravian and Augustinian systems did not allow Gregor Mendel to grow, breed, measure, and record the features of pea plants in the garden of his monastery, if they compelled behavior or placed restrictions on his actions that made such experiments impossible, the priest could not have uncovered the genetics that then provided the explanation for generational variation underlying Darwin's theory. So these syllogisms are true by degrees:

Diminish compulsion = increase possibility = increase discovery; therefore, diminish compulsion = increase discovery.

Increase compulsion = restrict possibility = reduce discovery; therefore, increase compulsion = reduce discovery.

The more a system compels behavior and reduces possibility, the more it inhibits discovery. The more a system reduces compulsion and increases possibility, the more it encourages discovery.

Here is the beneficent cycle produced by the system that expands possibility: new discoveries lead to new possibilities, which lead to new discoveries, which lead to new possibilities, and so forth. This is the vicious cycle produced by the system that limits possibility: fewer possibilities lead to fewer discoveries, which reduce future possibilities, which reduce future discoveries, until the system churns to a standstill.

Buoyed by competition, the system that acknowledges Reciprocity expands the possibilities for all its citizens. Riddled by conflict, the system that denies the fact that power is transferred through its own exertion lingers always in the shadow of force relations. By limiting oscillation, such a system limits movement, restricts possibility and imprisons its citizens (literally and figuratively, physically and mentally). Because the exertions required to restrict possibility do transfer power and lead to the redefinition of limits, systems that acknowledge Reciprocity naturally cultivate possibility and encourage discovery as they allow unacceptable restrictions to be redefined.*

So an understanding of Reciprocity reveals that drugs can only be discovered and produced in systems (or subsystems) that facilitate competition (as opposed to those that perpetuate conflict) because:

---

*   While I am raising this all in the context of drug development and distribution, it would be unconscionable to let this examination of discovery end at drugs. Taking the United States of America as one system (among many) that protects possibility for its citizens, ask yourself this important question: what is the source of America's history of discovery? Is it the abundance of natural resources or the system that was put in place? Is it the resources or the redefinition of limits that arises from the recognition of Reciprocity? When you travel to China, you see electric lights and airplanes and automobiles and many innovations that came from the United States, a society younger (by millennia) than China. Why is that? Why didn't the Chinese discover electricity? Or invent the airplane? Or the telephone? Develop the Internet? Manufacture the Model T? Discover numerous vaccines and lead the last century's medical breakthroughs? Or put a man on the moon? And why did Americans discover/accomplish these things in such rapid succession? Was it because America has a lot of trees and fertile dirt (resources)? Or is it because America's competitive/cooperative system encourages inquiry and requires ingenuity while China's has inhibited competition? Are African nations devoid of resources, or are they crippled by systems that restrict Reciprocity? Why do drugs move from America (an infant country) to Africa (mankind's genetic "Eden") and not vice versa? It is obviously not the seeds and soil that led to those breakthroughs—Africa has seeds and soil; and it is obviously not a superiority of people since "Americans," including *every* successful American doctor, scientist, and inventor hail personally or ancestrally from countries spanning the globe (China and every nation on the African continent among them); freed from the constraints imposed by fearful authorities (including that awfully fearful authority—ossified "culture"), America's immigrants have been provided possibility by a system that facilitates Reciprocity. And from possibility comes discovery.

     Now here's a footnote to a footnote: The USSR developed a relatively robust space program. How did that happen? It happened because they entered into competition (as opposed to force relations) with the United States, which increased—to a limited degree—co-operation between Soviet rulers and some of those whom they ruled (Soviet scientists). Ironically, in the end, it was precisely competition's requirement of cooperation that spelled the Soviet system's (inevitable) demise.

1. The presence of competition reflects the necessary co-operation that can only rest on some (even slight) underlying acknowledgment of Reciprocity. If a society were to declare, "In pursuit of discovery, we shall cooperate but not compete," the people attempting to perpetuate such a system would be incapable of navigating even the first fork in the road when, inevitably, various notions of how to proceed would arise. Faced with competing ideas but having foresworn competition, those people would either be compelled by circumstance to condone competition (i.e., allow multiple parties to pursue their separate hypotheses until the correct one won) or institute a top-down mechanism of resolution that would conflict with Reciprocity. Why couldn't they institute a democratic mechanism of resolution? Because the vote would be a competition. It is impossible to abandon conflict and pursue discovery without engaging in competition of some sort somewhere; thus, discoveries tend to emerge from competitive (as opposed to conflictive) systems.

2. The underlying acknowledgement of Reciprocity not only leads to the competitive system but also expands possibility by allowing for and facilitating resistance against restrictive measures (thus increasing possibility). As long as a system inhibits Reciprocity, it inhibits the possibilities that lead to discovery. And that explains why the world's drugs are generally developed inside countries that acknowledge Reciprocity—and then shipped into systems that resist it. In societies that don't recognize the fact that power is transferred through its own exertion (which also happen to be societies that discourage competition), the primary way by which drugs become available (if they become available at all) is through acquisition (i.e., import) rather than domestic discovery/production. The drugs must enter those systems from outside the system, often subsidized by the citizens of those systems that recognize Reciprocity.*

---

*   Such subsidization is also a form of altruism, and the recognition that competition is co-operation helps explain this apparently paradoxical phenomenon: today's great altruists emerge from the world's most competitive systems. Not only does competition allow for wealth-creation it also helps create the co-operative mind-set that leads the wealthy to willingly assist others. The fact that the world's most successful industrialists and entrepreneurs are also our most extraordinary altruists is not paradoxical once one understands the inherent nature of the competition (as opposed to conflict) that made those entrepreneurs/industrialists wealthy in the first place. It was not through separation—raiding others' castles and then hoarding what they looted (which is literally how the affluent

This economic application of the rule of Reciprocity—explaining why drugs are discovered/produced in systems that recognize Reciprocity and then shipped into systems that don't—reveals that the elimination of the dictatorship is the only way to initiate the co-operation necessary for self-sufficiency in those systems. Again, everything a government has to bestow upon its people comes from the people to begin with. Therefore, a government with little to bestow is a government that is not co-operating; it is either not co-operating in the creation, maintenance, and protection of possibilities that facilitate discovery/production in the first place; or it is not co-operating in just distribution of what it does collect, that is to say it is not allowing agreements that facilitate balancing/oscillation to determine distribution. Of course, most governments that resist Reciprocity do not co-operate at either end.

But this still leaves the question of distribution according to need in free-market societies, societies that *don't* distribute according to need.

So now, distribution.

Having considered the discovery part of the drug conundrum and keeping in mind that drugs that haven't been discovered can't be distributed, let's start this exploration of distribution in the free-market economy with two simple truths:

1. Drug companies exert.
2. Drug consumers (i.e., patients and their allies) exert.

Overexertions on the part of the drug companies (exertions that make it less possible for those who need the drugs to access them) will, by degrees, stymie distribution, which will lead to a reduction in production, restriction of possibilities, and ultimately diminishment of future discovery. Overexertions on the part of patients and their allies (exertions that inhibit competition/cooperation) will also, by degrees, stymie production, reduce possibilities, inhibit discovery, and lead ultimately to a reduction in distribution. Both parties—producers and patients—want their drugs distributed. The question, of course, is: under what conditions? So nowhere in free markets is power's pattern of exertion, transference, and redefinition (i.e., oscillation) more apparent (and important) than in this example.

---

accumulated wealth in the past)—but through unity (fidelity to the system), that is to say, not through conflict but competitive co-operation that the world's altruists acquired their wealth.

Reciprocity predicts that—through the oscillation of power which results from the competitive interactions between drug manufacturers as well as the exertions and transferences between manufacturers and patients/allies—rules will arise. And those rules (the progenitors of co-operation in competitive systems) will facilitate a market movement toward just distribution.

In order to expose that pattern in reality, I'll start with one example and then expand.

Our story begins in approximately 400 BC when the Greek physician Hippocrates prescribed "the bark and leaves of the willow tree (rich in a substance called salicin) to relieve pain and fever."[151] Our story ends (or arrives at present) with terms such as *patent, trademark, pharmaceutical bioequivalence, generic drugs, FDA,* and the *Hatch-Waxman Act.* The meat of the matter, of course, lies in the events that occurred between Hippocrates and Hatch-Waxman.

The "drug" that Hippocrates was harvesting is well-known today. It was the Bayer Company's chemist Felix Hoffman who "synthesize[d] a stable form . . . [that] later became the active ingredient in aspirin."[152] Aspirin quickly became Bayer's most important product, and the history of aspirin gives us more insight than we might imagine into Reciprocity's relationship to distribution, justice, and just distribution. It illustrates that capitalism's competitive/cooperative system pushes for greater distribution not less and outlines how a product with benefits to many can move from monopoly to ubiquity in an economic system that does not distribute according to need. Aspirin's story also leads us toward territory where we encounter broader agreements affecting drug distribution in the free-market economy, examples of just (balancing) distribution that emerge from the process of exertion, transference, and redefinition.

Let's begin this analysis of aspirin with the simple observation that salicin appears in nature. Thus we have encountered in fact a statement made earlier in theory: obviously, all capital ultimately traces back to natural resources and/or knowledge. Take salicin (a natural resource) add to it Bayer's knowledge of how to process it into aspirin, and you have a remarkable and marketable product.

Of course, aspirin was not the first product that came through the process of discovery, production, and distribution. That's why, by the time aspirin hit the market, those mature economic systems in which Bayer was operating had already formed the victim's doctrines of patent and trademark. Through the process of exertion, transference, and redefinition, those agreements (rules of the game) had been defined and recorded in order to encourage discovery by acknowledging and protecting the value of the inventor's efforts; that is to say, the victim's doctrines of patent and trademark were designed to preserve the possibility of ownership.

Were aspirin treated the same as salicin, as a substance that could simply be pulled from trees, then the value of Bayer's efforts and the production processes the company developed would be completely disregarded and systematically negated. In truth, aspirin is not just salicin; it is a chemical compound called acetyl salicylic acid; therefore, certain legal/economic systems allow it to be patented. Products that can be plucked from trees—apples, oranges—or pulled from the ground—potatoes, diamonds—cannot be patented. But the processes used in transforming them, as well as the final products of those transformations, can be. In recognizing the fact that possibility leads to discovery, we must also recognize that *possibility* includes the possible rewards *of* discovery. Patent law protects such possibilities: once aspirin was discovered and developed, if everyone could simply mimic its production, then some of the advantages of discovery and development would be greatly diminished while others would be altogether eliminated.

In addition, under the accumulations of agreements in which Bayer was operating, the terms and/or names applied to those processes/products could also be protected—by trademark, which is simply another victim's doctrine and manifestation of agreement that emerged from the pattern of exertion, transference, and redefinition. Trademarks also encourage discovery by protecting a number of possible motivations, including personal recognition and financial reward; if everyone can call their pill an aspirin, some of the advantages of discovering and developing a product called aspirin will be greatly diminished.

Here we see that the possibilities which encourage discovery exist at both ends of the process, and systems that recognize Reciprocity allow for the actions necessary to *pursue* discovery while protecting the potential rewards *of* discovery. Again, different people are motivated by different rewards—social contribution, personal recognition, and financial remuneration being paramount among them. If you diminish possibility, you diminish discovery and, therefore, reduce/eliminate distribution. Patent and trademark agreements are intended to encourage discovery and distribution by preserving the possibility of ownership, which in turn enhances the possibilities of social contribution, personal recognition, and financial remuneration.* But in the end, those patent and trademark agreements that protect ownership and encourage discovery are only agreements; they are not immutable phenomena of nature, and thus, they can be challenged, amended, broken, and/or abandoned as new events lead to new exertions, transferences, and (sometimes) redefinitions of limits.

Before we go forward, it is worth noting that these agreements (patent and trademark) were developed or adopted in part under relatively authoritarian regimes that did not fully acknowledge Reciprocity. Thus, these instruments are evidence of the exertions, transferences, and redefinitions that must occur under every system; that is to say, the fact that these limits were set reveals that oscillation exists everywhere (even under regimes that are not yet in full acknowledgment of Reciprocity).

---

*   Ownership's reinforcement of recognition and remuneration is obvious. But how does the possibility of ownership enhance the possibility of social contribution? Doesn't ownership encourage hoarding and therefore discourage communal benefit? No. In fact, communal cooptation inhibits discovery, which reduces social contribution. If everything you did was taken from your control and subsumed by or dispersed into communal proprietorship, then your individual vision would be perpetually jeopardized and generally fade away into the compromise that characterizes decision-by-committee. That statement is true by degrees: the more cooptation, the less contribution; the less cooptation, the more contribution. Over time, under the egalitarian pressures of communal cooptation, individual cogitation would be systematically discouraged. And people reared under such a system would feel the same sorts of conformist pressures as people reared under systems with highly ossified "cultures" (or strict, prefabricated notions of proper behavior). This is not merely theory. Individuals living under centralized (or centralizing) systems feel those effects in fact: "Elia López, a 22-year-old architecture student at UCV [University of Venezuela], worries that by the time she is designing buildings, the only client will be the state, limiting her creativity. 'Imagine if you started to do something creative, and suddenly you couldn't do it, or you could do it only if your ideas were the same as the government,' she said. Variations on that concern are almost universal among Venezuela's university students, whether they are majoring in sociology, dentistry or law" (Lyons, A12). In contrast, ownership protects the vision of the individual, encourages competition/co-operation, and therefore raises the possibility of social contribution. As long as the system recognizes Reciprocity, the potential ills of ownership will always be offset by the redefinitions that follow overexertions.

Back to aspirin: As Diarmuid Jefreys recounts in his study, *Aspirin: The Remarkable Story of a Wonder Drug*, when Bayer went to patent its product in Germany, the application was refused. "German law covered only new processes and not new products,"[153] and the German patent-office did not deem Bayer's process novel enough to warrant a patent. "[I]t soon became apparent that most other countries took the same view."[154] So we see at the outset that patent law establishes a competitive/cooperative approval process designed to engage in balancing (justice) and prevent conflict. In the end, "[i]t seemed that only two nations would grant Bayer the protection it sought. Fortunately, they were also the two largest potential markets: Britain and the United States of America."[155] On December 22, 1898, the British patent was filed "even before the new drug was named,"[156] and it was "[a]ccepted under the number 27,088."[157] Similarly, the US patent was filed on February 27, 1900.[158] "Bayer had managed to get a monopoly . . . over the production and sale of what was clearly a very popular new drug. And of course it had been able to obtain trademarks on the aspirin name everywhere because it was genuinely a new word."[159]

Now, monopoly is not a formula for just distribution (that's why I chose this aspirin example). And skeptics of the free-market's ability to achieve just distribution would consider such a situation dire. Consequently, one could easily understand how those with dictatorial inclinations (however benign or benevolent) might be tempted to dictate the distribution of such a beneficial product.* That is not, however, what happened. Aspirin's production was not seized, and the product was not distributed dictatorially. Yet just distribution of aspirin was reached. Today, aspirin is one of the most (if not the most) readily available drugs in the world. And this transformation from a unique, proprietary, and valuable drug to a near-universal commodity is precisely what makes aspirin an interesting example of distribution under systems that don't impose need-based judgments as the mechanism of distribution.

Here in brief is a tracing of the exertions, transferences, and redefinitions that led to today's condition—a world in which aspirin seemingly grows on trees:

---

* By considering such a simple example, one also sees this irony quite clearly: those who would act to take over aspirin from Bayer and distribute it according to their personal preferences would simply be replacing Bayer's monopoly with their own, which in the long-run would lead to monopoly's common consequence (and the outcome they feared in the first place)—diminished/unjust distribution. The logic that "the monopoly I run" will be more just than "the monopoly you run," while undoubtedly seductive, is also obviously false as it is based on the same sort of non-cooperative agenda that cannot lead to balancing.

The first redefinition of limits that would ultimately lead to just distribution of aspirin can be found in the details of patent law itself: "One day the US patent would run out and rival manufacturers would then be free to pounce."[160] Why would the patent one day run out? Because, while patent law is a victim's doctrine protecting the interests of discoverers and developers, those interests, if guarded too jealously, can also create new victims by denying others the utility of the invention/discovery; thus, patent law—itself a victim's doctrine that emerged from the process of balancing—has another victim's doctrine inscribed within it: patents expire. Why do patents expire? They expire in order to alleviate the victimization that might occur if certain products were forever controlled. Precisely the same motive/rationale that would guide some to make aspirin free to all at the outset guided patent law to prescribe end dates for patents. This was a systemic redefinition that had occurred before Bayer went into the aspirin business, and Bayer knew about it going in.

Now, it is worth noting that even though patent law was in place and even though Bayer's patent would one day expire, other manufacturers still fought (not literally, but competitively, since capitalism discourages violence) for the right to manufacture what could very well be considered the most important (and possibly profitable) new drug of their day: "Shortly before eleven on the morning of 2 May 1905, George Moulton KC stood up in the majestic oaken surroundings of London's High Court and prepared to fire the opening salvoes [not real salvoes, metaphorical salvoes] in one of the most significant intellectual property battles [not a literal battle] in medical-legal history . . . 'My Lord, said Moulton, 'this is an action for infringement of patent number 27,088.'"[161] "That two of Germany's leading chemical companies [Bayer and Chemische Fabrik von Heyden] should have been slugging it out in a British court might seem surprising at first, but the stakes were enormous."[162]

Bayer v. Chemische Fabrik von Heyden was no show trial. "Over the next eight working days [Justice Royce] was bombarded with facts and figures, chemical formulae, legal precedents, lengthy articles from German scientific journals and hours of expert but often conflicting testimony from some of Europe's leading chemistry professors, pharmaceutical scientists and doctors."[163] Of course, any examination of the details of that contest reveals numerous examples of Reciprocity-in-action, but foregoing a foray into the back-and-forth maneuvering that characterized the courtroom competition, we'll simply leave it at this: Bayer lost.

The same process of exertion, transference, and redefinition that enabled Bayer to patent aspirin in the first place (the same system that acknowledged

Reciprocity) also enabled others to challenge that patent. And the system, which would have moved in the direction of just distribution at the patent expire date anyway, moved that way even sooner.

The second redefinition came in connection with Bayer's ownership of the trademark *aspirin*. Unlike patents, trademarks don't expire because the word *aspirin* itself carries no utility. A rose by any other name would smell as sweet, and aspirin by any other name would work as well. Since no one can be victimized by another's ongoing ownership of a made-up word, the victim's doctrine has set no limits on such ownership. But the trademark does provide a distinct ownership and marketing advantage. So as the expiration date on aspirin's U.S. patent was nearing, Bayer made it clear that it would fight any rival attempting to appropriate its trademarked name. Bayer made those intentions clear in court—"It . . . filed suit against the United Drug company of Boston for trademark infringement"[164]—and it did so through this advertisement (broadcast) in the American Medical Association's journal: "The Trade-Mark 'Aspirin' (Registered US Patent Office) is entirely separate from the patent on Acetyl Salicylic Acid and will not expire with this patent. The Trade Mark 'Aspirin' remains our exclusive property and therefore only acetyl salicylic acid manufactured by the Bayer Co., Inc., can be marketed or sold as 'Aspirin'. Any violation of our trade-mark rights will be vigorously prosecuted."[165] There is no question that acetyl salicylic acid was about to experience a manufacturing bonanza as the American patent neared expiration. And given Bayer's preemptive defense of its trademark, competitive manufacturers would simply have had to call their aspirin by another name (just as Advil and Motrin are the same drug—ibuprofen— marketed under different names, and competitors market acetaminophen under brands besides Tylenol). Ultimately, Bayer's ongoing ownership of the word *aspirin* would have had no adverse consequence on distribution of the drug itself, and this examination of free-market pressures toward just distribution would have ended here. But then something remarkable happened, an event that casts a light all the way back to the beginning of this book, to the very definition and creation of power itself: the world fell back to force relations.

At the outbreak of World War I, in that descent from power relations to force relations, the agreements under which Bayer had been previously doing business were placed in serious jeopardy. And, upon declaring war "in April 1917, the United States [took] . . . control of all Bayer's American assets [i.e., abandoned the previously existing accumulation of agreements]."[166] Thus, the capitalists' competition—waged via the competitive techniques of courtroom "salvoes," marketplace "battles" and magazine ads—was followed by an actual war (a conflict waged with real salvoes, real battles, and magazines of ammunition). Germany abandoned the system. Then Germany lost the war. And in its subsequent surrender Germany had little choice but to accept certain redefinitions of limits, including a minor concession that must be considered a footnote to a footnote to a footnote among the many ramifications of the First World War—one of Germany's most prominent companies was forced to forfeit ownership of the word *aspirin*.

As World War I erupted, Bayer's participation in the American system that structured power relations between the countries was severed by force relations, and Bayer's trademark was swept away on the tides of war. This real-world example helps us see (again) the essential and unavoidable distinction between force and power. Bayer's trademark would not have been confiscated were it not for that falling back to force relations. So this particular example of the free-market's movement toward just distribution also holds within it an important illustration of the basic premise upon which much of this analysis has been based—power is the ability to influence another's actions; there is a difference between force and power; agreement creates power. Following the German/American abandonment of agreement, the Bayer Company was rendered powerless over the U.S. government's decision to release the word aspirin from its trademarked status.

Setting aside the odd (yet instructive) history of the word aspirin, Reciprocity shows us how acetyl salicylic acid moved from monopoly to ubiquity in a free-market economy: in the power relations that guide free-market distribution, just distribution is determined not by a single dictator, or dictatorial institution; instead, the economic system that acknowledges Reciprocity expands distribution through various forms of competition (including legal), each of which requires co-operation (abidance by agreements), and this primacy of the agreement in turn further elicits Reciprocity, which creates balancing, which leads to just distribution.

Of course, that is not necessarily true of every other available drug (yet). And the simple example of aspirin also leads us toward some of those more complex terms (and agreements) mentioned above. Here we have emerged onto that larger field wherein we encounter "pharmaceutical bioequivalence," "generics," "Hatch-Waxman," and other laws and concepts that have developed out of the process of exertion, transference, and redefinition, and which, when taken in scope, describe a movement toward just distribution in an economic system that acknowledges Reciprocity.

Returning to the earlier illustration of basic economic exchange (exchanging eggs for vegetables), it is clear that even such primitive barter rests on the implicit agreement that the goods being bartered are functional. The same foundational agreement also exists with regard to more complex products in more advanced markets: there is an implicit assumption that the drugs being distributed will do what the sellers say they'll do. Thus, as the U.S. drug market grew, the U.S. government (elected by the people and working on their behalf through the National Research Council of the National Academy of Sciences) undertook a thorough review of every drug that had been previously approved for use in the United States. This massive study, conducted under the name Drug Efficacy Study Implementation (DESI), evaluated the effectiveness of over three thousand medications. The result: a list of products that had been judged effective and which generic manufacturers could then file applications to produce.*

The point is not to debate the efficacy of DESI, but to explain why the study was undertaken. That exercise (itself an effort to facilitate just distribution) was not launched spontaneously on the whim of some potentate; it was the consequence of exertion (certain drug manufacturers overexerted by marketing ineffective drugs), transference (the victims and their allies took the power transferred by those exertions and used it to influence the actions of drug manufacturers), and redefinition (DESI was nothing if not an effort at redefinition). All of this occurred within a free-market economy, and again, it led toward just distribution: once the list of approved drugs was published, companies could produce "bioequivalent" or "generic" versions without first having to reproduce the studies that the original manufacturers had conducted.

But what about drugs approved for production post-1962? In 1984, the Drug Price Competition and Patent Term Restoration Act—aka the Hatch-Waxman Act—expanded the market for generic drugs ongoing. The Hatch-Waxman Act is nothing if not an example of the sort of co-operation that underlies and emerges from competition as well as an illustration of the

---

* This example highlights the necessity of Reciprocity in a just system. The U.S. government is accountable to the citizens it serves, and the politicians who spearheaded DESI would have lost their positions if the study were exposed as a mere mask behind which those leaders entered into corrupt agreements with drug manufacturers. In a system that does not recognize Reciprocity, a system in which the people are not able to exercise the power transferred to them through the exertions of their leaders (are not able to influence the actions of officeholders by voting them out of office), DESI would certainly have provided little more than a cover for corruption.

compromise that replaces conflict under capitalism. As a direct result of the Hatch-Waxman Act, "[g]eneric drug companies gained greater access to the market for prescription drugs, and innovator companies gained restoration of patent life . . . lost during the FDA's approval process."[167] In other words, the time it took from the date-of-patent to the date of FDA approval*would be tolled, and the clock would only start ticking toward expiration of the patent at the point of approval (I am simplifying this significantly—the details of patent restoration are far more complex; and they are also relatively irrelevant here, except for the fact that those details do also manifest the co-operation, compromise, and balancing that characterizes the competitive system and pushes producers toward just distribution). Now, along with that patent restoration concession to innovators came this advantage for generic manufacturers: companies seeking to manufacture generic versions of previously proprietary medicines would simply have to "submit an abbreviated new drug application (ANDA) for approval to market a generic product . . . [And, similar to DESI], [t]he ANDA process does not require the drug sponsor to repeat costly animal and clinical research on ingredients or dosage forms already approved for safety and effectiveness."[168]

Under Hatch-Waxman, the patent-period restoration recognizes and remunerates the innovator company for the effort and expense of testing; and the ANDA process makes it easier for competitors to manufacture the drug by freeing those manufacturers from the effort and expense of testing. Patents encourage discovery and distribution (again, drugs that haven't been discovered can't be distributed), and ANDA encourages distribution and (possibly) discovery by enabling competitors to generate revenue through the production of generic drugs, revenue they can then potentially redeploy toward research. This is not mere theory. The current accumulation of agreements—emerging directly out of the pattern of exertion, transference, and redefinition that characterizes Reciprocity-in-action—*has* encouraged efforts at discovery. According to the Congressional Budget Office's study entitled *How Increased Competition from Generic Drugs Has Affected Prices and Returns in the Pharmaceutical Industry*: "Between 1983 and 1995, investment in R&D as a percentage of pharmaceutical sales by brand-name drug companies increased from 14.7 percent to 19.4 percent. Over the same period, U.S. pharmaceutical sales by those companies rose from $17 billion to $57 billion (in current dollars). Overall, then, the changes that have

---

*   Note: The FDA itself as well as the regulations it enforces are all also products of exertion, transference, and redefinition of limits by victims and their allies.

occurred since 1984 (the Hatch-Waxman Act) appear to be favoring investment in drug development."[169] And the accumulation of agreements has also led to increased distribution: "Although generic drugs are chemically identical to their branded counterparts, they are typically sold at substantial discounts from the branded price. According to the Congressional Budget Office, generic drugs save consumers an estimated $8 to $10 billion a year at retail pharmacies."[170]

The point is not to declare a state of perfection with regard to drug distribution in the United States (nor even to enter into the details of the ongoing debate). Drug distribution under the U.S. accumulation of agreements remains subject to the future exposure of overexertions and the revision of the law by, or on behalf of, future victims. When those future redefinitions of limits will occur is unpredictable. Precisely how they will happen is unknowable. But that they will happen is inevitable. Why? Because drug companies exert; drug consumers (i.e., patients and their allies) exert; and the U.S. system acknowledges Reciprocity and facilitates oscillation. And that *is* the point: all of these pressures toward just distribution in the free-market system (the system that does not distribute according to need) stem from exertion, transference, and redefinition—a process that can only be facilitated by a system that acknowledges the fact that power is transferred through its own exertion.

Of course, Reciprocity's effect on economic interactions is not limited to the distribution of drugs. And were we to look, we would find countless examples of exertions, transferences, and redefinitions followed by further exertions, transferences, and re-redefinitions leading to the formation and adoption of new rules designed to achieve justice. Taking up one minor, non-drug-related example: in 1933, the Glass-Steagall Act separated the services of banks from the services of brokerages, making it illegal for commercial banks to own brokerages, sell stock, and offer certain other financial services to their customers. That act emerged out of the pattern of exertion and transference and the subsequent redefinition of limits on behalf of victims who had lost money with banks. In 1999, the Gramm-Leach-Bliley Act took down the Glass-Steagall wall, effectively redefining that 1933 redefinition and re-enabling banks to offer certain non-banking investment services to their customers. Why? Both banks and customers were being victimized by the inhibition of competition instituted by Glass-Steagall. Thus, the initial redefinition of limits was itself redefined when new victims emerged.

Here's another one: as a result of overexertions by the executives at Enron, WorldCom, and other publicly traded corporations, Congress passed the Sarbanes-Oxley Act, imposing more rigorous reporting requirements and making directors more directly liable for accounting errors and omissions. Subsequently, there was an uptick in companies going public in markets outside the United States as well as a high-profile trend toward taking public companies private; Goldman Sachs has even created "its own private system to trade the stocks of companies that don't want the scrutiny and regulatory burdens of going public . . . [and] Goldman's move partly reflects a business-community backlash against increased regulation of public-company accounting practices."[171] Sarbanes-Oxley may or may not have been an over-reaction (over-exertion) on the part of U.S. lawmakers who were acting on behalf of the significant number of victims created by the malfeasance of executives at Enron and elsewhere. If new victims emerge, the Sarbanes-Oxley Act (like Glass-Steagall) may also one day be revised.

Before we leave behind the general topics of economic exertion, transference, and redefinition as they relate to just distribution and the specific example of aspirin, let's select one sentence as the starting point for consideration of another reason why capitalism sustains itself; it is a sentence that we encountered earlier and could easily dismiss as ordinary: "That two of Germany's leading chemical companies should have been slugging it out in a British court might seem surprising at first, but the stakes were enormous."[172] And let's rewrite that sentence not only to explain why those companies were in that court but also to highlight another characteristic of free-market capitalism, an extraordinary quality that is directly related to Reciprocity: that two of Germany's leading chemical companies should have been seeking justice in a British court might seem surprising at first, but capitalism's agreements are capable of expanding.

We have seen how capitalism counters centralization's problems of discovery and distribution; now here's another reason why it survives—expansion. Two German companies were able to enter the English economic system because, as stated in the "System" section under the "Expansion of Agreements" subhead: "To hold people out, is to hold people in. To hold people out is to restrict those who are in the system from interacting with those who are outside the system. And people living within a system that acknowledges Reciprocity will not allow themselves to be held in. They will redefine such limits on interaction." And because every system's subsystems must eventually align (either recognizing or resisting Reciprocity), those two German companies were also able to enter the British legal system and pursue resolution of their disagreement because that system (pushed forward by acknowledgment of Reciprocity) was capable of engaging in the balancing that is justice. The notion of two companies willingly relying on the legal system of a foreign dictatorship to resolve their dispute is absurd.* A system that perpetuates the false notion that power comes from above cannot actively engage in the balancing/oscillation that results from Reciprocity since the entire point of such a regime is to inhibit the acquisition of power—not encourage it.

Here it becomes most clear why the earlier definition of expansion as a phenomenon distinct from the incorporation of land and people is vitally important. In common parlance, *expansion* refers to the dilation of borders. In the context of Reciprocity, *expansion* describes the phenomenon wherein previously less influential parties accumulate more power within a system. While such accumulation does unavoidably occur under authoritarian regimes with centralized economies, that accumulation is exactly what destroys (not sustains) those regimes. Despite the recurrent initiation of force relations by communists seeking to engulf new people and new lands, the fact that the system's agreements can't expand, that parties can't acquire more power as time goes on, led that system toward collapse.

The Soviet Union certainly expanded its borders, but its agreements could not expand to acknowledge the acquisition of power by individuals and groups interacting within the system. That inability to allow agreements to expand explains why, as it enlarged itself geographically, the Soviet Union (and this holds true for all systems that oppose the fact that power is transferred through its own exertion) had to construct barriers (legal and physical) against emigration and escape. Borders were blocked not to prevent outsiders from penetrating the Soviet state and availing themselves of a system in which all goods were distributed in perfect harmony with need. The walls were built to limit the people's possibilities, discourage exposure of exertions, and contain oscillation. And all three of those goals must inevitably lead to the dissolution, not continuation, of the system. Limiting possibilities inhibits discovery, which hobbles any society, particularly an isolated one. Discouraging the exposure of exertions (a priority for all rulers attempting to deny Reciprocity) becomes more difficult as the system grows in population and size; then as exposure of exertions becomes harder to control, oscillation becomes more difficult to contain. Ironically, the Soviet

---

*   It is worth noting that one of the first things that foreign companies do when they enter into agreements with Chinese companies is draft contracts with clauses stipulating that disputes will be resolved through arbitration—*not* through the Chinese legal system. Eventually, as the currently corrupt Chinese legal system aligns itself with its decentralizing (and therefore expanding) economic system, such clauses will no longer be quite so necessary.

policy of "expansion" highlighted the one thing that that system was truly incapable of accomplishing.

Resistance against Reciprocity leads to the construction of walls (both physical and metaphorical) because such systems need to contain whatever oscillation does exist; the rulers of such systems certainly cannot allow their people the possibility of leaving, so they must establish a physical end point ("this is as far as you can go") to parallel the strict ideological boundaries that they construct to resist Reciprocity. Metaphorically speaking, this works in much the same way inhabitants of a coastline erect breaker walls to contain the ocean. And it fails for the same reason: absent ongoing efforts by those wall-builders to reinforce their structure, the ocean's own oscillation always wins. But in the case of the containment wall surrounding a country, the wall-builders (rulers) face an even greater, and paradoxical, challenge: their efforts to reinforce the wall (exertions) actually weaken it by transferring power to the people who would tear it down.

Now, that metaphor of the coastal containment wall feels somewhat flawed because coastal residents are trying to contain the ocean from outside—they are trying to hold it out while the rulers who build walls around their people are attempting to contain the ocean from inside—they are trying to hold it in. And that is true. But there is another truth here as well. The rulers who refuse to recognize Reciprocity, those who make ongoing efforts to deny the transfer of power that their exertions create, are also trying to hold an ocean out, not an ocean of foreigners hoping to storm their system, but an ocean of co-operation that exists beyond their borders. They want to keep their people as blocked off as possible from external elements in order to avoid the formation of agreements that will inevitably let Reciprocity leak through. Just as to hold people out is to hold people in, to hold people in is also to hold people out.*

History has provided the data sufficient for us to conclude that holding the ocean of co-operation out is an impossible task. But now we know why cooperative/competitive interactions deteriorate both authoritarianism's foundation and façade and contribute to the crumbling of dictatorships. Once a system begins to engage in capitalism (an economic system based

---

* We see these truths to this day in the case of North Korea: "In Pyongyang's telling, 'ideological and cultural infiltration'—economic and other contacts with the outside world—brought down Soviet socialism; the masters of Pyongyang have no intention of allowing bourgeois infection to undo their own gulag paradise" (Eberstadt, A14).

on co-operation, not conflict), its legal and political systems must eventually align themselves with that co-operative/competitive (as opposed to conflictive) model. Because capitalism (based on the establishment of, and abidance by, agreements) recognizes Reciprocity, it naturally expands, empowering those who were previously less influential. As it expands—as previously less influential people acquire more power under the capitalist economic system—the pressure to reconcile a country's systems along competitive/co-operative lines of agreement (which employ non-violent mechanisms of resolution) necessarily builds (slowly and with setbacks); but no matter how such systemic alignment happens, it must happen, or else the regime must repeatedly fall back to fear-inducing exertions and ongoing isolationism (life confined behind walls).

Over time, as the citizens of countries whose political and legal systems do not recognize Reciprocity engage in capitalist/cooperative interactions with those that do, they unavoidably become entwined with those foreign legal and political systems (systems that are capable of balancing). This creates multidimensional pressures on the political/legal systems of regimes that do not recognize Reciprocity. Not only do the private citizens (workers) under dictatorial systems gain power through capitalist interactions with foreign nations, but the rulers themselves are also placed into circumstances in which they are forced to recognize Reciprocity. For example, a centralized economy that exports hazardous products will be influenced by its trading partners to remedy such errors (recall: under systems that recognize Reciprocity, "there are those who actually earn their living by exposing such abuse and seeking remedy. In a system whose agreements recognize Reciprocity and facilitate oscillation, victims turn to the law"). In other words, the rulers of a capitalist dictatorship will be held accountable for the quality of the products their country exports and will therefore be pressured toward economic decentralization, releasing themselves from responsibilities they cannot bear and setting their citizens free on the ocean of Reciprocity. In the alternative, the rulers will be forced to acknowledge they are subject to Reciprocity, that their exertions (exporting hazardous products) actually transfer power away and make others more able to influence their actions. Either way, the top-down model of power is toppled by the undercurrent of capitalist co-operation. As direct economic interactions between the citizens of these disparate systems becomes more common (and more essential to the citizens of those regimes that do not recognize Reciprocity), abandonment of the capitalist system will become more difficult, and these mounting internal and external pressures will push capitalist dictatorships to recognize Reciprocity throughout their legal and political systems as well.

Reciprocity cannot predict precisely when, where, or how this will happen, but it is unavoidable: as a result of direct economic interactions between citizens of systems that don't recognize Reciprocity and citizens of systems that do, capitalist dictatorships will be forced to align their systems either as a consequence of those international interactions or as the result of the power accumulated internally by their own citizens.

To outlaw capitalism is to severely restrict cooperation. That is why the elimination of capitalism "cannot . . . be effected except by means of despotic [i.e., non-cooperative] inroads."[173] But cooperation cannot be outlawed, though it can be disrupted by cement walls and "iron curtains." On the other hand, capitalist systems can't help but expand—can't help but allow initially less influential individuals to gain influence over time—because capitalism rests on co-operative rules (i.e., agreements); agreements create power, and power manifests Reciprocity, which generates oscillation and enables individuals/groups to acquire more power. Per Milton Friedman, "It is a striking historical fact that the development of capitalism has been accompanied by a major reduction in the extent to which particular religious, racial, or social groups have operated under special handicaps in respect of their economic activities . . . [T]he substitution of contract arrangements for status arrangements [the substitution of cooperation/competition for top-down, social coercion] was the first step toward the freeing of the serfs in the Middle Ages."[174] "[D]iscrimination against groups of particular color or religion is least in those areas where there is the greatest freedom of competition."[175] Today we can explain those observations—we have a theorem that underlies the data (those "striking historical fact[s]") connecting the rise of capitalism with the decline of systemic discrimination: Capitalism is competition; competition is cooperation; cooperation requires agreement; agreement creates power; power is transferred through its own exertion, and the oscillation that results from Reciprocity leads societies away from discrimination and toward systemic equalization.

It is simply impossible to have production without agreements. It is impossible to have agreement without power and impossible to have power without Reciprocity; therefore, it is impossible to have production without Reciprocity—no matter who controls the means of production. Once a system is established upon agreements that recognize and facilitate Reciprocity, the system is able to expand; once the system is able to expand (enabling initially less influential individuals to acquire more influence) it is able to endure indefinitely.

And with that statement, we can move out of economics and into the final analysis of power relations that makes up this "Power" section.

Democracy

Following a consideration of the resistance to Reciprocity, this section moved forward with a look at how power is maintained (and lost) within the theocratic system, took up the same question under the generic heading of authoritarianism, used the issues raised by the centralization of power in order to transition to the centralized economic system, compared the centralized economic system to the decentralized economic (free-market) system, a system that recognizes Reciprocity, and this "Power" section is now nearing conclusion at a consideration of the operation of power under democracy (a political system that acknowledges and allows for the fact that power is transferred through its own exertion).

Now, the statement that led into this subsection is as true for democracy as it was for capitalism—once a system is established upon agreements that recognize and facilitate Reciprocity, the system is able to expand; once the system is able to expand (enabling initially less influential individuals to acquire more influence), it is able to endure indefinitely. Oscillation sits at the genetic core of democracy, but oscillation is not a consequence of democracy—it is the cause. Reciprocity creates oscillation; oscillation leads to democracy. And democracy—because it recognizes the fact that power is transferred through its own exertion and facilitates the expansion of agreements—is able to endure.

Revolution is extinct in systems that recognize Reciprocity because the rulers are below the rules, and the rules themselves recognize the fact that power is transferred through its own exertion. Thus, when George Washington voluntarily ceded office at the end of his second term, when he handed over his sword at Annapolis, that act held more than symbolic value—it was more than the ritual representation of the abandonment of force (the surrender of the sword) as the system's mechanism of transference—it was an act with real consequence. Washington established the precedent that the system supersedes the president. And the stepping aside of America's first commander-in-chief became not a point of weakness for the country, but a point of strength, a foundation that made it not only possible for the country's future "commanders" to do the same but also impossible for them not to—if they were to maintain the same system. Washington correctly recognized "that his place in history would be enhanced, not by enlarging his power, but by surrendering it."[176] And one would have a hard time finding a single act reflecting more insight into Reciprocity.

When people discuss a government's legitimacy, they generally mean whether the leaders hold office with the consent of the people. And consent can only be reliably expressed and measured through elections. So legitimacy generally means democracy. But when one delves deeper, one discovers that what is really being discussed when the question of a regime's legitimacy arises is not only whether the leaders were elected but how/whether the government recognizes or resists the rule of Reciprocity. For example, Francis Fukuyama makes this statement: "Legitimate regimes have a fund of goodwill that excuses them from short-term mistakes, even serious ones, and failure can be expiated by the removal of a prime minister or cabinet. In illegitimate regimes, on the other hand, failure frequently precipitates the overturning of the regime itself."[177] Clearly, Reciprocity is woven throughout those words. Under regimes that recognize Reciprocity, cooperative/competitive procedures replace violence as the mechanism of resolution, and "failure can be expiated by the removal of a prime minister or cabinet." Under regimes that don't recognize Reciprocity, "failure frequently precipitates the overturning of the regime itself" (cf., once the ruler is below the rules, revolution is unnecessary, but if we invert this to consider the condition wherein the ruler remains above the rules, we see that under those circumstances revolution/coup is the *only* choice for people seeking to replace a ruler). Of course, the "failure" to which Mr. Fukuyama refers can only come through exertion, overexertion, misguided exertion, etc. Thus, that failure (being a consequence of exertion) transfers power to the people, and unless the system enables those people to exercise that power (unless the system recognizes Reciprocity), those people have no alternative except revolution to implement change. Today, the citizens of mature democracies are in the difficult position of watching the subjects of other systems struggle through the exertions and redefinitions that will lead to the systemic recognition of Reciprocity.

In addition to the fact that we now have a theorem explaining the data Mr. Fukuyama cites, we also know that it is not "goodwill" that preempts revolution under "legitimate regimes," nor is it solely "goodwill's" absence that prompts revolution under "illegitimate" ones. In both instances, it is the presence or absence of an acknowledgement of Reciprocity that leads to those disparate consequences (removal vs. revolution). So to the extent that "goodwill" is used as an explanation for the sustainability of democracy, "goodwill" is really a placeholder for Reciprocity. It is not goodwill, but the facilitation of Reciprocity that explains the survival of a system beyond even the sometimes severe "short-term mistakes." Taking up two examples touched on earlier, the citizens of the United States did not say, "Oh, our government has built up a fund of goodwill with us over the years, so we'll just excuse Presidents Nixon and Clinton of their crimes in office." And it would be hard to imagine either of those former presidents ever describing themselves as having been the beneficiaries of "goodwill." Instead, the system allowed the people (via elected representatives) to take the power those presidents transferred to them through their illegal exertions (exertions that exceeded the limits set by the relevant victim's doctrines) and use that power to influence the actions of those leaders.

It is pointless to delve too deeply into democracy's relationship to Reciprocity since so many of the examples provided throughout this study were drawn from the data produced by the experiences of democratic systems. Therefore, I'm not going to review all that has gone before in order to extract, highlight, and re-examine the examples that have had relevance to democracy. Instead, I am only going to consider two interesting (at least I hope they're interesting) democracy-related questions in light of what we now know of Reciprocity. The questions are: can democracy be imposed? and, what does Reciprocity tell us about the notion of "freedom"—a concept we have been circling throughout, have already directly encountered (under "free markets"), and one that is most often directly associated with democracy?

In taking up the question, can democracy be imposed? we must first fold in this ultimately unavoidable observation: given the fact that the acknowledgment of Reciprocity is inevitable, one would expect it to be relatively easy to establish a system that recognizes Reciprocity. Yet, history tells us it is not. So one must wonder, why is it so difficult to establish democracy? And the answer would appear to be that democracy can't be imposed. But that is false. Ironically, democracy is the only system that can be imposed and then hold with permanence. Any system can be introduced through force (even democracy). But none can be maintained that way (especially democracy). As we saw earlier in the case of Saddam Hussein's prewar "election," coercing people to the polls is not democracy (despite the Iraqi spokesperson's attempt to claim that it was a unique and superior form). Technically, any regime that seeks to achieve ongoing acquiescence will need to co-operate (since ongoing acquiescence is co-operation). So at some point, a system must be chosen by its people if it is to endure, and authoritarianism cannot be chosen because even if it were, Reciprocity would eventually undermine that choice. Even if a people were to explicitly state, "We agree to relinquish Reciprocity," that agreement would undermine itself because agreement *creates* Reciprocity. A country's citizens always constitute the system (that is to say, the people themselves create and/or abide, however begrudgingly, by the agreements); therefore, the system that does not acknowledge its citizens merely repudiates itself. People are sometimes duped or frightened into voting themselves out of the right to vote, but nowhere does the aspiring dictator proclaim: "A vote for me is a vote against the vote because I just want to be a dictator myself."

Democracy is the only system that can be imposed and hold because it is the only system that can be instituted through force that will then be able to sustain itself, independent of the original enforcers' own efforts. So we see that democracy actually presents a double advantage over authoritarianism (in any form): democracy can be imposed, but it doesn't have to be imposed. It can be introduced (and gain permanence) following conflict, but it can also develop out of co-operation. In fact, democracy is the only system that can be initiated through imposition *and* extended through invitation: "'Give me your tired, your poor, Your huddled masses yearning to breathe free, The wretched refuse of your teeming shore; Send these, the homeless, tempest-tost to me.'"[178] The idea of inviting someone into a system that does not recognize the rule of Reciprocity is, at worst, threatening and, at best, absurd. And no authoritarian regime would ever invite "the wretched refuse" (the "best and the brightest" maybe—but not "the huddled masses").

So given democracy's many advantages, why then is the system sometimes so difficult to establish? Reciprocity highlights two overarching answers intertwined with one another:

1. The imposition of democracy is undercut by (guess what?) Reciprocity.
2. Proactive/preemptive measures are difficult in systems that recognize Reciprocity because the acknowledgment of Reciprocity requires exertion for transference.

Surrender (i.e., acquiescence) is the birth of every system that acknowledges Reciprocity (since it is the birth of every system). If one is to introduce through force (i.e., war) a system that recognizes Reciprocity, then the war must be won. Surrender must be achieved. Many of whom it was once said "they will never surrender," did in fact do so: the Southern states at the end of the U.S. Civil War and Japan, Germany, Italy, etc., at the end of World War II. Some said of the Japanese that they would never surrender, and they could not handle democracy anyway. And yet the Japanese did both. The same is true of the Germans. Yet in neither of those cases was the defeated country subsumed into the system of the victors. Neither Japan nor Germany own votes in the U.S. Electoral College or seats in British Parliament. Regardless of how the current force relations between the United States and individuals in Iraq ends, Iraq will never enter the union as America's fifty-first state.

However, all the countries that were conquered by the Soviet Union were subsequently subsumed into that system and controlled by the same Politburo that operated in and from Moscow.*

Surrender starts system; it initiates agreement, power, cooperation, and, of course, balancing. Authoritarianism is not capable of handling that balancing, but democracy is. When a system that facilitates Reciprocity conquers one that doesn't, the people that were conquered can exercise their newly acquired power without further violence. So now we see that the basic question moves from "can democracy be imposed?" (yes) through "why is it difficult to establish democracy?" (because wars must be won) to "why don't democracies win every war they wage?" And this is where we see how Reciprocity itself can undercut the attempt to impose a system that recognizes Reciprocity.

Waging war entails what can quickly come to be perceived as (and sometimes is) an exertion against the system's own citizens (the very people who are fighting the war). As soldiers are killed (particularly today, as their deaths are broadcast immediately), the citizens of a system begin to view those deaths as exertions made against them by their own government, not as exertions made on their behalf. But if the system does not acknowledge Reciprocity, then the waging of war (and the consequent deaths of the country's soldiers) is simply one more among many exertions after which the regime must make efforts to preempt the potential exercise of the transferred power. In other words, it's business as usual for regimes that don't recognize Reciprocity. On the other hand, as we have seen throughout, democracy institutes competitive/co-operative (as opposed to conflictive) mechanisms of resolution, so war recedes toward last resort for the democratic system.†

In addition, democracies resist war as an option—and they retreat from force relations prior to victory (even when victory would be *assured* by the application of increased force)—because proactive/preemptive measures are

---

* In fact, nowhere have we seen this juxtaposition more clearly than in the adjacency of East and West Germany, divided by a containment wall that was constructed not by the system that recognized Reciprocity, but by the one that did not.

† The emphasis on agreement and systemic pressure against violence also explains why democracies prefer to impose economic sanctions as opposed to launching physical attacks (even when they are guaranteed military victory by virtue of their disproportionate strength). In order to have economic sanctions, one must have economic agreements (however loose or indirect they may be); democracies naturally pursue acquiescence through strategies that operate on agreement first before resorting to force relations.

difficult in systems that recognize Reciprocity. And such measures are difficult under systems that recognize Reciprocity because power requires exertion for transference.

That exact sentence first appeared within the discussion of the victim's doctrine earlier. And the concept has been inscribed throughout. Taking up this idea in its simplest form: think back to the schoolyard example of the child who had the toy snatched from her hand. As the teacher investigates the incident, what question is she very likely to ask? Answer: "who started it?" Absent an understanding of Reciprocity, the who-started-it question would seem nonsensical. One child snatched a toy from another; why does it matter what event(s) preceded the snatching? The act is wrong on its face. Yet the preceding acts are relevant once one recognizes that exertion instigates transference. If the one who had the toy snatched away actually initiated the conflict (e.g., through some taunt or tease or similar exertion), then she in fact might have transferred power, which the snatcher then chose (however immaturely) to exercise through snatching. This who-started-it question—as simple as it seems—becomes of paramount importance in systems that recognize Reciprocity.*

Absent an adversary's exertion (that is to say, absent the transfer of power by an enemy), citizens of a system that recognizes Reciprocity naturally feel powerless to initiate force relations. As was stated above, if a U.S. lawmaker had suggested placing anti-aircraft guns atop the World Trade Center for the purpose of shooting down passenger planes, he'd have been laughed (and voted) out of office. If that same lawmaker had introduced a declaration of war against Afghanistan on September 10, 2001, he would have met with a similar response. Why? No exertions. No victims. No transference of power to justify such extreme actions. Again, preemptive measures are difficult in systems that acknowledge Reciprocity because Reciprocity requires exertion for transference. That phenomenon, coupled with the fact that democracy introduces co-operative/competitive processes of resolution (the vote replaces violence) creates pressures against the use of force, and the

---

* Parallel with the fact that murder carries several different charges based on the severity of the exertion (involuntary manslaughter, voluntary manslaughter, first-degree murder, and second-degree murder), there are also defenses such as justified homicide and self-defense, which arise from and rest on the concept of "who started it?" That is to say, they also arise from and rest on an understanding of the fact that power is transferred through its own exertion; thus, sometimes even deadly exertions are justified by the exertions that preceded them.

leaders are—sometimes rightly, sometimes wrongly (I am presenting this as neither endorsement nor excuse for any particular instance, but merely as explanation)—reluctant to initiate or increase force relations. To make the point even stronger, the failure to launch (or fully pursue) force relations often rests on more than mere reluctance. The leaders of systems that recognize Reciprocity are, in many instances, systemically incapable of starting or escalating force relations. So Reciprocity reveals an irony at work here. Why don't those systems that acknowledge Reciprocity always win the wars they wage in an effort to introduce Reciprocity? The answer: Reciprocity.

The difficulty with imposing democracy exists at the outset: recognition of the fact that power is transferred through its own exertion will hinder and/or undermine the exertions of those who are attempting to impose a system that acknowledges the fact that power is transferred through its own exertion.* Therefore, it *appears* easier to impose an authoritarian regime, one that brutally denies Reciprocity, only because it is easier to initiate and fully pursue force relations under such a system. But Reciprocity will eventually undermine such imposition.

At base, the triumph of democracy can be explained by the fact that in order for any government to exist, agreements must always be formed, and when they are, all parties are vested with power (whether rulers acknowledge this or not). We found that fact in the very essence of human interaction where we also found that every system starts with acquiescence. With regard to the establishment of new systems, acquiescence is almost always a dramatically imbalanced beginning. But once acquiescence is achieved, balancing commences, and *balancing* is precisely the phenomenon democracy is capable of sustaining.

So here's where we are with regard to the imposition of a system that recognizes Reciprocity: authoritarianism can be initiated through force, but

---

*   As an aside, the fact that power is transferred through its own exertion helps us to understand why "smart bombs" (bombs that create *fewer* victims) have been developed and deployed. And based on the perspective Reciprocity provides, headlines such as this one come to make perfect sense: "Deadly Precision: To Fight Terrorists, Air Force Seeks a Bomb with Less Bang; It Cuts Collateral Damage By Using a Metal Powder Instead of Flying Shrapnel" (Jaffe, A1). From such data, one can either conclude that (for some unknown reason) people in democracies value life more than people in totalitarian regimes, or one can recognize that even in force relations, systems that acknowledge Reciprocity sometimes conclude that fewer victims will lessen the potential for transference of power.

it eventually runs up against Reciprocity. Reciprocity can be introduced through force, but it quickly runs up against a paradox: in order to impose democracy one must engage in a transaction that can be best expressed as "we've conquered you, you're free." Given the fact that the condition following surrender is a severely imbalanced one (although balancing begins immediately), no authoritarian ruler is going to come out and declare, "The power I wield really comes from you, the people I rule, as a result of your acquiescence." Yet that is effectively what conquering democracies have done, and they simply cannot do otherwise if they are to maintain fidelity to their own systems. (Again, neither Japan nor Germany participate in the U.S. Electoral College or British Parliament.)

There, in that strangely beautiful statement—"we've conquered you, you're free"—we directly encounter the concept we've actually been considering throughout: freedom. And what does Reciprocity tell us about freedom?

Setting aside the romantic (and impossible) notion of an individual roaming the plains (a là the Lone Ranger) or independently ruling the forest (a là Tarzan), actual human existence will always include human society (interaction), and therefore, human freedom must include an understanding of Reciprocity (the basic rule of human interaction). Because human existence requires human interaction, human freedom cannot mean you always get to do what you want. If freedom meant always doing what you wanted, then you would either have to live without interaction with others, interact only with people who always wanted to do what you wanted to do, or impinge on the freedom of those with whom you inevitably did interact (by making them always do what you wanted). Instead, human freedom is full participation in a system that acknowledges and facilitates Reciprocity.

In order to define freedom, one must also define bondage, and what is bondage but the condition of having been exerted upon (having had one's actions influenced) followed by the denial of the ability to exercise the transferred power? Milton Friedman has already made the same observation: "Political freedom means the absence of coercion of a man by his fellow men. The fundamental threat to freedom is power to coerce."[179] If freedom means "the absence of coercion," and if—as illustrated earlier—the absence of coercion requires recognition of Reciprocity, then freedom can only exist within a system that recognizes Reciprocity.

Here's another way to come at it: Freedom is life under a just system. What is a just system? A system that can engage in balancing. And how does a system engage in balancing? Through the recognition (and facilitation) of the fact that power is transferred through its own exertion.

We have already recognized that a *free* market is one involving the exchange of natural resources and/or knowledge under agreements that recognize Reciprocity. So can such a market include the exchange/sale of slaves? No. Why not? Because within such transactions, slaves are human beings who are being exerted against but are being denied the opportunity to exercise the power that is transferred to them by virtue of those exertions. As we will see in the "Broadcast" section, the slaves in the United States were not freed exclusively through the grace and efforts of enlightened Caucasians. They were freed in large part through their *own* exposure and exercise of the power that had been transferred to them.

When anarchists and communists launch campaigns in pursuit of visions of equality, what are they really envisioning? They're envisioning a condition in which they aren't *below* others. But upending (or even eradicating) the capitalist economic system doesn't level power; it simply institutes new imbalanced agreements under which new rulers gain influence. Again, the notion that "the dictatorship I run" will be more just than "the dictatorship you run" while undoubtedly seductive is also obviously false. How can one be just without being co-operative? How can one be co-operative without forming agreements? Once agreements are formed, power appears, and only the system that acknowledges Reciprocity can successfully facilitate the increase and decrease of power necessary to create systemic equality. A dictatorship cannot do that. The circumstance of not being held down is not only a necessary component of any valid definition of human freedom but also a condition that can only be achieved through systemic acknowledgement of the fact that power is transferred through its own exertion.

Finally, any definition of freedom must also describe a state of peace. Again and again we have encountered the fact that systems that recognize Reciprocity (be they political, economic, or legal) develop nonviolent mechanisms of resolution. Peace simply cannot be reached any other way than through the acknowledgment and facilitation of Reciprocity. Although that may seem to be a bold statement at first blush, it is neither a particularly profound nor radical notion once one penetrates to its core. In essence, stating that the acknowledgement of Reciprocity is the prerequisite of peace is the same as saying that acknowledgement of agreement (and its consequences) is the only way to eliminate disagreement. Wars are waged exclusively between regimes that do not recognize the fact that power is transferred through its own exertion or between regimes that do not recognize that fact and those that do. Historical data demonstrate that two systems that recognize Reciprocity have never gone to war with one another. And Reciprocity explains why: the recognition that exertion creates the potential for the transference of power (with extreme exertions creating greater potential) combined with the systemic ability (in fact necessity) to abide by agreements and underscored by the fact that citizens have a systematized influence over their leaders' actions all converge to create tremendous pressures against war. As human interaction continues, the recognition of Reciprocity will foster further recognition of Reciprocity. And once Reciprocity (encouraged by broadcast and carried out through exertion, transference, and redefinition) has moved the dictators of the world to their rightful place below the rules, political, economic, and legal disputes will be resolved through the various systems that *continue* to develop out of the redefinitions of limits Reciprocity makes possible.

This brings us now to another phenomenon we have encountered throughout: as we have seen repeatedly—from the mother's threatening to "file a report" against the bus driver to the broadcast of the beating of Rodney King to the formation of MADD to the Declaration of Independence—the redefinition of limits almost always begins with the exposure of exertions.

Broadcast

By order of the prophet
We ban that boogie sound
Degenerate the faithful
With that crazy casbah sound
But the Bedouin they brought out
The electric camel drum
The local guitar picker
Got his guitar picking thumb
As soon as the shareef
Had cleared the square
They began to wail

Shareef don't like it
. . .
Rock the casbah
. . .

—From the Clash, "Rock the Casbah" [180]

Up to this point I have studiously avoided any reference to works of fiction when illustrating Reciprocity-in-action, but now I've opened this section with the lyrics from a pop song. Why? First, we're in a section called "Broadcast," so it seems fitting to begin with an example *of* broadcast. But there are other reasons as well. "Rock the Casbah" is an act of broadcast *about* broadcast (broadly defined); that is to say, it is a song about the power of self-expression. As the Clash innately understand, that "banned boogie sound"—which is really the voice of free expression—does inevitably "rock the casbah" (i.e., disrupt the oppressive regime) as the guitar-picker picks up his guitar-picking thumb not only to strum that instrument but to thumb his nose at the oppressors. Expression is a form of resistance we have encountered throughout, and it is but one of the tools with which those upon whom power is being exerted work to define new limits (and those who are attempting to maintain power sometimes choose to exert).

Of course, the power of expression has been widely recognized. As the French philosopher Regis Debray presciently stated three years prior to the fall of the Berlin Wall: "Unfortunately, Americans are much more keen on the quantitative than the qualitative, and they focus more on Soviet military hardware than on their [the Soviets'] limited political prestige. That is responsible for your overestimation of Soviet power, as if power in history is the same as force of arms! What myopia and shortsightedness! There is more power in rock music, videos, blue jeans, fast food, news networks and TV satellites than in the entire Red Army."[181] Reciprocity is, of course, woven quite visibly into those words—"as if power . . . is the same as force!" And Mr. Debray's statement merely highlights the ability of expression to influence others' actions.

Power is the ability to influence another's actions. And there are only two ways by which one can exercise power: physical effort and communicative expression. That's it—effort or expression. Unless you've developed the ability to influence people's actions through thought alone (which you haven't), it is only by action and/or communication—speech, writing, photography, song (any of which may sometimes constitute broadcast)—that you can exert influence.

Throughout this work, I have been defining *broadcast* as communication intended to expose (and therefore facilitate) the transfer of power made possible by others' exertions. A weather report is a form of broadcast by broadcast's common definition, but that's not the type of broadcast I'm talking about here. In relation to the rule of Reciprocity, I am defining *broadcast* quite tightly as "the exposure of exertions." Given that this section will explore the role of broadcast in Reciprocity, it is worth repeating here what I have stated from the outset: broadcast itself is not an element of the rule in the way system and power are. Why not? First, our cavemen could have redefined limits without engaging in exposure of any sort; therefore, broadcast is not inherently part of the phenomenon (although broadcast is virtually omnipresent in today's efforts to redefine limits). Second, when broadcast is used to facilitate transfer, it is simply operating *on* Reciprocity. Absent the fact that power is transferred through its own exertion, the exposure of exertions would have absolutely no effect.

We have already encountered numerous examples of the efficacy of exposure in facilitating Reciprocity. What did Candace Lightner do but expose exertions? What did the tape of the Rodney King beating do but expose exertions? What did Abner Louima's injuries do but expose exertions? The Declaration of Independence exposed exertions. The investigations into the actions of Presidents Nixon and Clinton exposed exertions. Oliver Brown and his allies exposed exertions, and so on. Broadcast can take many forms, from an employee's private report to his employer to the worldwide broadcast of sounds and images gathered by news organizations.

On the other hand, what did Lenin, Minh, Mao, and Castro do? They made efforts to conceal exertions. Saddam Hussein concealed exertions. Chávez conceals exertions. Kim conceals exertions. Gadhafi conceals exertions. In denying freedom of speech and press, every dictatorial regime makes efforts to conceal exertions for the purpose of resisting Reciprocity and containing opposition. That is to say, by restricting broadcast, they erect impediments to both the exposure of their acts as well as the expression of resistance, all of which serves to under-gird such regimes' ongoing inhibition of oscillation. Again, why would anyone ever conceal exertions if not for the truth of Reciprocity? The answer is no one would. There is no reason to conceal exertion unless exposure can lead to loss. And how can exposure lead to loss unless the ability to influence another's actions is transferred through its own exertion? In other words, the exposure of exertions raises the potential for the transfer of power made possible by those exertions. So the real question quickly becomes not "why do oppressors ever conceal exertions?" but "why does broadcast facilitate transference?" What happens? Why *does* exposure trigger change?

There is an answer, and interestingly, the answer is found not in the act of exposure but in the *re*action to that act. People respond, "That's not fair." And what is fairness but justice? And what is justice but balancing? And what is balancing but the recognition of oscillation made possible through the facilitation of Reciprocity? So the exposure of exertions highlights the suppression of Reciprocity, and people react to it by pursuing the balancing that Reciprocity makes possible. That's why exposure works. What do people mean when they say, "That's not fair"? They mean that those to whom power was transferred as a result of exertions against them are not being allowed to exercise that power. Broadcast stands out as the effective mechanism to promote change because power is transferred through its own exertion and broadcast exposes the transfer.

Agreements accumulate and expand through exertion, transference, and redefinition, but the redefinitions can't occur unless the exertions are exposed. If people don't know what the exertions are, or even that the exertions exist, then they can't decide whether those exertions are beyond acceptable limits. Two cavemen interacting with one another are both aware of the exertions, so broadcast is not present. The same is true for the formation and redefinition of most agreements between husbands and wives, parents and children, employers and employees, etc.—broadcast is generally not necessary in those instances (though, undoubtedly, it sometimes is). But as more parties become subject to agreements, the exposure of exertions becomes necessary to facilitate justice. If a police officer beats a suspect and the suspect tells no one, then there is no transference of power. As soon as the policeman oversteps the agreed upon boundaries, the potential for transfer exists. But whether or not that transfer actually occurs depends upon whether the act is exposed; it depends upon broadcast. There were many victims of drunk drivers before Cari Lightner, but Candace Lightner (and those who quickly joined her) defined the girl's death not as an accident but as the consequence of an overexertion, and they broadcasted it. They demanded justice. Again, no one can predict when and where the next Candace Lightner will emerge. No one can explain why a Havel is a Havel, a Gandhi a Gandhi. But Reciprocity, assisted by broadcast, does explain why those people have been able to accomplish what they have.

In many ways (but not entirely), this "Broadcast" section is about the strategies of the berry bringers. How do those with less influence in a system pursue the balancing necessary to gain more influence? How do they take possession of the power transferred to them by the exertions of others? The redefinition of limits requires effort, and the details of such effort will differ from case to case. However, most instances will share one characteristic: they will begin with broadcast. As we have seen, both the proponents and opponents of freedom have relied on Reciprocity in order to pursue new agreements. And in both instances, they also generally began by exposing the exertions of the previous regime. Those who fight for freedom and those who fight against it understand the impact of broadcast in all its forms. And that fact brings us to a reiteration of this one: those who seek to deny Reciprocity will also suppress exposure and control broadcast.

In setting the scene and context for the coming subsections, I feel it is worthwhile to recall this earlier statement: "Today's wilderness exists in the space *between* the systems. This is the space where wars are waged. This is where people are killed. That wilderness is the most important topic of our time. And once we recognize the truth (and consequences) of Reciprocity, we begin to find answers as to how that void (absence of agreement) will be filled (or not)." Broadcast bears relevance to that statement because regimes that seek to deny Reciprocity make efforts to obscure their denial in order to suppress the development of agreements that recognize Reciprocity.

And at no time in human history have individuals the world over been as able as today to engage in the exposure that leads to freedom.

You can't walk into your bedroom, walk out fifteen minutes later, and announce, "Guess what? I just launched a newspaper with printing plants, delivery trucks, and vast distribution networks around the world." But you can walk out fifteen minutes later and say, "I just started a blog that has the potential to reach millions." You can e-mail news articles and pictures. You can pick up the phone and call someone on the other side of the world. You can send a text message. You can transmit a fax. You can start a Website. You can publish a print-on-demand book. And that only describes some of the options available to *individuals*. From this development, from the very recent and very real interconnectedness of communication (as well as the expanding foundation of capitalist co-operation) comes an entirely new set of possibilities, truly new in many ways and yet utterly familiar in one: as we will see, what once took shape as the heartrending narratives of slaves communicated in person and on paper now takes the form of data shot through fiber-optic cables and electronic images bounced from earth to space and back again. For those who understand Reciprocity and the freedom it makes possible, the opportunities to expose power-transferences are great—and growing.

But before we get swept up in Eutopian euphoria, let's concede that communicative interconnectedness (and its effects) will not proceed unimpeded: "Out of China this week came two telling news items. One is that Internet users hit 137 million, putting them on track to surpass their U.S. counterparts in a couple of years. The other is President Hu Jintao's plea that officials further regulate the Web."[182] "[I]n North Korea . . . Internet service is banned and possession of a VCR or DVD player is also a criminal offense. Even radios that aren't permanently tuned to the official government station are illegal."[183] Keeping in mind that broadcast itself forms a field upon which exertion, transference, and redefinition will play out, let's step back to investigate the phenomenon of broadcast and the complications it entails beginning with the fact that some expression, even some that purports to be exposure, is merely another form of exertion.

Expression as Exertion

If there are only two ways to influence another's actions—effort and expression—then what you say (expression) can also be exertion. In other words, if what one says can influence others' actions, then what one says can also potentially transfer power away from oneself. Thus, it is not surprising that an understanding of Reciprocity is often revealed in the ways people choose to express themselves. We encountered this earlier in MADD's alteration of its name from Mothers Against Drunk Drivers to Mothers Against Drunk Driving, and such examples exist all around us.

For instance, Reciprocity explains why countries have "defense departments" as opposed to "attack departments" even though the vast majority of any defense department's tools can be deployed only for attack, and an "attack department" would certainly make any country sound more formidable (in a world without Reciprocity). But because power is transferred through its own exertion, an attack department implies "power transferring" while a defense department implies a "power taking" institution.

In that same vein, Reciprocity also explains why the current abortion controversy in the United States is framed not as "pro vs. con"—as are most debates—but instead as "pro vs. pro": pro-choice vs. pro-life. To make an exertion against something is to potentially transfer power to it. The pro-choice faction would never choose to describe itself as anti-life, nor would the pro-life faction choose to describe itself as anti-choice. To make an overt exertion against fetuses is to potentially transfer power to those fetuses (and their allies). To make an overt exertion against choice is to potentially transfer power to those women (and their allies) whose choice you are restricting. So both factions implicitly emphasize their opponents' exertions (anti-choice, anti-life) in their own, positive self-descriptions. In point of fact, the pro-choice people are in favor of the destruction of fetuses under certain circumstances, and the pro-life people are in favor of restricting a woman's independence under certain circumstances. So an understanding of the rule of Reciprocity is clearly revealed in the language both sides have chosen.

Here's another example of Reciprocity's effect on language: earlier on, we encountered the fact that employees who form or join unions describe themselves as workers while they also describe the owners/employers/ executives as management. Why do this? Defining oneself as a worker emphasizes the fact that you *work* while also implying, by contrast, that managers don't (in fact, it implies that by making workers work, the managers are exerting against—and transferring power to—those workers).

And a final one: Reciprocity explains why the dirtiest possible human exertion—genocide—has been described as cleansing by those who engaged in it.

Even this quite cursory survey reveals that Reciprocity is often accounted for in the details of expression. And of course, expression encompasses a wide variety of social elements, including clothes, architecture, job titles, etc. (The clothes you wear do "say" something to others as does the architecture of a judge's bench, and so on.) But aesthetics, semiotics, and symbolism are not the topics at hand here. Here, I am focusing only on the finite and definable subject of *what* one says, not the extraordinarily complex (and perhaps infinitely nuanced) topic of *how* one says it.

So let's say you call up a colleague at work and ask him to do something for you; depending upon the agreements in place between the two of you (depending on whether you have influence over his actions), he may or may not do as you ask. Now, let's say he says no, at which point you scream, "Stupid bastard!" and slam down the phone. Have you hit him with a club? No. Have you touched him? No. But that speech of yours was an exertion, and it transferred power to him. And depending on how he defines limits (those upon whom power is being exerted define its limits) he may just let it go; or he may call his/your superior or even the human resources department and register a complaint against you for creating a hostile work environment. And then *your* actions will be influenced—not because of what you did (physically), but because of what you said. In other words, your words alone formed an exertion that transferred power to your colleague and made him more able to influence your actions.*

---

* Of course, the conditions I just described—a workplace with an HR department and/or supervisors willing to hear out and facilitate balancing with regard to inappropriate exchanges—all arise out of Reciprocity. In systems that don't recognize Reciprocity, no such structures exist. As an aside, it is interesting to note that based on that single utterance of "stupid bastard," your coworker would almost certainly *fail* in his efforts to establish a hostile-work-environment claim under Title VII of the U.S. Civil Rights Act of 1964. In order to establish such a claim, a plaintiff must show that his or her "workplace . . . [has been]

So expression can be exertion subject to Reciprocity. That's good to remember but not particularly fertile soil for new analysis. The fact that what you say can potentially transfer power to others was inscribed among the first sentences of this section: there are only two ways to exert power—action and expression. Therefore, expression can be an exertion subject to Reciprocity. That fact alone does not hold much significance relative to the concept of broadcast (except, perhaps, that we can now rewrite Reciprocity's third consequence to read, "When the purpose of an expression includes the maintenance of power, then power is maintained through calculated *conversation*). But there is a form of expression-as-exertion that bears significant relevance to broadcast as I'm defining it; that is to say, there is a form of expression-as-exertion that masquerades as exposure.

Let's look again at what your colleague did following that telephone outburst. He called his/your boss. He exposed the exertion. He did not, however, report that you screamed, "Stupid bastard, I'm going to kill you!" Obviously, if you did scream that, it would be a far worse exertion (an exertion that transferred more power away and opened up the potential for your actions to be influenced even more). But what if he *said* you said that even though you didn't? His report would then no longer be a simple act of exposure; it would become a form of expression-as-exertion. It would be an exertion masquerading as exposure, or a false broadcast—the intentionally

---

permeated with discriminatory intimidation, ridicule, and insult . . . Conduct that is not severe or pervasive enough to create an objectively hostile or abusive work environment . . . is beyond Title VII's purview. Likewise, if the *victim* does not subjectively perceive the environment to be abusive . . . there is no Title VII violation [emphasis added]" *Harris v. Forklift Systems, Inc.*, 510 U.S. 17 (1993). That brief excerpt contains (and confirms) a number of truths revealed by Reciprocity:

1. The law is the victim's doctrine.
2. The people upon whom power is being exerted define its limits ("If the victim does not subjectively perceive the environment to be abusive . . . there is no Title VII violation").
3. Power is transferred through its own exertion: a single incident would likely not transfer enough power to qualify for Title VII relief; however, as more or more extreme exertions occur, they transfer more power, and Title VII enables one to exercise that power in order to influence the actions of both the exerter(s) and/or the employer.

false or fabricated exposure of exertions. There is an obvious distinction here (one statement is true; one isn't), but the contrast between these two concepts (broadcast and false broadcast) draws out a less obvious yet profoundly important point regarding the nature of broadcast itself.

Consider this: what would your first instinct be following your colleague's accurate broadcast? Your instinct would be to find some way to diminish the transference: "I'm sorry, and I won't do it again" (the apology being a preemptive, self-imposed influence of your own actions and therefore a facilitation of Reciprocity); or: "I didn't mean it;" or: "I didn't say it;" or: "I was only joking,"* and so on. Following your colleague's exposure of your exertion, your instinct would certainly not be to find more people (witnesses) who heard you say what you said. But that is exactly what you would do following your colleague's false broadcast—you would go find witnesses that heard your outburst in order to expose (broadcast) your colleague's false report. Following your colleague's accurate exposure, you would not seek out witnesses. Why? Because you can't expose exposure. Following his false broadcast, you would seek out witnesses. Why? Because that false broadcast was not exposure; it was actually an exertion, and you can expose exertion even when such exertion attempts to conceal itself as broadcast.

And all of that serves to highlight this crucial point: Broadcast itself is not an exertion; it does not transfer power. It is a neutral act, a conduit to facilitate the transference of power made possible by the exertion that is being broadcast. Because power is transferred through its own exertion, the exposure of exertion doesn't transfer power back; it merely makes visible the underlying transference. In fact, rather than transferring power, broadcast often attracts additional exertions that, if exposed, can lead to an even greater transference.

It is important to open with the concept of false broadcast as a form of expression-as-exertion because broadcast itself is also pursued as precedent to the influence of others' actions. Those who expose exertions (and the power that has been transferred by exertions) do so for the consequent purpose of influencing the actions of the exerters (and their allies). Candace Lightner

---

* While the apology is a strategy designed to preempt or minimize others' influence over your actions (in other words, an effort on your part to facilitate balancing by influencing your own actions before someone else does), the I-was-only-joking defense is a tactic intended to reduce the exertion itself. Humor is a strategy that can be used effectively (or cynically—even desperately—misused) in order to diminish the transfer that might otherwise result from expression-as-exertion.

exposed exertions for the purpose of influencing others' actions, so did the authors of the Magna Carta and the Declaration of Independence.

The fact that false broadcast can have an effect (albeit a temporary one) identical to broadcast merely underscores the efficacy of broadcast. Charging others with exertion is a way of drawing power to oneself. The difference between false broadcast (ersatz exposure) and broadcast (accurate exposure) is, again, truth. And truth is, of course, sometimes quite difficult to discern (it can't even meet Justice Stewart's standard for pornography: "I know it when I see it"). But truth does exist. The bus driver reached truth with the girl's mother: the door-closing event did not warrant the filing of a report. Broadcast started the process by which truth was reached in the Abner Louima matter. Candace Lightner exposed and worked to codify truths. Truths were broadcast in the investigations of Presidents Nixon and Clinton. Oliver Brown and his allies acted on, exposed, and ultimately expanded preexisting agreements to better encompass truth. And as we will soon see, following the Rodney King verdict, broadcast led to truth regarding relations between the LAPD and large segments of Los Angeles' African-American community. So the question that bears fruit is not "what is truth?" but "how is truth determined?"

In science, the truth is reached through a controlled process that can be generally described as hypothesis, experiment, proof. Relative to Reciprocity, the truth regarding exertions and transferences is reached through the process of exposure that can generally be described as: revelations and rebuttals, or reports and reactions, or accusations and defenses. This overall process of exposure might also be called *scrutiny*.

Now, rather than lingering in abstraction, here's an example of how truth emerges through the process of scrutiny. It is a broadcast-related example that incorporates both false broadcast and broadcast, and it also raises the complication of having to distinguish between simple inaccurate reporting and actual ersatz exposure:

On September 8, 2004, *60 Minutes Wednesday* broadcasted a story exposing documents that raised serious questions about President Bush's service in the Texas Air National Guard, documents that revealed preferential treatment was given to the young lieutenant Bush (i.e., documents that, in effect, revealed unjust exertions). Following that broadcast, it was quickly revealed that the documents, allegedly typed in 1972, bore fonts available in Microsoft Word (a software program that obviously did not exist in 1972). How do we know about those fonts and the falsification of those documents? Almost immediately following the report, private individuals began using their own blogs to expose the font anomaly, and as they did, those "bloggers managed to put the network of Murrow and Cronkite firmly on the defensive."[184] The bloggers engaged in broadcast as I'm defining it here, exposing the exertions of CBS and the man who reported the story—Dan Rather. In so doing, some also asserted that Mr. Rather's broadcast was not merely inaccurate reportage but actually false broadcast, a report based, in part, upon obviously bogus documents aired with the explicit intention of influencing a presidential election that was less than two months away.

Mr. Rather engaged in broadcast (he exposed documents purportedly revealing that the president had been granted favoritism). But Mr. Rather's report transformed into inaccurate reportage upon the revelation of the forgery, and then it transformed again into false broadcast. What caused these transformations? The process of scrutiny I described above.

Following allegations that the memos were false, various parties examined the documents and engaged in a series of reports and rebuttals (accusations and defenses), including Mr. Rather who vouched for their veracity:

> Today, on the Internet and elsewhere, some people, including many who are partisan political operatives, concentrated not on the key questions of the overall story but on the documents that were part of the support of the story. They allege the documents are fake . . . The 60 Minutes report was based not solely on the recovered documents but on a preponderance of evidence, including documents, that were provided by what we consider to be solid sources and interviews with former officials of the Texas National Guard. If any definitive evidence to the contrary of our story is found, we will report it. So far, there is none.[185]

The process of scrutiny culminated ten days later with this statement by Mr. Rather:

> I no longer have the confidence in these documents that would allow us to continue vouching for them journalistically. I find we have been misled on the key question of how our source for the documents came into possession of these papers. That, combined with some of the questions that have been raised in public and in the press, leads me to a point where—if I knew then what I know now—I would not have gone ahead with the story as it was aired . . . We made a mistake in judgment, and for that I am sorry. It was an error that was made, however, in good faith and in the spirit of

trying to carry on a CBS News tradition of investigative reporting without fear or favoritism.[186]

Thus the truth was reached with regard to the veracity of the documents.

But is that merely an example of inaccurate reporting, or was there more—was it actually an act of false broadcast? Favoritism had been the topic all along, but by virtue of this error, the question was no longer whether Mr. Bush was the beneficiary of favoritism during the war, but whether Mr. Rather, in presenting evidence that laypeople were able to discredit so quickly, had revealed his own bias against the Republican incumbent (and by inference, favoritism for the Democratic candidate, Senator Kerry). Mr. Rather broadcasted a false report; the documents he held up as evidence were bogus. That's a truth. And it's a truth that was, itself, exposed through broadcast. But once the question of the documents' veracity was settled, the new question arose: what was Mr. Rather's intention? This brings us right back to the bus example and the identical distinctions applied there: "It was not clear whether the driver intentionally allowed the door to close on [the girl] or whether this was an honest accident." As stated at the outset, what was in operation on the bus that day is also in operation in the world at large, and so we see the same issue here: was Mr. Rather engaging in an act of concealment when he asserted that airing the documents was a mistake (or when he inferred that he was actually the victim, having been misled)?

Obviously, I can't answer the question of Mr. Rather's intentions. No one can (possibly not even Mr. Rather). There is no evidence that Mr. Rather intentionally reported a story that he knew with certainty to be false and fabricated. But by his own admission ("If I knew then what I know now"), there is also no doubt that he and his staff refrained from applying the scrutiny needed to reach the truth.

Book after book has been written about the biases of supposedly objective newsmen (and more will come), each of which is nothing more than the broadcast of the exertions of broadcasters. Unfortunately for Mr. Rather, this was not the first time his actions were exposed as exhibiting a bias against Republicans. The fact that the documents were false simply moved the conversation beyond the realm of inscrutable intentions and introduced tangible evidence. Prior exertions then came into play, and taken in sum, Mr. Rather's pattern of exertions ended up transferring a substantial amount of power to his opponents. As the *Washington Post* reported: "GOP critics as well as some media commentators demanded that the story be retracted and suggested that Rather should step down."[187] Ultimately, he did resign. Now, did he resign because he made a simple mistake or because he made exertions that transferred power? Reciprocity supplies the answer: Mr. Rather was forced to resign because his own exertions (which took the form of expression-as-exertion) transferred to others the ability to influence his actions. In other words, those upon whom Mr. Rather's power was being exerted—the president's allies and certain proponents of journalistic integrity ("GOP critics as well as some media commentators")—defined those exertions as beyond acceptable limits for a network news anchor; they took the power transferred by those exertions and used it to influence Mr. Rather's actions.

As with so many examples that have preceded this one, the point here is neither to condemn nor condone, but to explain what happened. News reporters sometimes exert (as opposed to report); their exertions transfer power, and those upon whom power is being exerted (and their allies) use broadcast to facilitate the transference. That is the process that describes Mr. Rather's demise as the anchor of the *CBS Evening News*. But can we conclude across the board that if an act of broadcast is pursued with a persuasive objective, then its content is not objective? No. Once again, it comes down to truth. The broadcasts that exposed the exertions against slaves in the United States certainly carried with them a persuasive objective: those who were exposing slaveholders' exertions were attempting to persuade others that the slaveholders had transferred immense amounts of power to the slaves and their allies. Yet those broadcasts were also exposing objective facts.

I opened with the Dan Rather example precisely because it's complicated, and I want to make the point up front that the distinction between "false broadcast" and "broadcast," while real, may not always be clear. In addition, false broadcast does not refer to plain old inaccurate reporting. The Jayson Blair scandal that tarnished the *New York Times*, though it clearly encompassed false reports, was not false broadcast in the sense I am defining it because the articles were not published with the implicit or explicit intention of exposing exertions. His was merely the misguided work-product of a troubled journalist. On the other hand, *Pravda*'s consistently and intentionally inaccurate reporting (purported exposure) of world events, especially the exertions of the Soviet Union's enemies, *was* false broadcast. Whether or not false broadcast can be easily distinguished from broadcast, one point is clear: without the fact that power is transferred through its own exertion, neither broadcast nor false broadcast would have any efficacy.

The distinctions between expression-as-exertion, exertion-as-broadcast (covered in the subsequent subsection) and broadcast as the trigger for transference cannot be organized into a clear-cut taxonomy (even though the distinctions are sometimes obvious). Instead, these concepts outline a spectrum of expression encompassing degrees and revealing numerous overlaps, which means there are examples that cannot be cleanly classified. In fact, false broadcast itself is a subset of a broader form of expression-as-exertion, a form generally referred to as propaganda.

But before I apply Reciprocity to propaganda and examine that wider form of expression-as-exertion, I want first to express an essential fact that has gone unuttered to this point, a basic premise that has been present throughout but which begins to take on the most relevance here in this consideration of expression: while system (agreement) creates power, communication forges agreement.

Quite simply, you can't reach agreement without communication, and you can't have system without agreement. Therefore, communication is the basis of system. Those simple facts are applicable to any system: one way or another the clubber had to communicate demands and consequences to the berry bringer before the other began bringing berries. Propaganda comes into play here because propaganda (for our purposes) is the communication of inaccurate information designed to influence the formation of agreements.

As covered above, Reciprocity is not concerned with static agreements such as "we agree the sky is blue" or "we agree our neighbor is weird." Instead, Reciprocity concerns action-oriented accords that contain future components (e.g., "I will bring berries if you won't club/kill me;" "go on green, stop on red;" "don't trade stocks based on inside information"). But there are always other (very basic) agreements that precede and underlie every agreement affecting future conduct. For instance, the agreement that I'll bring berries if you don't club me would rest on the agreement that you are actually able to club me; in other words, I would have to see the club and your ability to wield it before I acquiesced to your demand. Broadcast facilitates those sorts of basic prerequisite agreements. Agreeing that the sky is blue or that our neighbor is weird does not create power, but it does lay the groundwork for subsequent agreements that do (e.g., given the actions of the green-sky faction, let's pass a law against saying the sky is green; or, given the weirdness of our neighbor, let's create and enforce restrictions on his movements).

Taking a closer look, broadcast could inspire a chain of foundational agreements such as: we agree that certain events are occurring; we agree that these events should not be happening; we agree that X is the victim, and we agree that Y is the injuring party. Now, none of those agreements contain future components, but they can form the foundation for, and influence the formation of, subsequent agreements that do hold future components. In other words, given our agreement that Y's exertions have gone beyond acceptable limits, we can now also agree that we will work to define new limits on Y's future exertions and exertions similar to Y's. Of course, in order for people to agree that X is the injured party and Y is the party committing the injury, Y's exertions must be broadcast.

In order to understand *what* propaganda is, it is necessary to step back and consider *why* it is—why does propaganda exist at all? Without the fact that agreement creates power, propaganda would not exist. Why attempt to mold someone's opinion (why try to reach the basic prerequisite agreements) unless such opinion might form the foundation for agreements with future components? Taking our hypothetical example a step further, let's say it is true that Y is injuring X. In that scenario, who is more likely to engage in the communication of *inaccurate* information designed to influence the formation of agreement? In other words, who is more likely to confuse or confound broadcast with propaganda? The answer: Y. And why is Y likely to do that? Y would employ propaganda for one reason: to establish or maintain agreements that are favorable to Y's retention of power.

Expanding this out into reality, we see that rulers looking to establish or maintain agreements out of sync with the exertions and transferences that are actually transpiring will disseminate propaganda (engage in this form of expression-as-exertion) in order to influence the formation of agreements bearing future components and thus influence others' actions. While propaganda can be (and is) used by institutions within systems that recognize Reciprocity, this form of expression-as-exertion is a particularly useful tool for those seeking to deny Reciprocity. Propaganda helps prop up a system that denies Reciprocity by perpetuating the sort of "unsettled circumstances" that dictators rely on in order to justify their ongoing suppression of oscillation. In other words, if we all agree that the present circumstances are sufficiently unsettled (an agreement without a future component), we will be more likely to acquiesce to laws that resist Reciprocity (victim's doctrines that project the dictator into the position of potential victim). If we now define Y as a ruler seeking to deny balancing, we see that such a ruler would spread propaganda justifying his exertions in order to create the illusion that his enemies had transferred power to *him*, and that his own exertions were then merely exercising that power. In other words, the dictator will try to make it appear as though *he* is now engaged in balancing, and that far from denying Reciprocity, he is actually acting on it.

Propaganda is an exertion (taking the form of expression-as-exertion) that is designed to lessen the likelihood of power transference. And it lessens the likelihood of such transference by diminishing exertion and exaggerating (or inventing) and thus increasing the exertions of the opposition while also erecting this obvious complication: under circumstances in which power is being exerted through propaganda, one must first determine the truth in order to expose the exertion (expose the propaganda). That can sometimes present a seemingly (if not actually) insurmountable obstacle. This is especially true given the restrictions on expression and exposure that are generally in place under systems that regularly pursue the propagandistic strategy of expression-as-exertion. How are you going to expose the truth if you don't have a right to free speech, free assembly, or a free press? In addition, beyond the system's borders, the task of exposing propaganda is often made more daunting by (ironically) the very propaganda which one is attempting to expose.

For example, Ion Mihai Pacepa, "the highest-ranking intelligence official ever to have defected from the Soviet bloc,"[188] has not only exposed the false broadcast campaign (dubbed *dezinformatsiya*) of his former bosses but, in doing so, has also described its efficacy: "During the Vietnam War we spread vitriolic stories around the world, pretending that America's presidents sent Genghis Khan-style barbarian soldiers to Vietnam who raped at random, taped electrical wires to human genitals, cut off limbs, blew up bodies and razed entire villages. Those weren't facts. They were our tales, but some seven million Americans ended up being convinced that their own president, not communism, was the enemy."[189]

Now, more than fifty-eight thousand American soldiers/citizens were killed in the Vietnam War. That is a fact. Many citizens who survived defined this not as an exertion against the enemy but as an exertion against themselves. That is also a fact. How each citizen reached his or her own definition is an open (and realistically unanswerable) question, and whether or to what extent propaganda (whatever its provenance) helped form the opinion that preceded their call for the war to end (their redefinition of limits) is a question upon which people continue to apply significant scrutiny (revelations, rebuttals; accusations, defenses). If Lt. Gen. Pacepa's account is accurate, then it demonstrates the power of propaganda; if his allegations are exaggerated, then his own exertions will be exposed. Regardless of the truth that scrutiny uncovers, Reciprocity provides us with an overarching understanding of the enduring framework within which any such exertions and transferences will proceed: it explains the use of propaganda, the exposure of propaganda, the search for truth, and how that search is conducted.*

Of course, as stated above, propaganda does not take only the form of false broadcast (ersatz exposure). The communication of inaccurate information designed to influence the formation of agreements may take many shapes, including (perhaps especially) the language one uses to define one's enemies. We encountered this earlier in the expressions Marx and Engels employed to describe bourgeois capitalists: "Modern bourgeois society . . . is like the sorcerer who is no longer able to control the powers of the nether world which he has called up by his spells."[190] Again, by employing such damning language, Marx and Engels were making exertions designed to mold opinion in order to reach the agreement that the bourgeoisie should be overthrown and to establish a system that outlawed capitalism. In pursuit of their specific agenda, they utilized propagandistic expressions in order to draw others toward the communist system. Having created the foundation for agreements containing future components and then having actually formed those agreements, propagandists continue to disseminate false information in order to perpetuate the system that resists Reciprocity. These ongoing campaigns

---

* Reciprocity also sheds light on this sad, sometimes dangerous, but not uncommon phenomenon: some who live in free countries—systems wherein Reciprocity is acknowledged and where balancing occurs—want desperately to believe that *balance* is possible. They want to believe it so much that they ignore (i.e., actively choose *not* to scrutinize) the encroachments upon freedom (and often horrible atrocities) that occur in those countries whose leaders claim to be pursuing or to have achieved such balance. The fantasy of a balanced society is based entirely on a misunderstanding of power—those who harbor such a fantasy don't understand that power is in constant oscillation. They see power as a substance that can be distributed evenly throughout a society. And they believe the lies (propaganda) that tell them such distribution is being pursued, or has been achieved, elsewhere in systems to which they are not subject. Of course, the fact that power is in constant oscillation in no way means that a "just society" is impossible—far from it. Once again, the recognition and pursuit of Reciprocity (rather than its elimination) is *more* likely to lead toward political, legal, social, and economic justice because, quite simply, you can't have any justice without the recognition that power is transferred through its own exertion. By attempting to impose balance, dictators eliminate the balancing that is necessary to reach the ends truly desired by those who innocently, but mistakenly, support those dictators.

can take a negative form (our enemies are to blame for our problems) as well as a positive one (we have achieved a glorious society far superior to others, one that is free of crime, unemployment, inflation, etc.), all of which is nothing more than the effort to maintain the static agreements (we agree that capitalism is the problem; we agree that communism is the solution) that underlie and help sustain ongoing acquiescence.*

Today, certain Middle Eastern textbooks allegedly present maps that redact the state of Israel. Clearly, this is an example of propagandistic expression-as-exertion. Regardless of whether one is Israel's ally or enemy, Israel does exist. That's a truth. And we can easily locate the cartographic erasure of Israel in the category of propagandistic expression-as-exertion for two reasons: first, it's blatantly false; second, it has been exposed.†

Recently, the American Jewish Committee published an advertisement bearing the headline: "How can there be peace in the Middle East if Israel isn't even on the map today?"[191] Under that headline were displayed graphical excerpts from a Syrian fifth grade schoolbook, a Palestinian Authority schoolbook, a Saudi Arabian sixth grade schoolbook, and a map from the Lebanon Ministry of Tourism. Each of these graphics showed Palestine filling the entire space between Egypt and Jordan. Now, without a doubt, the American Jewish Committee took out this ad for a purpose; it had an objective. But if its ad is accurate, then that was an act of broadcast—exposing the exertions of the Syrians, Saudis, Palestinians, and Lebanese who published those materials. If what the American Jewish Committee published is inaccurate, then that is a propagandistic form of expression-as-exertion, one that others could easily broadcast by simply producing the materials to refute the allegations.

Reciprocity readily explains the purpose of such schoolbooks. Clearly the communication of inaccurate information is designed to influence the static opinion that forms the basis for agreements with future components. Such propaganda is designed to produce the foundational agreement that Israel is illegitimate, which must precede any agreement to oppose and destroy the state

---

* In the spirit of simplicity, we can see this phenomenon just as clearly when it takes shape as gossip. Gossip is the communication of information (often inaccurate) specifically intended to influence the formation of static agreements (e.g., "our neighbor is weird") that may then form the basis of action-oriented agreements with future components (e.g., "let's shun him").

† Remember, you cannot expose exposure; you can only expose exertion, even when it takes the form of expression. If Israel actually did not exist, then exposing maps that did not show Israel would be pointless.

(an agreement with a future component). Publishing schoolbooks that contain intentionally inaccurate maps is clearly an example of the broader form of propagandistic expression-as-exertion. And this particular example helps to uncover another important point regarding communication's relationship to power. In order to create agreement one must engage in communication, but in order to sustain the acquiescence that forms the basis of agreement, one must maintain a shared memory (i.e., one must remember the agreement), or to state the same point in a more ominously impressive manner, one must control history.

This concept of controlling history leads us into another essential (but to this point unexpressed) premise because, in actuality, what we've been talking about throughout—going all the way back to the point when the berry bringer met the clubber—is memory. Communication precedes agreement, and memory perpetuates it. Without memory one can't have any form of enduring agreement. To the extent that *memory* and *history* are synonymous, then one can't have enduring agreement without history. Therefore, anyone attempting to mold the opinions that form the foundation for agreements will seek to control history. This is not an original observation (innumerable people have made similar statements); what is original is the underlying theorem that explains *why* parties seeking power also seek to control history: memory (e.g., history) contains and perpetuates the understanding of initial acquiescence that underlies ongoing agreement; therefore, anyone seeking to maintain power will also seek to control the history that defines that initial acquiescence. In short, history (be it in the form of written victim's doctrines or oral accounts) holds agreement, and agreement creates power.*

---

* In this context, the fact that power is transferred through its own exertion helps explain the Holocaust-denial that is common among enemies of Israel. If Israel's enemies reduce or eliminate the exertions that transferred power to Israelis in the first place, then they weaken the foundation of the Jewish nation and move closer to their desired destruction of the state itself. The same holds true for conspiracy theorists who attempt to blame the U.S. for the events of September 11, 2001. By eliminating the transfer that occurred through those extreme exertions, they also undermine the legitimacy (created by Reciprocity) of America's subsequent actions. Revising history would not make any sense, or have any effect, were it not for the truth of Reciprocity and the fact that history (one kind of static agreement) forms the basis for agreements with future components.

Now, the extent to which the caretakers of any given system need to actively control history correlates directly with the facts of that system's history itself. For instance, if a system was formed through efforts intended to empower its people, then its history can stand on its own. But if a system was formed through efforts intended to seize power for despots (and if those despots wish to maintain the illusion that the system was established for the common good), then that false history will not stand on its own—it will need to be maintained with effort. To the extent that a given history is accurate, it will require less effort to maintain. To the extent that a given history is fabricated, it will require more effort to maintain. Anyone who has attempted to perpetuate a falsehood knows this: lies require vigilant tending while truths exist independent of anyone's efforts to maintain them.*

Systems that recognize and facilitate Reciprocity (in part by protecting free expression), allow truths to emerge through the revelations and rebuttals that scrutiny comprises. On the contrary, the rulers of systems that resist Reciprocity must make efforts to confound or control the formation of memory. That applies retrospectively (revising history) as well as prospectively (controlling the broadcast of current events). To the extent a scene is constructed, it forms an exertion, one that potentially transfers power to the people against whom the exertion is being made. To the extent a scene is simply recorded and presented, it is an act of broadcast; it does not form an exertion, and it does not transfer power. Those statements, as with so many that have preceded, are true by degrees: The more fabrication is present in any purported act of broadcast (either in the form of false facts or selective reporting), the more power can be potentially transferred. The less fabrication is present in any purported act of broadcast (the more objective and less selective the reporting), the less power can be potentially transferred.

Expression-as-exertion, exertion-as-broadcast, and broadcast as the trigger for transference all translate events into some manner of communication, which can, in turn, help mold the basic agreements ("we agree these things are happening") that then form the foundation for agreements with future components ("here's what we're going to do about it"). Communication forms the basis of agreement, and memory sustains it; agreement equals system; system creates power; thus, communication—and its control—is central to the creation and maintenance of power. This "Broadcast" section opened by

---

* For example, if every explanation of—and reference to—evolution and gravity were completely eradicated, evolution and gravity would still exist. They would simply resume the form of truths waiting to be described.

describing the dichotomy of physical exertion vs. expression, but we must now recognize that those two forms of influence, while generally distinct, are not entirely exclusive. Instead, expression (communication) can also take the form of physical exertion. In fact, some exertions, even violent, forceful ones, are actually acts of broadcast intended to expose injustice (intended to expose the suppression of Reciprocity and facilitate its fulfillment).

Exertion as Broadcast

Riots, protests, and boycotts are the three most prominent forms of exertion-as-broadcast (physical exertions designed to draw attention to injustice). And I will apply Reciprocity to all three, beginning here:

Sometime during the week that included Wednesday, April 29, 1992, (the day that the verdict in the Rodney King case was announced) a photographer for the *Washington Post* captured this odd image—a thin, somewhat dazed woman, stumbling through the dust and debris of a ransacked store in South Central Los Angeles, clutching two four-packs of toilet paper, one in each hand. Now, did that woman really want those eight rolls of toilet paper so much that she was ready to rob a store to get them? Or was something else going on there? Obviously, there was something else going on. And the answer to what was going on has already been provided much earlier in the context of these other events: Adam Fortunate Eagle Nordwall and his allies did not seize Alcatraz in 1969 because they actually wanted that rock; Indian activists did not barricade the Bureau of Indian Affairs in 1972 because they had a burning desire to inhabit that building. And that anonymous woman did not grab those rolls because she desperately needed toilet paper. Those individual exertions were all parts of larger acts of broadcast designed to expose earlier exertions and facilitate the transfer of power.

The woman's act of looting, while seemingly silly in light of the significant death and destruction that the King riots wrought ("During five days of violence, 54 died, 2,328 were injured"[192]), is actually of a piece with the overall expression of lawlessness (riot) intended to highlight a condition in which balancing had failed not just incidentally but—from the perspective of the rioters—systematically. The riots themselves actually began with a similar incident: "Shortly after 4:00 [on the afternoon of April 29, 1992], five young black males made a beer-run to the Pay-less Liquor and Deli at Florence and Dalton Avenues, a Korean-owned store . . . known in the neighborhood as 'Mr. Lee's.' Their beverage of choice was Olde English 800, the malt liquor consumed by Rodney King in quantity before his fateful drive nearly fourteen months earlier. At the store each youth scooped up four or five bottles . . . and walked toward the entrance, where their path was blocked by David Lee, son of the owner. One of the youths struck Lee in the head with a bottle, and two others hurled bottles at the glass door of the store . . . 'This is for Rodney King,' one yelled. From behind a bullet-proof counter Lee's father, Samuel, pushed a silent alarm button that alerted the 77th Street Station of the robbery. It was 4:17 p.m., and one of the deadliest urban riots in the nation's history had begun."[193]

Like the woman who stole the toilet paper, the men who took the beer did not want the beer; they wanted to make a statement against the system, and the statement they wanted to make can be roughly expressed as: "The exertions of white police officers against the black community transferred power not only to Rodney King (power that you have just denied him), but to us, and we're going to expose that transference (and exercise that power) whether the system that surrounds us acknowledges that transference or not. If the law (victim's doctrine) won't protect the victim, then we won't accept the law. If the law defines those officers' exertions as within acceptable limits, then we, the people, upon whom that power is being exerted, do hereby demand a redefinition of those limits."

During the course of the officers' trial, prosecutor Terry White had stated, "At some point you have to look at that tape and say enough is enough."[194] That is precisely what the rioters were saying: "Enough is enough." "You've gone too far." "You've crossed a line." "The situation is unacceptable." And, "This is for Rodney King!"

In opening my analysis of the King incident in the "System" section, I stated that "it is difficult to decide where to start with an event as complex as the Rodney King episode." And for our purposes, I began with the night of his arrest. But in making their own analysis of the incident, many members of the African-American community in Los Angeles (and elsewhere) did not begin with the night of Rodney King's arrest. They did not agree that Mr. King made the first exertion when he took the wheel in an intoxicated condition—instead, they began their own analysis of the interaction by taking into consideration events that had occurred well before that night.

Many members of the African-American community came to view the King episode not as an isolated volley of exertions and transferences that took place one night between the police and an intoxicated motorist, but as part of a broader pattern of interaction between the LAPD and African-Americans (and possibly between whites and blacks in general). From the viewpoint of the African-American residents of South Central LA, this wasn't just about

Rodney King. The King riots took place within the context of a community rife with ethnic animosity and memories/perspectives shaped by the Watts riots, Operation Hammer, and the overall ongoing tension between police and LA's African-American community[195]—"Blacks, particularly young males, complained they were often stopped by police and 'proned out'—made to lie face down with legs and arms spread and palms up—for minor traffic violations or for no reason at all."[196] Thus, the rioters' actions in response to the King verdict were not merely intended to express displeasure at what they considered to be a miscarriage of justice (a lack of balancing) in this particular instance but also to expose the overall transference—to draw attention to a broader pattern of abuse that consistently manifested itself in an application of the victim's doctrine that actually created more victims within their community.*

During the course of the riots, literally countless individual crimes (some quite severe) were committed. And the fact that these acts were pursued for the overall purpose of broadcast did not absolve the actors of responsibility for their actions. Exertion-as-broadcast is not a get-out-of-jail-free card. Those individual crimes were exertions that transferred power. And to the extent possible, those who committed the crimes were arrested, and whatever power their individual exertions transferred was then used to influence their actions. But when viewed in sum, the grand combination of those lawless acts were treated not as an exertion, but as an exposure of exertions on the part of the police. Following the Rodney King riots, balancing did occur. But whose actions were most influenced? When the Rodney King episode is taken in full scope (from arrest to riot), we see that it was the Los Angeles Police Department's actions that were most affected by the event. The institutional remedies put in place following the riots were directed not at the community but at the police for the benefit of the community.

---

* To support the notion that the riots did not erupt in response to a single incident of perceived injustice, it is perhaps interesting to note that, although a large proportion of Caucasians in the Los Angeles community considered O. J. Simpson to be guilty of double-homicide, we did not witness a riot following his acquittal. The difference in those reactions has only to do with the history of exertions and the general lack of balancing that preceded the specific lack of balancing manifested by the King verdict. Were a pattern to develop wherein wealthy African-Americans were repeatedly acquitted of murdering whites, you would—without a doubt—eventually see white riots intended to expose exertions and facilitate balancing.

Here are some of the initiatives undertaken in the aftermath of the Rodney King riots:

1. "As the disorders spread, President George Bush and Attorney General William Barr swiftly set in motion the process that led to the federal indictment [on civil rights charges] of the four white LAPD officers who had been acquitted of using excessive force against Rodney King."[197] Ultimately, Officers Koon and Powell were convicted of violating Mr. King's civil rights, and each was sentenced to thirty months in prison (Officers Briseno and Wind were acquitted).
2. "Diversity training for recruits was intensified."[198]
3. "[T]he Police Commission chose Katherine Mader, an experienced prosecutor, as the LAPD's first inspector general."[199]
4. "[T]he Police Academy . . . devised a new program for teaching police recruits how to arrest resistant suspects without using unnecessary force."[200]
5. "The Police Academy expanded cultural-awareness and language training."[201]
6. "The banner of the new LAPD became 'community policing' . . . [which] replaced the *Dragnet* model of gung-ho policing."[202]
7. "[C]ommunity advisory boards were established in each of the city's eighteen police divisions, co-chaired by an LAPD captain and a civilian."[203]
8. "[T]he LAPD obtained permission to use pepper spray and other non-lethal weapons and virtually abandoned the side-handled metal baton that . . . [was] called 'the caveman's weapon of choice.'"[204]

The riots served as a form of broadcast that ultimately facilitated balancing. And the exposure of police exertions and transferences actually moved the LAPD away from that club wielded by our caveman and further into tactics employed by policemen operating under an accumulation of agreements.

Today, we can understand the riots to be broadcast for two reasons:

1. They exposed exertions; it is unlikely the changes enumerated above would have been implemented, the police department's actions would not have been influenced in those ways, without the riots (without the fact that exertion-as-broadcast drew attention to the precedent transfer of power to L.A.'s African-American community).

2. They facilitated the exercise of the power that had been transferred; had the riots been purely an exertion, then the remedies would have been imposed upon the community, not upon the police. But after the conflagration, administrative offices weren't established to teach Los Angelenos not to riot. The law is the victim's doctrine, and the new laws/policies recognized the African-American community as the victim—*following* the riots. The conclusion of the overall episode was not "hey, we have a problem with black rioters;" it was "hey, we have a problem with our police department's relations with the African-American community."

Exertion-as-broadcast is underscored by Reciprocity's second consequence: the people upon whom power is being exerted define its limits. People will work to redefine limits even if the system itself is inhibiting their redefinition. Riots are not revolutions, but they're related. They are efforts to expose the fact that the rules are being applied unevenly (this is as true for soccer riots as it is for the Rodney King riots). The Rodney King rioters were, in effect, saying, "The more powerful elements of our system are not hearing our voices, so we'll now take action to make certain we're heard." Those who riot are obviously resorting to violence, but they are not falling back to force relations. Rioters don't seek an abandonment of the system (that would be a revolution), but simply a certain justice (balancing) with regard to the application of rules. This fact was expressed in the words shouted by those who protested the King verdict in New York: "Prosecute the cops . . . justice now."[205] No one, however, called out to jettison the U.S. Constitution (just as rioters on a soccer field don't cry out to eliminate the ball). The rioters were not trying to destroy the system, but fix its operation; they were seeking justice within the same system that they felt had failed them. The acknowledgement of Reciprocity preempts a falling back to force relations, so riots are not revolutions. They are extreme expressions of protest. And protest is our second, less extreme form of exertion-as-broadcast.

Right up front, we must recognize that any form of resistance will manifest some degree of exposure because resistance, on its own, necessarily calls attention to the exertion(s) against which one is resisting. But refusal becomes protest en masse, and protest becomes exertion-as-broadcast: a physical effort (the gathering, the march, the strike) intended to expose the exertions of (and facilitate the transfer of power from) those against whom the protest is being held. It also must be acknowledged from the outset that while riots, by their nature, are *dis*-organized, protests are always organized;

yet (despite their surface-unity) protests also hold within themselves multiple factions—groups of actors acting similarly but for separate reasons. So any picture of a protest that ascribes a single, unifying motive to all the protesters is going to be (more or less) inaccurate.

Before I apply Reciprocity to the interesting question of why we need—or desire—to paint such unified pictures of protest, I want to examine what Reciprocity can tell us about the more basic question of why those component factions exist in the first place. Reciprocity's causes and consequences provide an explanation: the fact that power is disbursed throughout a system means that it is never exerted uniformly from a central authority, which, in turn, means that it is exerted in different ways in different places; this, in turn, means that protestors (while in general agreement that exertions have exceeded acceptable limits) may not agree about the ways in which power has been exerted or the remedies for such exertions. The protesters have, most likely, experienced different exertions in different ways and are, therefore, moved forward by different motivations.

Now, accepting the fact that activist-factions exist within any protest, the need—or desire—to paint unifying pictures of protest can be explained in three ways. The first explanation arises from the overarching truth that protests *are* unified on the surface—they do move in coordinated fashion. So the protestors' coordinated exertion naturally draws descriptive accounts and explanations that provide a singular story to match the surface singularity of the action.

The second explanation for unifying depictions arises from practical limitation: it would be impossible to accurately portray every elemental motivation of any protest without somehow reliving the entire event from every perspective.*And the third explanation for the ascription of a single unifying motive for protest arises from Reciprocity and the Reciprocity-related elements that were just covered: communication precedes agreement, and

---

* In addition to the vast array of *relevant* motivations underlying the participation of various protestors (or even rioters), any time one atomizes a group effort down to the level of individual impulses, one will also find numerous causes for participation that have nothing to do with the target of the protest or Reciprocity. Such motivations can include everything from "I don't have anything better to do," to peer-pressure, to impulsive ("mob-mentality") participation, to self-centered opportunism (the woman who stole the toilet paper may have been acting on any or all of those motivations), to basic (or even sociopathic) malcontentedness. But regardless of the motivation, each individual's participation still contributes some component to the larger act of broadcast.

memory perpetuates it. Without memory, one can't have any form of enduring agreement. To the extent that *memory* and *history* are synonymous, then one can't have enduring agreement without history. Therefore, anyone seeking to create, take, or maintain power will also seek to control (communicate) the history that precedes agreement and/or defines the already extant acquiescence. Because the point at which power is exerted is the point at which there exists the greatest potential for its transfer, focusing on and exposing a single point of exertion (e.g., they told Rosa Parks to move to the back of the bus) as the impetus for redefinition will heighten the potential for transfer even more than if one were to broadcast a hundred, a thousand, or a million points of plight. By exposing (communicating the story of) a single unacceptable exertion (e.g., the beating of Rodney King) and raising it up as the point of protest to redefine the limits on all similar exertions, one is more likely to gain the ability to influence the actions of the exerters and their allies (i.e., facilitate the transfer of power needed to eradicate such exertions).

As Bret Stephens of the *Wall Street Journal* has observed: "Successful democratic revolutions tend to have iconic figures: Think of Nelson Mandela in South Africa, Václav Havel in Czechoslovakia, Lech Walesa in Poland and Viktor Yushchenko in Ukraine. These men not only led their movements to victory but also, through their personal suffering, became emblems of the suffering of their people."[206] By fixing the focus on a single, definable, understandable individual or event, the broader goal of a widespread redefinition of limits is more likely to be reached. But right off the bat, we must recognize that this is not a recipe. The anointing of such an emblem is as subject and susceptible to scrutiny as any other form of expression, and given the stakes in play (given the fact that systems may rise and fall on the shoulders of such emblems), the scrutiny that will be applied makes the development of these catalytic actors and actions (e.g., Gandhi and colonial occupation, Havel and communist oppression) highly resistant to contrivance. In other words, we find here (in the protest form of exertion-as-broadcast) the same truths regarding expression-as-exertion that we encountered earlier: To the extent that a given history (or story) is accurate, it will require less effort to maintain. To the extent that a given history (or story) is fabricated, it will require more effort to maintain.

Acknowledging the fact that any retelling of an event will contain some manufactured facets—that is to say, any narrative will necessarily possess structural elements (choices made regarding beginning, middle, end, elisions, and emphases throughout), stylistic ingredients (such as the recurrent use of parentheses) as well as rhetorical devices (simile, metaphor, metonomy) that affect the telling and diverge (to greater or lesser degrees) from absolute fact—we can see that underlying all of those details will sit a core of exposure or exertion. The closer the expression sits to truth (exposure), the more it will survive as an act of broadcast (an act that does not transfer power away); the closer it sits to fiction (exertion), the more susceptible it will be to scrutiny, and the more power it will potentially transfer to those against whom the fiction is being deployed. In other words, while the emblem that arises organically out of events (exertions and transferences) can become a potent catalyst for change (i.e., it can become a point-of-exertion prone to the sort of exposure that triggers the transfer of power and subsequent redefinition of limits), the wholly manufactured "emblem" is pure exertion, subject to Reciprocity and likely to redound upon the actions of those who render it.

For example:

"In November of 1987, a 15-year-old girl named Tawana Brawley was found in upstate New York, covered in feces and [with] racial slurs written in charcoal [on her body]. Brawley, who is black, claimed to have been abducted and raped by six white law enforcement officers."[207] Those were explosive charges alleging extraordinary exertions, which would have undoubtedly transferred to Ms. Brawley an immense amount of influence over the actions of those officers—had the charges been true. But the Tawana Brawley matter was thrown out following careful scrutiny by, and the report of, "a grand jury [who] determined that her case was not credible."[208]

Here are a few of the problems with Ms. Brawley's story as outlined by the grand jury in its findings: Prior to the discovery of her body, "[Ms. Brawley] was . . . observed stepping into a large plastic garbage bag and pulling it up around her. She remained stationary for a couple of seconds, looked around, hopped a few feet, and then, while still inside the bag, lay on the ground;"[209] "[w]hen discovered, Tawana Brawley was not suffering from exposure. If an individual had been outdoors continuously from Tuesday evening, November 24, to Saturday afternoon, November 28, when the temperature several times dropped to the freezing point, there is a high probability the individual would have suffered from exposure;"[210] "[w]hen discovered, Tawana Brawley was not malnourished. If an individual had been deprived of food for four days, there is a high probability that there would have been evidence of malnourishment;"[211] "[w]hen discovered, Tawana Brawley did not have a bad odor to her breath. If an individual was prevented from practicing oral hygiene for a four day period, there is a high probability that there would have been a bad odor to the breath;"[212] "[w]hen discovered, there were no burns on any part of Tawana Brawley's body. The jeans that Tawana Brawley was wearing when found had been burned in the crotch area. If an individual had been wearing the jeans in which Tawana Brawley was found when the jeans were burned, there would be burns on the body;"[213] "[t]here was no medical or forensic evidence that a sexual assault was committed on Tawana Brawley. If a 15-year-old girl had been forcibly raped or sodomized by multiple assailants over a four day period, there is a high probability that medical or forensic evidence would have been found;"[214] "[a]ll of the items and instrumentalities necessary to create the condition in which Tawana Brawley appeared on Saturday, November 28, were present inside of or in the immediate vicinity of Apartment 19A"[215] (an apartment "Tawana Brawley had significant contact with and spent a period of undetermined duration in"[216] between the time of her alleged disappearance on "Tuesday evening, November 24, and the time she was found on Saturday, November 28"[217]).

In the context of Reciprocity, the grand jury's findings support the notion that someone attempted to turn Tawana Brawley into a transcendent emblem for African-American victims of racism. It is not known who did or did not help Ms. Brawley manufacture the evidence of her alleged abuse. But as the case became public, three men stepped up as high-profile allies of the fifteen-year-old girl and champions of her status as a single, understandable point-of-exertion that serves to encapsulate a broader pattern of exertion and transference. The Reverend Al Sharpton, attorney Alton H. Maddox, Jr., and attorney C. Vernon Mason put themselves forward as Ms. Brawley's representatives (both in court as well as in the court of public opinion). And they made concerted efforts to elevate her into an emblem of racist abuse by the white law enforcement establishment. Their efforts to establish Ms. Brawley as an icon representing—and somehow connected to—broader injustices did work to a degree: "Many people . . . believe . . . that to question her story is to betray all the black women who were raped and disbelieved throughout American history."[218] But while attempting to raise Tawana Brawley into an icon of the most brutal form of racism, the Reverend Sharpton and his colleagues also attempted to demonize Prosecutor Steven Pagones: "According to the Associated Press, Sharpton and Brawley's lawyers asserted 'on 33 separate occasions' that a local prosecutor named Steven Pagones 'had kidnapped, abused and raped' Brawley."[219] The strategy (conscious or not) was to create a negative co-emblem alongside Ms. Brawley, erecting Mr. Pagones as a lightning rod for anti-establishment sentiment and turning him into the symbol of broader prosecutorial abuses: "Sharpton took up Brawley's cause and defended her refusal to cooperate with prosecutors, saying that asking her to meet with New York's attorney general (who had been asked by Gov. Mario Cuomo to supervise the investigation) would be like 'asking someone who watched someone killed in the gas chamber to sit down with Mr. Hitler.'"[220]

As I stated at the outset, a clear-cut taxonomy of expression-as-exertion, exertion-as-broadcast, and broadcast as the trigger for transference cannot be created, and what we've done here is slip from the topic of exertion-as-broadcast (protest) into expression-as-exertion (the fabrication and false broadcast of a "point-of-exertion" intended to serve as the emblem of a larger transference). In the end, the grand jury found the broadcast of Ms. Brawley's assault to be an act of contrivance, an act that was itself exposed through the questions and answers, revelations and rebuttals, reports and reactions, accusations and defenses that constitute scrutiny: "To issue [its] report, the Grand Jury heard from 180 witnesses, saw 250 exhibits and recorded over 6,000 pages of testimony."[221] And of course, the more fabrication is present in any purported act of broadcast, the more power can be potentially transferred.

The ultimate conclusion of the Tawana Brawley matter reveals that those who allied themselves with her and acted on her behalf were (whether they knew it or not) engaged not in exposure but in exertion, which ended up transferring substantial power away from them and to those upon whom they were exerting. Following their attempts at emblemization, Sharpton, Maddox, Mason, and Brawley (who has since changed her name) all experienced a significant influence of their actions as a direct result of the power transferred by their own exertions. A jury found them all guilty of defaming Prosecutor Pagones, and the judge imposed both compensatory and punitive damages. Rev. Al Sharpton was ordered to pay $65,000.[222] Alton H. Maddox was ordered to pay $95,000[223] and also had his law license suspended.[224] C. Vernon Mason, who "was disbarred after his public role in the Brawley case,"[225] was ordered to pay $185,000.[226] And Ms. Brawley was also ordered to pay Mr. Pagones $185,000 in compensatory and punitive damages.[227] In addition, "Brawley and her family left the State of New York . . . having intentionally failed to cooperate with the grand jury process and having refused invitations (and/or disobeyed subpoenas) to testify under oath,"[228] and "the attorneys C. Vernon Mason and Alton Maddox . . . have since fallen off the edge of the world of political influence."[229] Clearly, power (the ability to influence another's actions) is transferred (and lost) through its own exertion.

Tawana Brawley engaged in a purported act of broadcast (with her injuries providing the supportive testimony); others attempted to lift her up as an emblem of racist exertions suitable for use as a flashpoint of protest (in his defamation-case decision, Judge Hickman noted "[t]he Court was appalled that Brawley would see fit to travel from the Washington, D.C. area to a rally in Brooklyn [a rally at which she again asserted that her story was true], but did not see fit to travel to Poughkeepsie to testify under oath before the jury"[230]); the contrivance was exposed, and Ms. Brawley's act—along with the actions of some who associated themselves with her—transferred away significant power.

But the point of analyzing the Tawana Brawley affair is not merely to present yet another example of Reciprocity-in-action. In examining the technique of protest (which is one form of exertion-as-broadcast), we encountered the phenomenon of the emblem that arises from exertions and comes to stand as a flashpoint for resistance. We have just finished considering the fact that such emblems are not easily manufactured, and we can now turn our attention to another Reciprocity-related aspect of the emblem-of-exertion: just as it is useful for those attempting to effect change to focus on a single, understandable, definable act or actor as the point of transference that represents a larger pattern, it is equally important for the rulers making efforts *against* Reciprocity to discourage the development of such icons.

As stated earlier, three of the four men on our short-list of liberators—Mohandas Gandhi, Nelson Mandela, and Václav Havel—were all jailed but not killed by their governments. That *restraint* was motivated by the desire to maintain power. Because power is transferred through its own exertion, the rulers of those systems actively sought to avoid the transference that would have certainly erupted had they executed those emblematic men. And the reasoning behind their reluctance to murder those men (their fear of forging an emblem) may also go a long way toward explaining this: At 3:00 p.m. on the afternoon of May 13, 1989, "up to 1,000 students [some of whom had already been demonstrating for approximately two weeks] began a hunger strike at Tiananmen Square"[231] in Beijing, China. By the following evening, "visitors and observers at the Tiananmen Square exceeded 100,000."[232] On May 17, "[t]he number of hunger strikers [had] increased to 3,000."[233] And on May 18, "[t]he afternoon march and demonstration involved about 1 million people."[234] Yet despite the sheer, almost incomprehensible numbers who participated in the Tiananmen Square demonstrations, a single image has emerged as the emblem of those protests; it is not the picture of an awesome but indistinguishable mass of one million protestors on the march, but the vision of one man standing entirely, almost eerily alone in the middle of a deserted city street—and single-handedly halting the progress of a long column of armored tanks as they attempt to make their way along Beijing's Avenue of Eternal Peace.

If we take the time to consider that transcendent image, we see that Reciprocity—and particularly our understanding of the effectiveness of the emblem—provides us with an explanation for these two, key facts:

1. The man was not run over.
2. You do not know his name.

To begin this analysis, it is necessary to recognize that Chinese party leaders (rulers of a system wherein the rulers aren't yet below the rules) are not entirely adverse to killing citizens who resist the system—in fact, only seventeen *days* after troops had cleared Tiananmen Square (far too short a time for any legitimate trials to take place), formal "[e]xecutions of arrested 'hooligans' and rioters began."[235] * But China's rulers did not dispatch those tank pilots onto the city streets under orders to run everyone over. In response to the Tiananmen protests, a great debate roiled China's Politburo as some Chinese leaders were loath to use physical exertion against the protesters: "One faction, headed by General Secretary Zhao Ziyang, wanted to [restore control] by negotiating with the demonstrators [i.e., acknowledging their power by acquiescing/acceding to certain demands], which would have opened a path to some sort of accommodation between regime and society. A military crackdown was the hard-line course advocated by Premier Li Peng and eventually preferred by Deng Xiaoping and his colleagues among the Elders."[236] Predictably, the party leaders who favored the use of physical exertion against the protestors fell back on the old "stability" argument as their excuse for impeding the very reforms they professed to support.

Deng Xiaoping: "Of course we want to build a socialist democracy, but we can't possibly do it in a hurry . . . If our one billion people jumped into multiparty elections, we'd get chaos like the 'all-out civil war' we saw during the Cultural Revolution. You don't have to have guns and cannon to have a civil war; fists and clubs will do just fine. Democracy is our goal, but we'll never get there without national stability."[237]

---

* Chinese law, a victim's doctrine that protects rulers by preempting the actions that could potentially make them the victims of revolt, applies the death penalty to numerous crimes. "The death penalty [is] . . . used extensively to punish around 68 crimes, including economic and non-violent crimes" (Amnesty International). And the rulers do impose such penalties: "[A]t least 1,010 people were executed and 2,790 sentenced to death [in China] during 2006" (*Ibid.*).

To achieve such "stability," Deng and his allies advocated the imposition of martial law (martial law is a limbo between power relations and force relations). The inclination to impose martial law reveals it was not true stability (balancing) that they were seeking, but the reestablishment of an indurate control that could only be achieved by forcing the demonstrators back into acquiescence. The response to that martial law approach (the argument against military action) hinged on a recognition of Reciprocity, a recognition that such forceful exertions might lead to a *total* loss of power: Zhao Ziyang "persisted in arguing that the forcible suppression of the students might prove to be a mistake of such magnitude as to destroy the legitimacy of the regime."[238]

Zhao Ziyang: "Let me tell you how I see all this. I think the student movement has two important characteristics. First, the students' slogans call for things like supporting the Constitution, promoting democracy, and fighting corruption. These demands all echo positions of the Party and the government. Second, a great many people from all parts of society are out there joining the demonstrations and backing the students . . . This has grown into a nationwide protest. I think the best way to bring the thing to a quick end is to focus on the mainstream views of the majority . . . That way we can avoid a sweeping characterization of the protests as an antagonistic conflict. We can concentrate on policies of persuasion and guidance [i.e., minimize exertions/transference] and avoid the sharpening of conflict."[239]

Zhao recognized that stability comes from balancing whereas the denial of Reciprocity leads to a tense and brittle system that is *more* apt to topple.

Ultimately, the "Elders" opted for the military solution. They resisted Reciprocity, and they succeeded. But the details of their success, the specific manner in which they proceeded—particularly regarding the way they managed broadcast—demonstrates that they understood the truth of Reciprocity even as they attempted to deny it. Even after martial law was declared, after Chinese citizens were dropped into that limbo between power relations and force relations, "Yang Shangkun, who was responsible for the implementation of martial law, could only say, 'We must be equally firm about stopping the turmoil and about avoiding bloodshed in doing so."[240] In other words, to maintain our power, we must carefully calculate our exertions.*

---

* Interestingly, *turmoil* is a translation of "the Chinese word *daluan*, which has a very loaded meaning; it indicates chaos following the breakdown of government"

In developing a fuller understanding of point number one above—the fact that the tanks did not mow down that man in the street—we now see that such exertive thrift was not due to an underestimation of the seriousness of the situation; on the contrary, it was the very nature of the Tiananmen protests, the fact that those protests directly threatened the Chinese Communist system (the fact that the demonstrators were "calling" the bluff promises of party leaders), which led to a more careful calculation of exertions on the part of China's rulers. Unlike the Rodney King rioters, who took action and pursued balancing within a system that recognizes Reciprocity, the protestors at Tiananmen Square were not crying out for justice alone, not seeking merely a better balancing within the existing accumulation of agreements. Instead, they were attempting to redefine limits in a way that would bring into existence many entirely new agreements, including these democratic reforms that reveal Reciprocity, its consequences, and its effects woven throughout:

"(1) a fair assessment of Hu's administration [per Reciprocity: a history that moved closer to the truth and further from propaganda*];

(2) complete retraction of the antispiritual pollution and antibourgeois campaigns [per Reciprocity: revision of the static, statist agreements that supported agreements with repressive future components];

(3) public enumeration of properties owned by each of the government and Party leaders [per Reciprocity: an inventory of all those "houses on the hill"];

(Gray, 419). In the context of Tiananmen, the term was first applied to the protests in a high-profile editorial issued by the party itself. So why would a regime attempting to hold off systemic breakdown decide to imply that such a breakdown had *already* occurred? Reciprocity provides the answer: through their choice of words, Chinese rulers were attempting to draw propagandistically on the rule of Reciprocity by implying that their future forceful exertions would be justified by (i.e., an act of balancing against and utilization of the power transferred by) the prior exertions of the demonstrators.

* The "Hu" referred to here is Hu Yaobang, a former secretary general of China's Communist Party and proponent of democratic reforms, who was dismissed from his post after "Deng Xiaoping ordered Hu to stop the [pro-democracy] protests [that had erupted in 1986, three years prior to Tiananmen Square] and he refused" (Gray, 412). The protests that led to the events at Tiananmen Square began the day Hu died (April 15, 1989). Thus, in attempting to manage the Tiananmen Square demonstrations, China's rulers were also contending with (and suppressing) efforts to elevate Hu Yaobang to the status of emblem.

(4) permission for a private press and lifting of media restrictions [per Reciprocity: permission to establish mechanisms of broadcast];

(5) increases in the educational budget and wages and benefits for intellectuals [per Reciprocity: a stronger position for those who communicate the facts that help mold agreements];

(6) abolishment of the unconstitutional ten-point restrictions against public demonstrations passed by the People's Congress executive committee [per Reciprocity: placing the rulers (the committee) below the rules (the Constitution)] and

(7) fair and precise reporting [per Reciprocity: broadcast] of the current demonstrations in Party and government newspapers."[241]

In other words, the protestors were seeking human freedom by demanding the implementation of institutional mechanisms to facilitate balancing and establish life under a system that acknowledges Reciprocity.

So with this understanding of the protestors' demands comes a recognition that the Chinese government was attempting to stop a revolution, not start one; therefore, due to Reciprocity's third consequence (when the purpose of an exertion of power includes the maintenance of power, then power is maintained through calculated conservation, not unlimited exertion) the regime had to carefully calculate its own exertions—not wantonly crush Chinese citizens in the streets. Because the communist system attempts to centralize power and does not institutionally recognize the fact that power is disbursed throughout, it does not provide systemic mechanisms for oscillation, and therefore, those seeking to exercise the power they have acquired through the regime's exertions have no alternative but to take action outside the system. Revolution (by definition) entails an abandonment of current agreements (otherwise revolution is unnecessary), and revolution almost always requires the falling back to force relations in order to achieve such abandonment. Had the government used its tanks to openly and callously crush that man standing alone on the Avenue of Eternal Peace, it would have also increased quite significantly the potential for the falling back to the very force relations (abandonment of the system) it was attempting to avoid.

Now, what is perhaps most remarkable of all about the emblematic picture of that man and those tanks is not that the tanks stopped, but that the image was captured one day *after* troops had violently confronted citizens in the streets of Beijing and cleared the protestors from Tiananmen Square in the early-morning hours of June 4. Despite the fact that such violence had already occurred, Chinese officials were still doing all they could not to create an emblem, not to manifest that single, unacceptable point-of-exertion that, when broadcast, would serve as the flashpoint for full-blown revolution. In truth, the efficacy of the emblem (be it an individual or event) was clearly understood by both sides. As tensions mounted, "student leader Wang Dan expressed the hope that a Walesa figure would appear in China."[242] So we can ask, what was the difference between the violent clashes that took place in the early-morning hours of June 4, and the confrontation between man and tank the next day? Death is death—so why kill in one instance and not in the other?

Whether one takes into consideration the diminished number of citizens on the streets, the masking element of darkness or the absence of cameras, one recognizes that the main difference between 1:00 a.m. on June 4 (when the troops cleared the square) and daytime on June 5 (when the man stopped those tanks) is the difference in the overall potential for broadcast. As the pictures of that man and those tanks prove, cameras were there on June 5; that is to say, broadcast was present—and the Chinese rulers knew it. On the other hand, "[w]hen the army entered the Square in the middle of the night, the lights were cut off for a time. What may have been done in the dark we will probably never know."[243] Chinese troops cleared the square under the cloak of night and *after* clearing all broadcast agencies from the area. In the end, the country's rulers were able to resist Reciprocity for the same reason any regime is able to resist it: because the people (whose acquiescence creates power) defined the government's well-calculated exertions as within acceptable limits (i.e., they acquiesced). Why did the military take action in the dark? To conceal exertions, of course. And that question was already answered even more specifically at the very outset of this section: if people don't know what the exertions are or even that the exertions exist, then they can't decide whether those exertions are beyond acceptable limits.

So Reciprocity and the role of broadcast explains this apparently paradoxical juxtaposition: the Chinese army proceeded against a mass of protesters under cover of darkness, but one man stopped a line of tanks in broad daylight. Remarkably, the fact that those killing machines did not kill that man in cold blood and plain sight relates to every aspect of Reciprocity and its consequences: Power is transferred through its own exertion; the point at which power is exerted is the point at which there exists the greatest potential for its transfer; the people upon whom power is being exerted define its limits; when the purpose of an exertion of power includes the maintenance of power, then power is maintained through calculated conservation, not unlimited exertion. And the role of broadcast is also vividly illustrated: broadcast stands out as the effective mechanism to promote change because broadcast exposes the exertions that create the transfer; people react, "That's unjust," but if they can't see (literally or metaphorically) the injustice, then they won't seek the balancing that Reciprocity makes possible. Thus, Reciprocity and broadcast explain why that lone man was not flattened. But Reciprocity and broadcast also explain the second point enumerated above: you don't know that man's name.

To this day, the single most iconic individual to emerge from the protests at Tiananmen Square remains anonymous, known only as the Tank Man by those who have investigated the incident and attempted to discover his identity. Furthermore, (and even more remarkably), in China, "[t]he regime has managed to erase the Tank Man's image, famous throughout the world, from Chinese memory."[244] Thus, when filmmaker Antony Thomas traveled to China in search of the Tank Man and showed "the iconic picture to undergraduates at Beijing University, the nerve center of the 1989 protests, none of them recognize[d] it."[245] "Captured on film and video by Western journalists, this extraordinary standoff became an icon of the struggle for freedom around the world."[246] But not in China.

Why would the Chinese government attempt to "erase the Tank Man's image . . . from Chinese memory?" We have the answer already: memory sustains agreement, and memory of the Tank Man's success would maintain the static agreement that one, unarmed individual can halt a convoy of tanks, which would, in turn, inspire confidence in the fact that power comes from below and support the static agreement that we can oppose our government. And all of that would then serve as the foundation for new agreements with future components: "Let's utilize our power to redefine limits and establish the democracy that the Tank Man (and his allies) failed to establish before." Reciprocity shows that agreements are redefined by those upon whom power is being exerted if they define the exertions as beyond acceptable limits. If, in the midst of such an attempt at redefinition, the regime kills the resisters, then the regime risks a falling back to force relations if members of the surviving population then act to redefine those deadly exertions as beyond acceptable limits. Creating an emblem-of-exertion, such as the one that would have been created had the Tank Man been crushed, increases the likelihood that survivors will act to redefine limits. But if the regime doesn't kill the resisters, if one man can halt a line of tanks, then the regime risks revelation that power comes from below, is disbursed throughout, and is transferred by its own exertion. Thus, the Tank Man's image has to be censored by a regime that does not yet recognize Reciprocity (a regime that, as Reciprocity predicts, controls the institutional means—and takes actions to suppress all forms—of broadcast).

Chinese communist rulers killed far fewer citizens in and around Tiananmen Square than they've killed in secret, yet Tiananmen Square presented a far greater potential for the loss of power. Why? Because of the broadcast that the protestors accomplished and attracted (Zhao Ziyang: "The fasting students feel themselves under a spotlight"[247]). As evidenced by the events at Tiananmen Square, exertion-as-broadcast not only attracts additional broadcast but often additional exertion and, therefore, increases both the potential for exposure as well as the power that is potentially transferred. The anonymous Tank Man's singular act of defiance attracted a significant amount of broadcast. And both his immediate survival and subsequent cultural erasure provide us with an iconic episode that vividly encapsulates the rule of Reciprocity, the role of broadcast, and the importance of the emblem.

In the past few pages, we entered an analysis of protest, came to the phenomenon of the emblem that can help bring protest to its successful consummation (i.e., help with the redefinition of limits that is protest's purpose), examined the complications associated with the emblem, and now, with those underlying insights in place, we can take up an instance (one among many) in which the emblem-of-exertion was effective in facilitating the transference of power pursued through protest. I opened this book with a bus story, the brief account of an insignificant incident I happened to have once witnessed, and before we leave the Tank Man's memory behind, let's take him with us onto another bus and into a much better-known story. The anonymity of the Tank Man becomes all the more remarkable (yet understandable) when we seat him aside another icon who refused to move, the high-profile Rosa Parks.

First and foremost, the juxtaposition of Beijing, China, against Montgomery, Alabama, highlights significant advantages for those seeking to redefine limits within a system that acknowledges Reciprocity: the demonstrators in Beijing ran up against the need for revolution; the demonstrators in Montgomery did not. The rulers of the first system can't admit that a single individual can effect change (i.e., power comes from below); the leaders of the second system must.* The rulers of the first system must control broadcast; the leaders of the second system can't. Agreements cannot expand in the first system; they can expand in the second. And even this: because any recognition of Reciprocity also requires the recognition that power (including economic power) cannot be centralized, Reciprocity requires a decentralized economic system, and the competition/cooperation that such decentralization requires creates additional opportunity for nonviolent economic resistance (boycott).

Before we examine boycott through the events that followed Rosa Parks's arrest, it is worthwhile to establish some important points. First, Rosa Parks's refusal to move to the back of the bus was an act of resistance, not protest (resistance becomes protest en masse), but she and her allies did broadcast her arrest as that single instance of exertion-and-transference, exposing it as the understandable flashpoint around which others could rally; that is to say, America's emerging civil rights leaders directed their attention to Rosa Parks (as an effective emblem that grew organically out of events) in order to broadcast broader injustices. Second, Rosa Parks's allies knew quite well what power is and how it works. Here, we can add Martin Luther King to our list of liberators who understood and utilized the rule of Reciprocity.

---

* As Natan Sharansky explains, "Had Mahatma Gandhi [and I would add, Martin Luther King in his own context] been facing the regime of a Stalin or a Hitler, his struggle . . . would have ended before it began. Fortunately for him, he confronted a British society that, while imperialist, was also liberal and democratic" (Sharansky, 47). Here I would point out that democracy is a product of Reciprocity, and "liberal" is a placeholder for the system that has recognized the fact that power comes from below, is disbursed throughout, and transferred through its own exertion. Both Gandhi and King were resisting against/within systems that had already had their own revolutions, had already placed the rulers below the rules. As explained earlier, the hunger-strike strategy that Gandhi pursued works directly on Reciprocity and broadcast: the hunger strike both increases the exertion of power (by virtue of the fact that the regime's refusal to redefine limits may now end in the protestor's death) and attracts broadcast (no one conducts a hunger strike in secret—that's called suicide). Confronted by a hunger strike, a nascent authoritarian regime (such as Stalin's or Hitler's) would simply take the opportunity to kill or deport the hunger striker ("Make sure that Gandhi guy books passage on the next Philosophy Steamer") as a chance to invoke more fear.

Martin Luther King: "Power is the ability to achieve purpose . . . Power is the ability to effect change . . . and I want you to stick it out so that you will be able to make Mayor Henry Loeb and others say 'Yes' even when they want to say 'No.'"[248]

Power is the ability to influence another's actions, and it is created by acquiescence/agreement (it is created by that "yes" to which the Reverend King referred). Martin Luther King and his allies moved forward from that single moment in Montgomery and other emblematic exertions and transferences that preceded and followed (e.g., the murder of Emmett Till, the Little Rock Nine, the Greensboro Four, Freedom Riders, the events of Bloody Sunday), and they took the power that had been—and was being—transferred to them through the exertions of their opponents in order to: 1. institutionalize/codify the power which had been transferred (i.e., memorialize more "yeses" in the form of the Civil Rights Acts of 1964 and 1968, the Voting Rights Act and other, relevant victim's doctrines) and 2. achieve greater access to power that had already been memorialized (i.e., *expand* agreements such as the overturning of the "separate but equal" doctrine that had recently resulted from the "yes" decision in *Brown v. Board of Education*).

Overall, what are the images one most readily associates with the nonviolent civil rights movement led by Martin Luther King? 1. The broadcast accomplished by Rev. King's speeches. 2. Black men being blown over with water cannons, attacked by dogs, confronted by police, screamed at by fearful, hate-filled whites, or marching past armed troops. In each and every instance, those protests drew both exertion and broadcast. In truth, all protesters use the combined phenomena of broadcast and Reciprocity, relying on exertion-as-broadcast both to expose exertions and possibly draw more transference. If protesters drew neither broadcast nor exertion to themselves—that is to say, if they were merely ignored—they would be left crying out powerless (unable to influence the actions of their adversaries).

Now, despite the efficacy of nonviolent resistance in certain circumstances, Reciprocity does not lead logically to the conclusion "don't exert." Quite the opposite, we must exert. But we must exert with an understanding of Reciprocity and the potential transfer of power that accompanies any exertion. Ultimately, an understanding of the rule of Reciprocity helps us better understand when and how to exert, how to take the power transferred to us through others' exertions, and how to use that power in order to institute new limits. Thus, Reciprocity can guide both our actions and inaction.

So with regard to the strategies of exertion (the action and inaction) surrounding Ms. Parks, we find that the pulpits of Montgomery's ministers became the platforms for broadcast as those ministers spread word of Rosa Parks's resistance and in so doing also exposed the inherent injustice of the exertions made against her (and the congregations to which the ministers were preaching). Then those ministers, Ms. Parks, and their allies all moved forward from static agreements—what Rosa Parks did was right/what was done to her was wrong—to an agreement with a future component: we will boycott the buses in Montgomery, Alabama.

As stated at the outset of this subsection, boycott is our third and final form of exertion-as-broadcast. It incorporates economic resistance into the discussion, and it brings back to mind those "million little dictators" each exposing, exerting, resisting, competing, and cooperating in their own way. In other words, it highlights another advantage of capitalism as well as another instance in which capitalism allows for nonviolent remedy. As was already proven, one cannot maintain a centralized economic system without centralized political and legal systems (since such overlapping systems must align or separate). Political and legal authoritarianism is inevitable in a centralized economy, and therefore, boycott would be deemed revolutionary (and quashed) at the get-go. Why would boycott be deemed revolutionary? Simple: "From each according to his ability, to each according to his needs" means that people who need to take the bus should be able to take it whether they pay for it or not; thus, a bus system that shuts down as the result of nonpayment would reveal the fact that production (the fares of riders), not need, was defining distribution. Moreover, an admission of influence by (or defeat at the hands of) a boycott would also be an admission of failure in the centralized system—it would reveal, beyond a shadow of a doubt, that power was not centralized.

The statement that a centralized system cannot abide boycott is true by degrees. The more centralized a system, the less able it will be to allow boycott; the less centralized a system, the more boycott will begin to appear. Boycott requires broadcast. Centralized systems must inhibit broadcast. Boycott requires economic influence. Centralized systems must inhibit economic influence. Therefore, one can predict that as Reciprocity moves a system toward decentralization, boycott will become more plausible. And we do find that prediction borne out in reality. As this recent news article clearly illustrates, boycott is being pursued in present-day China (and please note, it is being pursued via the world's newest form of broadcast): "Blogger Hits Home By Urging Boycott of Chinese Property . . . Since he posted an open letter on his Internet blog . . . urging Shenzhen residents to stop buying property, [Zou Tao] says, he has been deluged with more than 150,000 pledges of support nationwide."[249] And as predicted, boycott is also being suppressed by the rulers of a system that cannot acknowledge Reciprocity: "In challenging developers, Mr. Zou recognizes he has crossed the line from consumer advocacy to political activism [we have already seen this is inevitable since the overlapping economic/political systems must align or separate, and therefore, economic protest cannot be tolerated in a centralized system that prohibits political protest] . . . [but] [h]e wasn't prepared for the resistance to his latest crusade. He says plainclothes security agents seized him at the Shenzhen airport last month . . . The agents grilled him overnight but let him go the next day."[250] Once again, China's odd and unsustainable, capitalist-dictatorship hybrid (an authoritarian system in which some citizens have the personal broadcast capabilities of blogs) has emerged because of capitalism's requirement of co-operation.

To fully understand the efficacy of boycott in the capitalist system, consider this paradox: In Montgomery, Alabama, whites didn't want to sit next to negroes at all, so, once the boycott began, not having *any* negroes on the buses should have been cause for celebration, not concern. But that was not the case. Montgomery's white political elite were gravely concerned. Absent economic considerations, the white reaction to the boycott was inherently illogical. And that recognition brings us back to the nature of capitalism: capitalism is competition. Competition is cooperation. Therefore, capitalism is cooperation. The white bus owners needed the co-operation of the negroes. In short, they needed blacks on the buses. And Montgomery's African-American community knew it. The Montgomery bus boycott began on Monday, December 5, 1955, following the distribution of thirty-five thousand handbills (i.e., broadcast), which read in part: "Negroes have rights, too, for if Negroes did not ride the buses, they could not operate."[251]

Well, the buses could certainly operate; drivers were perfectly capable of driving near-empty vehicles through the streets. But they could not sustain such operation in a capitalist system: "A month after the boycott started, on January 5, 1956, Montgomery City Bus Lines transportation superintendent James H. Bagley sat in his office at 701 North McDonough Street in downtown Montgomery. In a telephone conversation with his home office in Chicago, he reported that company business was down so much that expenses far exceeded income during the past month. Although few people had been riding the buses, drivers had to be paid and gasoline had to be purchased. According to his estimation, it cost between forty and forty-four cents every mile to operate a bus. Since the boycott had started, he estimated that the company had lost about twenty-two cents for every mile of operation. Multiplied to its fullest, with twelve buses operating sixteen hours a day, the company was losing at least four hundred dollars every day . . . Because the company had a contract [i.e., capitalist agreement] with the city to provide public transportation, buses had to continue to run their regular routes."[252]

In a centralized system, there would have been no contract and no authentic cooperation, just a coercive government attempting to maintain the illusion that it had something to bestow upon its people that did not come from its people to begin with and rulers who would quickly equate economic resistance with revolutionary activities (crossing that "line from consumer advocacy to political activism"). Again, the Montgomery bus boycotters were not trying to incite a revolution; they were trying to gain more power by expanding agreements within the same system (specifically, they were attempting to expand the desegregation decision of *Brown v. Board of Education*).

Now, in Montgomery, the intransigent nature of the protestors' opponents (the fact that this particular conflict involved deeply held racist beliefs and much emotion) meant that the economic pressure of the boycott was not sufficient to inspire compromise, and the resolution had to come from an external authority (a decision by the Supreme Court). Thus, the boycott ended a bit over one year after it began, on December 20, 1956, the day after the boycott's leaders in Montgomery received the Supreme Court's written order affirming the lower court's finding that "the enforced segregation of Negro and white passengers on motor buses operating in the City of Montgomery . . . violates the Constitution."[253]

When the boycott began, blacks couldn't sit where they pleased on Montgomery's buses. When it ended, they could. The fact that power is transferred through its own exertion (plus the consequences of that fact) sparked, sustained, and carried the black activists' legal, political, and economic efforts to successful consummation. The bus boycott served as the high-profile platform upon which Montgomery's African-American community broadcasted the unjust nature of the segregationists' exertions.

Of course, there was a subtext to the Montgomery bus boycott. It was the same subtext that lurked beneath *Brown v. Board of Education*, the King riots, the Louima assault, the ersatz emblemization of Tawana Brawley, and every other instance of black-white race conflict in the United States. That subtext is slavery. In moving from exertion-as-broadcast to broadcast as the trigger for transference, we will move backward many years before Rosa Parks and Rev. King to the initial exertions and transferences that made black activists and leaders necessary (and possible) in the first place. We will go straight into the belly of the beast in order to examine the circumstance that constitutes a systematic clubber-berry bringer correspondence. As I stated in the opening pages, those who do not accept the fact that power is vested throughout a system might understandably ask, "What about slaves? What power could they possibly have?" That is the question we will now address directly. And I hope this comes as no surprise: Reciprocity and broadcast provide the answer.

Broadcast as the Trigger for Transference

Continuing in the spirit of simplicity, here's another introductory example similar to the toy-snatcher scenario considered earlier. This one is a true story, also drawn from a playground (and recounted to me). Picture a schoolyard at lunchtime recess. To be more precise, picture the schoolyard of a New York City public school at lunchtime recess. Now, imagine this: from among the frantic pandemonium and deafening cacophony of children run amok, rises a single, unusually loud voice to boldly exclaim, "I told you not to do that. That's called bullying."

And that—plain and simple—is called broadcast.

No need for the teacher to sort out "who started it," no question about who exerted and who had the power to influence the other's actions. "I *told* you not to do that" means this is not the first time I've spoken to you about your behavior; and it also shows that I have not exerted back; I've merely asked you to stop. "That's called *bullying*" means the exertion was predefined as unacceptable even before any judge engaged the case. Needless to say, the situation was resolved in favor of the boy who undertook that simple act of broadcast (without any further effort on his part). In short, the boy who raised his voice took the power transferred to him through the exertions of the other child and used broadcast to trigger the transference.

It's a simple example, but as with most of its kind that have gone before, it shines light across a much broader landscape. We have met "the boy who raised his voice" in many of the events already analyzed: Václav Havel was the boy who raised his voice; Mohandas Gandhi was the boy who raised his voice; Candace Lightner was the girl who raised her voice. Rosa Parks raised her voice when she refused to rise, and the silent Tank Man's voice, suppressed in China, rose to reach beyond the country's borders. Martin Luther King raised his voice. Nelson Mandela raised his voice. The barons on Runnymede raised their voices. The opponents of Presidents Nixon and Clinton raised their voices. American Indians raised their voices. In addition, many other major figures who did not make it into the scope of this study have also raised their voices: Lech Walesa, Ronald Reagan ("Mr. Gorbachev, tear down this wall!"[254]), Winston Churchill. And countless lesser-known yet no less important individuals have taken on the role and responsibilities of "the boy who raised his voice."

Of course, the most interesting aspect of this example is not simply that the boy raised his voice, not merely that he said *something*, but more precisely, what he said. "That's called bullying" pretty much explains why Castro jams Radio Martí: he doesn't want outsiders (or anyone) defining him as a bully to his people (on the other hand, one can say anything one wants about a president of the United States, and one will either expose truth or expose oneself as an unreliable source; that is to say, one will either facilitate the transfer of power away from the president or transfer power away from oneself through one's own expressive exertions). The exposure inherent in "that's called bullying" also helps explain why the Chinese government requires search engines to censor results, why Saudi Arabia bans books, and why every dictator seizes control of his country's press (it explains why you can't start a newspaper in North Korea).

From this, and so much that has gone before, we now directly encounter another counter-intuitive truth. It was touched on indirectly before (in the recognition that broadcast itself is not an exertion, that it does not transfer power away), and we can now state it even more succinctly as the common cause for every dictatorship's suppression of expression: broadcast is a taking, not a giving.

Power exists throughout every system, but it is not distributed everywhere equally—it survives in a condition of give-and-take (oscillation). And the strategy for those who want to take power (i.e., gain greater influence over another's actions) is first to expose the exertions that are opening up the potential for the transfer of power. To be sure, broadcast is an outwardly directed report. And it can assume the form of any evidence revealing an exertion: a crying child, a black eye, a burnt house, a body hanging limply from a tree, or it can come as testimony from those who witnessed or experienced the acts that rendered those results. But the broadcast itself, while assuming the form of an offering of evidence, actually serves the purpose of taking power.

We can perhaps better understand broadcast as a taking, not a giving when we consider the act and intent of *surveillance*. Normally, we would consider surveillance (the taking in of images) to be the opposite of broadcast (the putting out of images), but really, surveillance is a form of broadcast as I've defined it since its sole reason for existence is to expose exertions. In short, surveillance without the threat of exposure is not surveillance; it's voyeurism.

In *Discipline and Punish: The Birth of the Prison*, Michel Foucault examines and explains "the disappearance of torture as a public spectacle"[255] within certain systems. And in explicating punishment's overall, internalizing movement ("punishment . . . will . . . become the most hidden part of the penal process"[256]), he draws upon the Panopticon (and Panopticism) as a transcendent example, overarching model, and in some ways, metaphor for the technique of surveillance that today replaces the spectacle of punishment-on-display as the main mechanism of social discipline in most societies. In other words, Foucault traces in detail precisely the movement that we encountered under the "Justice" subhead in the first section: once a punitive system (accumulation of agreements) is formed, Reciprocity predicts that the emphasis will naturally shift from force to power (influencing the convict's actions through various degrees/techniques of incarceration as opposed to those forceful exertions that will tend to transfer power away from the party imposing punishment).

Bentham's Panopticon, the architectural invention from which Foucault derives Panopticism as his model for the broader surveillant society, is a circular prison-structure with a tower at its center from which a guard (who is not visible to the prisoners in the cells that encircle him) may see directly into each and every cell. Clearly, the tower that stands in the center of the carceral mechanism is charged with the potential for exposure. Its stone-silent presence whispers the constant threat of discovery and broadcast. Thus, it is not the surveillance itself that influences the prisoner's actions but the threat of exposure (even more specifically: the potential for the transfer of power that would result from such exposure) that keeps him under control. And Foucault demonstrates conclusively that the thread of this threat leads out far beyond the Panopticon's walls.

As Foucault reveals, the most impressive characteristic of the Panopticon is that no one need sit in the tower. It is the mere threat of surveillance (we would say, the potential that their exertions will transfer power away from them) that influences the actions of those situated within the structure. Thus, Foucault's broader concept of Panopticism describes the masterful method by which a society exerts control without actually making an exertion:

> He who is subjected to a field of visibility, and who knows it, assumes responsibility for the constraints of power [i.e., he influences his own actions]; he makes them play spontaneously upon himself; he inscribes in himself the power relation in which he simultaneously plays both roles [i.e., clubber and berry-bringer]; he becomes the principle of his own subjection.[257]

That is an accurate and sophisticated account of the end-effect of the evolution of discipline. But why has discipline evolved at all? Why does punishment move out of sight? Why do systems make this shift from punishment-on-display to Panopticism? Reciprocity, its consequences, and effects provide the most concise answer: surveillance is a quintessential form of calculated conservation—it is an act without *action*. Thus, it is inevitable that surveillance would emerge in systems that recognize Foucault's own truth ("power comes from below") as well as the fact that power is transferred through its own exertion. In short, Reciprocity reveals the impetus for such an evolution: punishment-on-display equals exertion-on-display equals the transfer-of-power-on-display. Thus, in order to minimize the potential for transfer, punishment must be internalized (in every sense).

Consider this fact regarding the spectacle of torture: the criminal usually came from the community as did the crowd that came to view his brutal execution. As he was basically one of them—a fellow citizen and subject of the sovereign—the crowd naturally identified with him, and so they became the ones upon whom the king's power was being exerted. This is not my theory, but Foucault's own observation rendered in Reciprocity's vocabulary. Per Foucault, the scaffold, the structure upon which the convict was tortured and killed (i.e., the point of the sovereign's own exertion), also became the point at which the most dramatic declarations regarding unacceptable limits were voiced: "If the crowd gathered round the scaffold, it was not simply to witness the sufferings of the condemned man . . . it was also to hear an individual who had nothing more to lose curse the judges, the laws, the government and religion [i.e., decry unacceptable definitions of limits while drawing attention to the exertions and exerters] . . . Under the protection of imminent death, the criminal could say everything and the crowd cheered."[258] In other words, under such circumstances, the criminal's expressive exertions were immune from transfer since it had already been decided that he had transferred all.

As the efforts of countless dictators vividly prove, broadcast becomes a core commodity in power relations. By erecting the scaffold and executing citizens upon it, the sovereign himself was providing his enemies with a singularly effective broadcast-platform (while simultaneously exposing his own extreme exertions). Power is exposed through exertion. Thus, at the point of exertion, power is identified and defined, but in that very attempt at definition (that is to say, as the exerters attempt to define their own power), power becomes subject to redefinition. At the point of exertion, power becomes tangible and therefore subject to the changes we've witnessed: redistribution, reduction, loss. Hence, over time (as limits are redefined) exertions are also reduced, and surveillance/broadcast emerges as the primary mechanism of social control both as a result of those redefinitions as well as the effort to minimize the potential for future transference. Interestingly, by applying our concept of broadcast to Foucault's analysis of the history of disciplinary influence, we see that Foucault actually describes a history that moves from broadcast to broadcast—from the sovereign's deterrent display of his own exertions (broadcast) to the surveillance and exposure of the exertions of subjects (broadcast).

The phenomenon of surveillance is useful to us in understanding broadcast as a taking, not a giving. And the movement of punishment from corporal to carceral is a helpful illustration of the process Reciprocity predicts and explains. But there is another important point here, one that takes us directly into an examination of the systematic movement of slaves from captivity to freedom. By placing convicts upon the scaffold, the king gave his enemies the chance to tell their own story, to raise their own voices, literally, above the crowd. And it is precisely that voice—the voice of the voiceless—that pierces the oppressive veil and sets transference in motion. That voice is the one thing the clubber cannot confiscate from the berry bringer (unless the clubber kills him, and thus destroys the system he seeks to maintain). And that voice is also the mechanism of exposure for real-life slaves who redefine limits in part by engaging in broadcast and telling their own stories. In this vein, Henry Louis Gates, Jr., a preeminent scholar of the American slave narrative, has observed that: "One of the most curious aspects of the African person's enslavement in the New World is that he and she *wrote* about the severe conditions of their bondage within what, with understatement, came to be called 'the peculiar institution.' In the long history of human bondage, it was only the black slaves in the United States who—once secure and free in the North, and with the generous encouragement and assistance of northern abolitionists—created a *genre* of literature that at once testified against their captors and bore witness to the urge of every black slave to be free and literate. Hundreds of ex-slaves felt compelled to tell their tales on the anti-slavery lecture circuit in the North and in the written form of the autobiographical narrative [emphasis in original]."[259]

The experience of the American slaves provides much of interest regarding the role of broadcast in Reciprocity (i.e., how exposure helps facilitate transfer). But it is important to clarify that the efforts to expose the injustices exacted within that institution are not particularly curious if one takes *curious* to mean uncommon or hard to explain. There is nothing uncommon about oppression (slavery is, of course, an uncommonly extreme form of oppression, uncommon partly because Reciprocity makes it impossible to maintain), and members of every oppressed people have written and spoken of (i.e., broadcasted) their experiences. To make that point abundantly clear: Havel's *Power of the Powerless* and Marx and Engels' *Communist Manifesto*—utterly antithetical in their content—*both* fall squarely into this genre of broadcast: oppressed people exposing their oppression. Today, certain citizens of China, Iran, Cuba, North Korea, and other dictatorial regimes around the world use every available means to broadcast the exertions made against them and in the process begin to take (bit by bit) the power transferred to them. To be sure, the extraordinarily imbalanced nature of slavery gives us a singularly powerful example of Reciprocity-in-action, and the uniquely consistent form and unusually concentrated collection of slave narratives belies important influences and explicit objectives. The emergence of a definable "*genre* of literature" is unarguably unique, but from Reciprocity's perspective the existence of this type of broadcast (the voice of the voiceless) is not.

When viewed from the perspective Reciprocity provides, however, there is something quite curious about the events surrounding the emancipation of the slaves in the United States of America, and this curiosity arises not from the act of broadcast but from the bifurcation of the United States' system, the very split that led the country into war with itself. Here is the prelude to the Civil War as described by President Lincoln (with Reciprocity's explication interpolated): "One-eighth of the whole population were colored slaves, not distributed generally over the Union, but localized in the Southern part of it. These slaves constituted a peculiar and *powerful* [i.e., capable of influencing others' actions] interest. All knew that this interest was, somehow, the cause of the war [emphasis added]."[260] "Both parties [North and South] deprecated war; but one of them would make war [i.e., fall back to force relations] rather than let the nation survive [i.e., rather than continue to co-operate in a system wherein oscillation was leading unavoidably to abolition]; and the other would accept war rather than let it perish [i.e., the North would not acquiesce to the South's demand for secession, but would pursue the force relations the South initiated in order to achieve the South's own surrender and acquiescence]."[261] In point of fact, the U.S. Civil War is a strikingly strange illustration of Reciprocity-in-action. Whereas in every other example we have taken up, the rebels were the ones *resisting* oppression, Southern rebels were not rebelling against the denial of Reciprocity (as their forefathers had); they were fighting to *maintain* a system that denied Reciprocity. It is a rare circumstance indeed wherein a group opposes its own government in order to preserve obvious oppression. But that is what happened. And it is precisely in the South's own resistance to Reciprocity that we begin to find answers as to how and why slavery failed in the United States.

I began this study by positing the first agreement between our now-familiar and highly theoretical cavemen: the clubber and the berry bringer. And now we have come full-circle to meet these far-too-familiar and not-at-all-theoretical real men: the master and the cotton picker. Here we see there is no difference between theory and reality, between the clubber-berry bringer and master-cotton picker correspondences; each presents an instance of initial extremely imbalanced acquiescence. And therefore, in examining how and why slavery was eradicated in the United States, we also see that we already know *why* slavery failed. The reason was stated previously in the "Power" section, under the "Oscillation" subhead: Slavery fails because it attempts to oppose Reciprocity as well as *all* of Reciprocity's consequences. Slavery survives exclusively on the attempted denial of oscillation. And it is for this reason (the fact that oscillation cannot be avoided) that we see, empirically, that wherever slavery appears, the slaves eventually achieve freedom. So oscillation is the reason slavery fails (it is the "why" part of "how and why"), but what are the details of its failure? How did the slaves work to redefine limits? It is in this "how" part where we see broadcast playing a significant role.

Before we look in detail at the role of broadcast in the emancipation of the American slaves, it is important to note that there is—as Reciprocity predicts—a basic story (or hegemonic history) of the abolition of slavery in the U.S., and it goes something like this:

Abraham Lincoln and his assorted generals led a courageous group of white men from the North into bloody battle against the secessionist South and, in the process, delivered emancipation to the slaves.

And there is a great deal of truth to that history. That account could not possibly have endured as long as it has (under the intense scrutiny to which it has been subjected) if there weren't substantial amounts of truth in it.* According to generally accepted estimates, over 2,500,000 men enlisted in the Union Army; approximately 110,000 lost their lives in battle, and approximately two hundred fifty thousand died of disease and other causes.[262] Lincoln did render slavery unlawful in the South when he signed the Emancipation Proclamation. And the president himself lost his own life as a direct result of both his uncompromising perseverance against the dissolution of the Union as well as his endorsement of that proclamation, each of which were positions he took (and held) in the face of strong resistance from numerous and varied factions. Here we can easily add Abraham Lincoln to our growing list of liberators who understood Reciprocity and all it entails:

> I am naturally antislavery. If slavery is not wrong, nothing is wrong. I cannot remember when I did not so think and feel, and yet I have never understood that the Presidency conferred upon me an unrestricted right to act officially upon this judgment and feeling. It was in the oath I took that I would, to the best of my ability, preserve, protect, and defend the Constitution of the United States. I could not take the office without taking the oath. Nor was it my view that I might take an oath to get power, and break the oath in using that power.[263]

So Lincoln understood much about Reciprocity. He saw the injustice in a system that denied balancing; he also understood that agreement creates power, that the ruler is below the rules and that co-operation is the essence of true authority (as he said on a separate occasion: "With public sentiment, nothing can fail; without it, nothing can succeed. Consequently he who molds public sentiment goes deeper than he who enacts statutes or

---

* Of course, every battle over who controls the history of the U.S. Civil War—and Lincoln's legacy—is explained by and arises from the role of memory in agreement and the importance of agreement to power. But, again, truth does exist, and anyone looking to construct a history out of whole cloth will inevitably run up against this dilemma: "Every image of the past . . . virtuous and vicious, is a construction, uninterpretable outside its selective, narrative framing; yet the materials going into the image consist of facts (assertions of varying reliability and generalizability), whose interpretation is constrained by rules of evidence" (Schwartz, x).

pronounces decisions"[264]). Lincoln knew innately that conflicting systems cannot be sustained simultaneously: "I believe this government cannot endure permanently half slave and half free"[265]; and he understood that memory underlies agreement as well: "The mystic chords of memory, stretching from every battlefield and patriot grave to every living heart and hearth-stone all over this broad land, will yet swell the chorus of the Union."[266]

But there are many other truths—stories with significant consequence for emancipation—that exist beneath the broad Lincoln-freed-the-slaves summary. By his own admission, Abraham Lincoln did not wake one morning and say, "Hmm, I think I'll free the slaves today." The soldiers of the North did not all suddenly stand up in miraculous moral synchronicity and march forth onto the plains at Manassas, then forward into ferocious battles at Shiloh, Antietam, Fredericksburg, Chancellorsville, Gettysburg, Chickamauga, Spotsylvania (and numerous points between)—until the South surrendered at Appomattox. Without question, after the South fired on Fort Sumter, secession became the prime mover for the Northern men who then enlisted. But as Reciprocity tells us, the power to achieve emancipation along the way, the ability to influence others' actions in such dramatic fashion, could not simply come from the president; power does not come from above—it comes from below. It had to have been transferred through exertion, and it had to come from the people upon whom the exertions were being made. In other words, power had to come from the slaves as a result of the exertions of slaveholders. To take this point from the inverse: had the slaves themselves not resisted, had they not sought the redefinition of limits, had they been truly content with their lot in life (as many did argue they were), then the effort to free them would have stalled before it even started. Lincoln knew that as well: "John Brown's effort [his failed raid at Harper's Ferry] was peculiar. It was not a slave insurrection. It was an attempt by white men to get up a revolt among slaves, in which the slaves refused to participate."[267]

The slaves did not fall back to force relations (although a significant number of free blacks did eventually join the Union forces). Instead, it was the South itself that started the conflict, and in so doing expedited the end to which Reciprocity was already leading; without the war, slavery would have ended later rather than sooner—but it would have ended. That point can be underscored rhetorically: why would the South have seceded in the first place if not for fear of this inevitability? And the point can be proven by Reciprocity: the eventuality of abolition is dictated by the facts that agreement creates power, that power is disbursed—unevenly—among all parties in a system and that power is transferred through its own exertion (all of which is consolidated into the term *oscillation*). The agreements that constituted the United States' system made it impossible for the North simply to impose emancipation upon the South (had it even wanted to), so emancipation would have come slowly, over time.

Here are the broad-stroke events of the Civil War viewed through the lens of Reciprocity: as oscillation moved slavery toward abolition, the South seceded in order to divorce itself from the accumulation of agreements that were leading to that redefinition of limits on behalf of the slaves. And upon secession, the South did remove itself from the scope of those agreements; the two sides then fell back to force relations, and in the midst of those force relations, Lincoln's Emancipation Proclamation eradicated slavery in the secessionist states. This proclamation had no immediate effect on slavery anywhere, since the South was no longer subject to the North's accumulation of agreements; that is to say, Lincoln's proclamation did not influence the actions of Southern slaveholders because power is created by acquiescence, and the South had not yet acquiesced. The Emancipation Proclamation did, however, make clear that this term of surrender would not be negotiated. When the South did surrender, it had no choice but to accept emancipation as part of the accumulation of agreements to which it was acquiescing, and the proclamation then influenced the actions of Southern slaveholders. In short, the slaves won their freedom within a system that recognized Reciprocity (a system to which their captors were not subject), and when the South acquiesced to that system, the door to freedom was opened to Southern slaves (and slaveholders). At that point, the entire Southern population—masters and bondsmen alike—benefited from that same extraordinary phenomenon described above: "We've conquered you; you're free." Technically, of course, the slaves weren't truly freed until they—more precisely, their posterity—accomplished the expansion of agreements that brought them into and secured them all the rights of citizens living under a system that acknowledges Reciprocity.

Given the truths that Reciprocity describes, there can be no question that Africans in America, who were discouraged (though, following the Emancipation Proclamation, not fully excluded) from taking up arms in their own cause, had to be active and essential agents in facilitating the power transferences that led to their freedom. But if the slaves did not launch a full-fledged revolt, how did they participate in the facilitation of their freedom? As has been rightly observed of the fugitive slave and influential orator, Frederick Douglass: "In the Civil War between the North and the South, Frederick Douglass was not a soldier, not a politician. Yet, he is a major figure in the coming of the Civil War and in the way the war is fought."[268] So how should we describe this influential man if he was neither soldier nor politician? Our answer is clear: he was a broadcaster (he raised his voice).* The slave named Isabella, who changed her name to Sojourner Truth, was neither soldier nor politician; she was a broadcaster (she raised her voice). Solomon Northup (who was born a free man in New York, then enslaved in the South) and Harriett Jacobs (who published her narrative under the pseudonym Linda Brendt) and William Wells Brown (who also wrote novels and plays) and Moses Roper (a mulatto slave) were neither soldiers nor politicians; they were broadcasters (they all raised their voices). And the long list goes on to include countless individuals (emblems of transference) who spoke (and sometimes wrote) openly of the injuries they and others incurred at the hands of their "masters." The slaves participated in their own emancipation in large part by broadcasting exertions that had been made against them and thus highlighting the power that had been transferred, power that their allies (Lincoln and the Union Army) then took up on their behalf.

In a field as well-trodden as the U.S. Civil War, this general point (the slaves participated in their own emancipation) has been made before. What is original here is not the empirical observation that the slaves helped facilitate their own freedom, but the theorem that underlies that fact, the *explanation* for why (which we already have) and how they were able to win freedom at all. The Civil War took shape across thousands of instances of human contact and conflict, but without the exposure of the exertions made against

---

* In a pattern that recalls the century-long correspondence between Marx and Havel (and ironic as it may be), Frederick Douglass fled for a time back *to* England, the country against which his own oppressors had previously rebelled. Thus, as with communists and those who later resisted their regimes, the exertions of slaveholders (dissenters in their own day) transferred power away from them and to the new dissidents (the slaves and their allies). And in the end, the American revolutionaries' own exertions became the ones against which these later dissidents dissented. In point of fact, Douglass's life encapsulates many of the concepts we are encountering: he was born a slave, learned to read, escaped, and connected with an ally, William Lloyd Garrison (also a broadcaster and publisher of the *Liberator*), who recognized Douglass's power as an emblem. Douglass then went on to publish his own paper, the *North Star*, and later, in an act that once again underscores the importance of the emblem, Douglass dropped the symbolism, dispensed with metaphor (and modesty) and changed the name of his newspaper to—what else?—*Frederick Douglass' Paper*.

the slaves (if no one knew the extraordinary transference of power that was taking place), the ultimate emancipation could not have occurred. And if the slaves themselves did not expose those exertions, then no one would have known really what was going on.

It is generally accepted that the first African slaves were carried to North America in the 1600s. Reciprocity tells us that resistance was available immediately, but agreements had to accumulate and communication capabilities had to develop (and mature) before slaves could work to (re)define the limits that would eventually result in their own freedom. Of course, as communication was increasing and agreements were accumulating, those who were seeking to resist Reciprocity (even though they were not explicitly aware—or inclined to admit—of Reciprocity's existence) were also making efforts to inhibit communication at all stages of slavery's development. Taking up just one example of the requisite inhibition of communication, our understanding of the rule of Reciprocity and the role of communication in the formulation of both static and dynamic agreements provides the most basic explanation for this historical fact: "[A] Virginia state law, passed in 1831, [forbade] schooling for blacks, whether slaves or free, and a subsequent statute [barred] from the state any black who left Virginia to learn to read or write. (Other Southern states had similar laws)."[269] Why were the slaveholders so adamantly opposed to the education of their slaves? The answer: Outlawing education encumbers participation in the system while also retarding communication (which in turn inhibits the accumulation of agreements). And the excommunication of those who do seek education is but another example of the containment wall constructed to keep out co-operation. As Reciprocity predicts: the Southern system had to hold blacks in (and out); the North could be more porous.

Having now navigated every preliminary tangent, and as we proceed with this analysis of the role of broadcast in the emancipation of the American slaves, it is important to reemphasize the extraordinary imbalance of influence that slavery presents. Of course, when we look directly at the acts of broadcast themselves, we find that the slaves' own words provide the most compelling illustrations of the horrors they survived (i.e., the exertions they endured at every stage).

At abduction:

"One day, when all our people were gone out to their work as usual, and only I and my sister were left to mind the house, two men and a woman got over our walls, and in a moment seized us both; and without giving us time to cry out, or to make any resistance, they stopped our mouths and ran off with us into the nearest wood. Here they tied our hands, and continued to carry us as far as they could, till night came on."[270]

In the hold of the slaveship:

"[N]ow that the whole ship's cargo were confined together, it became absolutely pestilential. The closeness of the place, and the heat of the climate, added to the number in the ship, being so crowded that each had scarcely room to turn himself, almost suffocated us . . . This deplorable situation was again aggravated by the galling of the chains, now become insupportable; and the filth of necessary tubs, into which the children often fell, and were almost suffocated. The shrieks of the women, and the groans of the dying, rendered it a scene of horror almost inconceivable."[271]

On the plantation:

"I have often been awakened at the dawn of day by the most heart-rending shrieks of an own aunt of mine, whom [the master] used to tie up to a joist, and whip upon her naked back till she was literally covered with blood. No words, no tears, no prayers, from his gory victim, seemed to move his iron heart from its bloody purpose. The louder she screamed, the harder he whipped; and where the blood ran fastest, there he whipped longest. He would whip her to make her scream, and whip her to make her hush; and not until overcome by fatigue, would he cease to swing the blood-clotted cowskin. I remember the first time I ever witnessed this horrible exhibition. I was quite a child."[272]

In the master's house:

"I now entered on my fifteenth year—a sad epoch in the life of a slave girl. My master began to whisper foul words in my ear. Young as I was, I could not remain ignorant of their import . . . He was a crafty man, and resorted to many means to accomplish his purposes . . . He peopled my young mind with unclean images, such as only a vile monster could think of. I turned from him with disgust and hatred. But he was my master. I was compelled to live under the same roof with him . . . He told me I was his property; that I must be subject to his will in all things."[273]

It would hardly seem possible to find more compelling examples of broadcast. And absent the rule of Reciprocity, it would hardly seem possible that any group could lift itself up from the depths of such a severe imbalance. These descriptions help us not only to see broadcast at work but also to understand how powerful an example of Reciprocity-in-action emancipation provides. "Slavery was an institution where one human being had absolute control over another human being. They [the slaves] might be here tomorrow; they might be sold the next day . . . They could not control where they went, what they did, what they ate, who they would marry."[274] Slavery manifests the clubber-berry bringer relationship at its most extreme, grotesque and, unfortunately, real. The slaves had no vote. They had no citizenship. They had no rights whatsoever. But they had acquiesced; they had formed agreement; they had created power; and they had been exerted against in extraordinary fashion. They used broadcast to expose the exertions made against them—and in the process, they exposed the power that had been transferred to them.

To be sure, the slaves didn't talk their way out of slavery. But broadcast was the most effective effort that they undertook. The Underground Railroad could not have spirited away each and every slave. So those that made it out had to stand up, speak up, and be held up as emblems of the exertions being made against them. Allies had to be inspired to say that's not fair, and then to pursue the balancing that Reciprocity makes possible. And that is precisely what did happen as this quote from 1845 so clearly demonstrates: "Startling incidents, authenticated, far excelling fiction in their touching pathos, from the pen of self-emancipated slaves do now exhibit slavery in such revolting aspects, as to secure the execrations of all good men."[275] And this similar statement from 1849: "This fugitive slave literature is destined to be a powerful lever. We have the most profound conviction of its potency. We see in it the easy and infallible means of abolitionizing the free States."[276] So the slave narrative was recognized and utilized as an explicit tool, a "lever" for abolishing slavery. But broadcast is a lever that works only if power is transferred through its own exertion and if the broadcast of exertions facilitates that transfer. After all, what is that lever of broadcast leveraging if not the power that has been transferred through exertions? Without Reciprocity, exposure would, at worst, foster morbid fascination and simply feed schadenfreude or, at best, raise a moral indignation that would then run impotently up against a wall of immovable power.

But power is transferred through its own exertion, and the slaves themselves, in partnership with white abolitionist allies and free blacks, broadcasted their experiences and exposed the transferences that had been made. Harriett Beecher Stowe was not slave, soldier, or politician; she was a broadcaster (she raised her voice). Wendell Phillips was not slave, soldier or politician; he was a broadcaster (he raised his voice). William Lloyd Garrison was not slave, soldier, or politician; he was a broadcaster (he raised his voice—and others'). Dr. James McCune Smith was not slave, soldier, or politician; he was a broadcaster (among his other remarkable accomplishments—he raised his voice). And that extremely truncated list goes on (and on) as well.

Ultimately, the impact of the slaves' acts of broadcast can be measured in many ways, including this objective accounting: "[S]lave narratives were extraordinarily popular texts. Here is just a sampling of how well they sold: . . . Frederick Douglass's *Narrative* (1845) sold 5,000 copies in the first four months of publication; between 1845 and 1847, it sold 11,000 copies; in Great Britain, nine editions were printed in these two years; and by 1860, 30,000 copies had sold. Solomon Northup's narrative sold 27,000 copies in its first two years of publication. Moses Roper's text went into ten editions between 1837 and 1856. William Wells Brown's book reached its fourth edition in its first year of publication."[277] *

---

*   These sale statistics now force us to face this important question: wasn't it capitalism that set the slaves in chains? Isn't slavery the most egregious manifestation of the point made much earlier—people will destroy nature, produce dangerous products (and by-products), privilege the profit-motive, and harm/exploit others in the process of transforming natural resources into wealth? Certainly, one must blame capitalism for American slavery. The desire to render natural resources into wealth while incurring the lowest possible cost-of-production was slavery's motivating force. But if one is to maintain intellectual integrity, one must also credit capitalism's role in abolition as well. After all, the North was capitalist too. And the capitalist system itself did help set the slaves free, not just through the sale of slave narratives (although a centralized economic system paired—as it must be—with a centralized political system could never have tolerated the production and distribution of such tracts), but also through the ongoing accumulation of capitalist agreements. So if capitalism was both the problem and the solution, then we must consider the possibility that there was something else at work. Upon such consideration, one quickly sees that it was not a fault of the capitalist system, but a suppression of Reciprocity that held those slaves in chains. Reciprocity reveals why, in the long run, capitalism and slavery are incompatible. Capitalism, being competition based on rules/agreements (as opposed to conflict held in check by dictate and fear-inducing exertions, which is, ironically, a description of slavery itself) cannot help but recognize the fact that power is transferred through its own exertion—as the numerous failed efforts to defy this truth frequently attest. Capitalism led these slaves into bondage, but the recognition of Reciprocity—as manifested in both the political (democratic) and economic (capitalist) system of the North—led them out. Thus, it was not capitalism, but a refusal to recognize Reciprocity that held the slaves in chains. Ironically, the only way the slaveholders could have *kept* their slaves in chains would have been to destroy the very system for which they were exploiting those slaves in the first place. To maintain slavery they would have had to destroy the competitive/cooperative capitalist accumulation of agreements and replace it with a severe, centralized system.

As one would expect, given our understanding of the role of memory in agreement, those slave narratives and other acts of broadcast (recall: "Hundreds of ex-slaves felt compelled to tell their tales on the anti-slavery lecture circuit"[278]) not only exposed the prior and continuing transferences, but also played a crucial role in shaping the memory that formed the foundation for (future) agreements with future components: "[Frederick Douglass] spoke at anniversary after anniversary, at GAR reunion after GAR reunion . . . where he tried to forge a kind of black-abolitionist memory of the Civil War."[279]

In the end, what we're talking about when we consider slaves as broadcasters is the whistleblower writ large. Whether the exertions take place on plantations or in corporations, in classrooms or in the shadowy corners of church vestries—broadcast exposes exertions and facilitates the transfer of power that those exertions make possible. Here again we see a truth we have encountered throughout: it is not the *exposure* of the authoritarian regime's refusal to engage in balancing that creates instability; it is the refusal to engage in balancing itself that creates such systemic fragility. The broadcast of the exertions of oppressors (those who refuse to recognize Reciprocity) only makes the instability more visible and triggers the transference.

What I have presented here is merely a portion of a portion of the relevant history. But it is enough. At the outset and throughout much of what finally became American slavery, the slaves acquiesced. They acquiesced to the lowest possible level, and then they slowly rose again. In the United States, free men (American revolutionaries) who freed themselves based on an innate understanding of Reciprocity (and secured their own freedom upon laws and institutions that recognize and facilitate the rule) then went on and (to their eternal shame) did enslave others. And those others, in turn, worked to free themselves—by employing the same truths and consequences of Reciprocity on which their captors had also relied. This is not an exclusively American history (life under a system that recognizes Reciprocity is not reserved for people who inhabit a land marked off between certain lines of latitude and longitude). In that same vein, the events that took place on the field at Runnymede are not exclusively English; Gandhi's Satyagraha is not exclusively Indian; the Velvet Revolution is not exclusively Czech; the fall of the Berlin Wall is not exclusively German, and so on. Instead, these events have produced data that reveal a phenomenon applicable and extant everywhere anyone interacts. These are all human histories, and together they form one history. Freedom emerges from the agreements that arise out of the interactions between parties with unequal power. The rule of Reciprocity, its causes, and its consequences reveal that this was, is, and will always be true.

Works Cited in Footnotes

Amnesty International, *Amnesty International Report 2007: China*, http:// thereport.amnesty.org/eng/Regions/Asia-Pacific/China

Batson, Andrew, "China Builds Commerce Codes, Beijing Fashions Measures to Underpin Fast-Changing Economy, *The Wall Street Journal*, March 2, 2007.

Eberstadt, Nicholas, "Nuclear Shakedown," *The Wall Street Journal*, July 6, 2006.

Farzami, Farouz, "Iranian Moolah," *The Wall Street Journal*, October 26, 2006.

Foucault, Michel, "The Subject and Power." James D. Faubion, Ed., Paul Rabinow, Series Ed., *Michel*

Foucault: Power. Essential Works of Foucault 1954-1984 (New York: The New Press, 1994).

Fukuyama, Francis, *The End of History and the Last Man* (New York: Perennial, 2002).

Granier, Marcel, "Remote Control," *The Wall Street Journal*, January 24, 2007.

Gray, Jack, *Rebellions and Revolutions: China from the 1800s to 2000* (Oxford: Oxford University Press, 2002).

Harris v. Forklift Systems, Inc., 510 U.S. 17 (1993). Available at http://www. law.cornell.edu/supct/html/92-1168.ZO.html

House Concurrent Resolution 108, *U.S. Statutes at Large*, 67: B132. Cited at http://www.digitalhistory.uh.edu/native_voices/voices_display. cfm?id=96

Indian Gaming: The National Information Site of the American Indian Gaming Industry, www.indiangaming.com

Jaffe, Greg, "Deadly Precision: To Fight Terrorists, Air Force Seeks a Bomb with Less Bang; It Cuts Collateral Damage By Using a Metal Powder Instead of Flying Shrapnel," *The Wall Street Journal*, April 6, 2006.

267

Kirsch, Adam, "Lenin's First Purge," *The New York Sun*, August 22, 2007.

Kirsch, Adam, "Twilight of the Ideologies," *The New York Sun*, February 28, 2007.

Lyons, John and De Córdoba, José, "To Oppose Chávez, Youth in Caracas Rally Behind Stalin . . . That's Ivan Stalin González, Student-Movement Leader; A Broad Dissent on Campus," *The Wall Street Journal*, November 24-25, 2007, p.A12.

Mussomeli, Joseph A., "'The Worst Genocide Ever,'" *The Wall Street Journal*, August 1, 2006.

Schwartz, Barry, *Abraham Lincoln and the Forge of National Memory* (Chicago: The University of Chicago Press, 2000).

Sharansky, Natan, and Dermer, Ron, *The Case for Democracy: The Power of Freedom to Overcome Tyranny & Terror* (New York: PublicAffairs, 2004).

Endnotes

1   Michel Foucault, *The History of Sexuality Volume I: An Introduction.* (New York: Vintage Books, 1990), p.94.

2   Lou Cannon, *Official Negligence: How Rodney King and the Riots Changed Los Angeles and the LAPD* (Boulder: Westview Press, 1999), p.21.

3   *Ibid.*, p.39.

4   *Ibid.*, p.25.

5   Grand Jury Indictment, *U.S. v. Volpe, et al.* http://www.courttv.com/archive/legaldocs/newsmakers/louima.html.

6   Lou Cannon, *Official Negligence: How Rodney King and the Riots Changed Los Angeles and the LAPD* (Boulder: Westview Press, 1999), p.20.

7   "Trial Story: The Rodney King Case: What the Jury Saw in CA v. Powell." Court TV, Broadcast 1992.

8   *Ibid.*

9   *Ibid.*

10   *Ibid.*

11   *Ibid.*

12   Brian Z. Tamanaha, *The Rule of Law* (Cambridge: Cambridge UP, 2004), p.3.

13   Jean-Jacques Rousseau, *The Social Contract* (New York: Penguin Books, 1968), p.79.

14   MADD Online: Really MADD: Looking Back at 20 years. http://www.madd.org/aboutus/1686.

15   MADD Online: MADD Milestones. http://www.madd.org/aboutus/1179.

16   Robert Service, *Lenin: A Biography* (Cambridge: Harvard UP, 2000) p.395.

17   Ho Chi Minh, *Ho Chi Minh Selected Works Vol. III* (Hanoi: Foreign Languages Publishing House, 1961), pp.17-20.

18   *Ibid.*, pp.26-27.

19   *Ibid.*, *Vol. IV*, p.450.

20 Mao Zedong, *The Writings of Mao Zedong: 1949-1976* (Armonk: M.E. Sharpe, Inc., 1986) p.4.

21 Robert E. Quirk, *Fidel Castro* (New York: W.W. Norton & Co., 1993) p.274.

22 *Ibid.*, p.240.

23 Joseph J. Ellis, *Founding Brothers: The Revolutionary Generation* (New York: Vintage Books, 2000), p.152.

24 Yogesh Chadha, *Gandhi: A Life* (New York: John Wiley & Sons, 1997) p.457.

25 Nelson Mandela, "Address to the People of Cape Town, Grand Parade, on the Occasion of His Inauguration as State President." http://www.anc.org.za/ancdocs/history/mandela/1994/inaugct.html

26 Václav Havel, *The Power of the Powerless* (Armonk: M.E. Sharpe, Inc., 1985), p. 93.

27 Brian Z. Tamanaha, *The Rule of Law* (Cambridge: Cambridge University Press, 2004), p.25.

28 A.E. Dick Howard, *Magna Carta Text and Commentary* (Charlottesville: UP of Virginia), pp.7-8.

29 *Ibid.*, p.45.

30 *Ibid.*, p.4.

31 Henry Bracton, *On the Laws and Customs of England, vol. III* (Cambridge, Mass.: Harvard UP, 1968), pp.305-06. Quoted in Brian Z. Tamanaha, *The Rule of Law*, p.26.

32 Arthur R. Hogue, *Origins of the Common Law*, (Indianapolis: Liberty Fund, 1986), p. 57. Quoted in Brian Z. Tamanaha, *The Rule of Law*, p.27.

33 Brian Z. Tamanaha, *The Rule of Law* (Cambridge: Cambridge UP, 2004), p.26.

34 Robert Francis Harper, *The Code of Hammurabi King of Babylon: About 2250 B.C.* (Chicago: The University of Chicago Press, 1904), p.11.

35 *Ibid.*, p.37.

36 *Ibid.*, p.95.

37 *Ibid.*, pp.99-101.

38 *The Constitution of the United States of America*, Article I., section 2.

39 *Ibid.*, Article I., section 3.

40 *Ibid.*, Article II., section 4.

41 Joseph J. Ellis, *His Excellency George Washington* (New York: Vintage Books, 2004), p.189.

42 "President Nixon's Resignation Speech." http://www.pbs.org/newshour/character/links/nixon_speech

43 *The Declaration of Independence of the Thirteen United States of America*, July 4, 1776.

44 *Ibid.*
45 *Ibid.*
46 *The Constitution of the United States of America*, Amendment III.
47 *The Declaration of Independence of the Thirteen United States of America*, July 4, 1776.
48 *The Constitution of the United States of America*, Article I., section 8.
49 *The Declaration of Independence of the Thirteen United States of America*, July 4, 1776.
50 *The Constitution of the United States of America*, Article III., section 2.
51 Viktor E. Frankl, *Man's Search for Meaning* (Boston: Beacon Press, 2006), p.134.
52 Natan Sharansky and Ron Dermer, *The Case for Democracy: The Power of Freedom to Overcome Tyranny & Terror* (New York: PublicAffairs, 2004), p.41.
53 *The Random House College Dictionary*, "Equilibrium" (New York: Random House, 1982), p.446.
54 *Brown v. Board of Education*, 347 U.S. 483 (1954).
55 *The Constitution of India.* http://indiacode.nic.in/coiweb/welcome.html
56 Francis Fukuyama, *The End of History and the Last Man* (New York: Perennial, 2002), p.296.
57 Joseph J. Ellis, *His Excellency George Washington* (New York: Vintage Books, 2004), pp.123-124.
58 Stephen Greenblatt, *Shakespearean Negotiations* (Berkeley: University of California Press, 1998), p.29.
59 *Ibid.*, p.30.
60 Francis Paul Prucha, *American Indian Treaties: The History of a Political Anomaly* (Berkeley: University of California Press, 1994), p.1.
61 *Ibid.*, frontispiece.
62 *Ibid.*, p.5.
63 *Ibid.*, p.7.
64 *Montana v. Blackfeet Tribe*, 471 U.S. 759 (1985), available at: http://caselaw.findlaw.com.
65 Antonin Scalia, *A Matter of Interpretation: Federal Courts and the Law* (Princeton: Princeton University Press, 1997), p.27.
66 Laurence M. Hauptman, "Finally Acknowledging Native Peoples: American Indian Policies since the Nixon Administration." From Philip Weeks, ed., *"They Made Us Many Promises": The American Indian Experience, 1524 to the Present* (Wheeling: Harlan Davidson, Inc., 2002), p.214.
67 Francis Fukuyama, *The End of History and the Last Man* (New York: Perennial, 2002), pp.xvii-xviii.

68 Václav Havel, *The Power of the Powerless* (Armonk: M.E. Sharpe, Inc., 1985), p.23.

69 Jeffrey McCracken, "Detroit's Symbol of Dysfunction: Paying Employees Not to Work," *The Wall Street Journal*, March 1, 2006, p.A1.

70 Jean-Jacques Rousseau, *The Social Contract* (New York: Penguin Books, 1968), p.83.

71 Maurice Cranston, "Introduction," *The Social Contract* (New York: Penguin Books, 1968), p.26.

72 *Ibid.*, p.34.

73 Jean-Jacques Rousseau, *The Social Contract* (New York: Penguin Books, 1968), p.53.

74 Maurice Cranston, "Introduction," *The Social Contract* (New York: Penguin Books, 1968), p.30.

75 Brian Z. Tamanaha, *The Rule of Law* (Cambridge: Cambridge University Press, 2004), p.47.

76 Maurice Cranston, "Introduction," *The Social Contract* (New York: Penguin Books, 1968), p.38.

77 Jean-Jacques Rousseau, *The Social Contract* (New York: Penguin Books, 1968), p.55.

78 *Ibid.*, p.80.

79 *Ibid.*, p.57.

80 Henry Bracton, *On the Laws and Customs of England, vol. III* (Cambridge, Mass.: Harvard UP, 1968), pp.305-06. Quoted in Brian Z. Tamanaha, *The Rule of Law*, p.26.

81 Friedrich Nietzsche, *The Birth of Tragedy and The Genealogy of Morals* (New York: Doubleday, 1956), p.219.

82 Michel Foucault, *The History of Sexuality: An Introduction. Volume I.* (New York: Vintage Books, 1990), pp. 92-93.

83 Michel Foucault, "The Subject and Power." James D. Faubion, Ed., Paul Rabinow, Series Ed., *Michel Foucault: Power. Essential Works of Foucault 1954-1984* (New York: The New Press, 1994), p.343.

84 Friedrich Nietzsche, *The Birth of Tragedy and The Genealogy of Morals* (New York: Doubleday, 1956), pp.180-181.

85 Bruce Feiler, *Abraham: A Journey to the Heart of Three Faiths* (New York: HarperCollins, 2002), p.9.

86 Jeffrey Moses, *Oneness: Great Principles Shared by All Religions* (New York: Fawcett Columbine, 1989), pp. 4-5.

87 *Ibid.*, pp. 40-41.

88 *The Declaration of Independence of the Thirteen United States of America*, July 4, 1776.

89   *1936 Constitution of the USSR*, http://www.departments.bucknell.edu/russian/const/36cons01.html.

90   Robert Service, *Lenin: A Biography* (Cambridge: Harvard UP, 2000) p.395.

91   Ho Chi Minh, *Ho Chi Minh Selected Works Vol. III* (Hanoi: Foreign Languages Publishing House, 1961), pp.17-20.

92   Mao Zedong, *The Writings of Mao Zedong: 1949-1976* (Armonk: M.E. Sharpe, Inc., 1986), p.4.

93   Robert E. Quirk, *Fidel Castro* (New York: W.W. Norton & Co., 1993), p.274.

94   Václav Havel, *The Power of the Powerless* (Armonk: M.E. Sharpe, Inc., 1985), p.27.

95   Antonin Scalia, *A Matter of Interpretation: Federal Courts and the Law* (Princeton: Princeton University Press, 1997), p.113.

96   "Saddam 'wins 100% of vote.'" http://www.cnn.com/2002/WORLD/meast/10/16/iraq.elections.ap/index.html.

97   *Ibid.*

98   *Ibid.*

99   Joseph J. Ellis, *Founding Brothers: The Revolutionary Generation* (New York: Vintage Books, 2000), p.152.

100   Yogesh Chadha, *Gandhi: A Life* (New York: John Wiley & Sons, 1997), p.457.

101   Nelson Mandela, "Address to the People of Cape Town, Grand Parade, on the Occasion of His Inauguration as State President." http://www.anc.org.za/ancdocs/history/mandela/1994/inaugct.html

102   Václav Havel, *The Power of the Powerless* (Armonk: M.E. Sharpe, Inc., 1985), p. 93.

103   Francis Fukuyama, *The End of History and the Last Man* (New York: Perennial, 2002), p.24.

104   "Saddam's Lidice," *The Wall Street Journal*, March 8, 2006, p.A20.

105   "We Will Bury You." http://www.time.com/time/magazine/article/0,9171,867329,00.html

106   Arnold Tsunga, "'Yes, You Will Be Thoroughly Beaten,'" *The Wall Street Journal*, November 2, 2006, p.A12.

107   Eason Jordan, "The News We Kept to Ourselves," *The New York Times*, April 11, 2003, p.A25.

108   Stephen Greenblatt, *Shakespearean Negotiations* (Berkeley: University of California Press, 1988), pp.136-137.

109   Michel Foucault, *Discipline and Punish: The Birth of the Prison* (New York: Vintage Books, 1995), p.49.

110   *Ibid.*, p.53.
111   *Ibid.*, p.60.
112   Francis Fukuyama, *The End of History and the Last Man* (New York: Perennial, 2002), p.32.
113   Stephen Greenblatt, *Shakespearean Negotiations* (Berkeley: University of California Press, 1988), p.37.
114   *Ibid.*
115   Václav Havel, *The Power of the Powerless* (Armonk: M.E. Sharpe, Inc., 1985), p.27.
116   *Ibid.* p.23.
117   *Ibid.* p.29.
118   *Ibid.*, p.23.
119   *Ibid.*
120   *Ibid.* p.27.
121   *Ibid.* p.28.
122   *Ibid.*
123   *Ibid.* p.26.
124   *Ibid.* p.28.
125   Farouz Farzami, "Iranian Moolah," *The Wall Street Journal*, October 26, 2006, p.A18.
126   *Ibid.*
127   James Hookway, "As Vietnam Grows, So Does Graft," *The Wall Street Journal*, April 20 2006, p.A4.
128   Gordon Fairclough, "In Chinese Province, Bling from Bribes Goes Up for Bid," *The Wall Street Journal*, March 21, 2007, p.A1.
129   Li Jinsong, et al., "Blind Injustice," *The Wall Street Journal*, September 13, 2006, p.A18.
130   Ho Chi Minh, *Ho Chi Minh Selected Works Vol. III* (Hanoi: Foreign Languages Publishing House, 1961), pp. 26-27.
131   Milton Friedman, *Capitalism and Freedom* (Chicago: The University of Chicago Press, 2002), p.187.
132   Karl Marx, *The Communist Manifesto*, David McLellan, Ed., *Karl Marx: Selected Writings* (Oxford: Oxford University Press, 1977), p.222.
133   *Ibid.*, p.226.
134   *Ibid.*, p.221.
135   Václav Havel, *The Power of the Powerless* (Armonk: M.E. Sharpe, Inc., 1985), p.23.
136   Karl Marx, *The Communist Manifesto*, David McLellan, Ed., *Karl Marx: Selected Writings* (Oxford: Oxford University Press, 1977), p.237.

[137] Karl Marx, "Critique of the Gotha Programme," *Marx, Engels, Lenin: On Historical Materialism* (Moscow: Progress Publishers, 1972), p.165.

[138] Milton Friedman, *Capitalism and Freedom* (Chicago: The University of Chicago Press, 2002), p.134.

[139] Thomas C. Schelling, *Micromotives and Macrobehavior* (New York: W.W. Norton & Co., 1978), p.21.

[140] *Ibid.*

[141] *The Compact Oxford English Dictionary, Second Edition,* J.A. Simpson and E.S.C. Weiner (New York: Oxford University Press, 2004), p.266.

[142] Brian Z. Tamanaha, *The Rule of Law* (Cambridge: Cambridge UP, 2004), p.69.

[143] Milton Friedman, *Capitalism and Freedom* (Chicago: The University of Chicago Press, 2002), p.18.

[144] Edward Taylor, http://online.wsj.com/home/us, May 3, 2007, 4:32 p.m.

[145] Milton Friedman, *Capitalism and Freedom* (Chicago: The University of Chicago Press, 2002), p.39.

[146] *Ibid.*, p.13.

[147] *Ibid.*, p.166.

[148] Benjamin Graham, *The Intelligent Investor* (New York: HarperCollins, 2003).

[149] Milton Friedman, *Capitalism and Freedom* (Chicago: The University of Chicago Press, 2002), pp.14-15.

[150] *Ibid.*, p.166.

[151] "The History of Aspirin," www.bayeraspirin.com/pain/asp_history.htm

[152] *Ibid.*

[153] Diarmuid Jefreys, *Aspirin: The Remarkable Story of a Wonder Drug* (New York: Bloomsbury, 2004), p.78.

[154] *Ibid.*, p.79.

[155] *Ibid.*

[156] *Ibid.*

[157] *Ibid.*

[158] *Ibid.*

[159] *Ibid.*

[160] *Ibid.*, p.83.

[161] *Ibid.*, pp.84-85.

[162] *Ibid.*, p.85.

[163] *Ibid.*, pp.86-87.

[164] *Ibid.*, p.115.

[165] *Ibid.*, p.116.

[166] *Ibid.*, p.121.

167 "What Are Generic Drugs?", U.S. Food and Drug Administration Center for Drug Evaluation and Research, http://www.fda.gov/cder/ogd/

168 *Ibid.*

169 "How Increased Competition from Generic Drugs Has Affected Prices and Returns in the Pharmaceutical Industry," Congressional Budget Office, http://www.cbo.gov/ftpdoc.cfm?index=655&type=0&sequence=1

170 "What Are Generic Drugs?", U.S. Food and Drug Administration Center for Drug Evaluation and Research, http://www.fda.gov/cder/ogd/

171 Randall Smith, "Goldman Takes 'Private' Equity to a New Level," *The Wall Street Journal*, May 24, 2007, p.C1.

172 Diarmuid Jefreys, *Aspirin: The Remarkable Story of a Wonder Drug* (New York: Bloomsbury, 2004), p.85.

173 Karl Marx, *The Communist Manifesto*, David McLellan, Ed., *Karl Marx: Selected Writings* (Oxford: Oxford UP), 1977, p.237.

174 Milton Friedman, *Capitalism and Freedom* (Chicago: The University of Chicago Press, 2002), p.108.

175 *Ibid.*, p.109

176 Joseph J. Ellis, *His Excellency George Washington* (New York: Vintage Books, 2004), p.143.

177 Francis Fukuyama, *The End of History and the Last Man* (New York: Perennial, 2002), p.18.

178 Emma Lazarus, "The New Colossus," displayed upon the pedestal of the Statue of Liberty. Also available at http://www.nps.gov/stli/historyculture/index.htm

179 Milton Friedman, *Capitalism and Freedom* (Chicago: The University of Chicago Press, 2002), p.15.

180 The Clash, "Rock the Casbah," *Combat Rock*, Epic/Legacy Records, January 25, 2000.

181 "The Third World: From Kalashnikovs to God and Computers: An Interview with Regis Debray," *New Perspectives Quarterly* 3:1, Spring 1986.

182 Emily Parker, "'I Know Who My Comrades Are,'" *The Wall Street Journal*, January 27-28, 2007, p.A8.

183 *The Wall Street Journal*, "Dictators and the Internet," October 8, 2007, p.A18.

184 Howard Kurtz, "After Blogs Got Hits, CBS Got a Black Eye," *The Washington Post*, September 20, 2004, p.C01.

185 Dick Thornburgh and Louis D. Boccardi, "Report of the Independent Review Panel on the September 8, 2004 *60 Minutes Wednesday* Segment 'For the Record' Concerning President Bush's Texas Air National Guard Service," January 5, 2005, Exhibit 1D, http://wwwimage.cbsnews.com/htdocs/pdf/complete_report/1D.pdf

186 "Dan Rather Statement on Memos," CBS News, http://www.cbsnews.com/stories/2004/09/20/politics/main644546.shtml

187 Howard Kurtz, "Rather Concedes Papers Are Suspect.," *The Washington Post*, September 16, 2004, p.A01, http://www.washingtonpost.com.

188 Ion Mihai Pacepa, "Propaganda Redux," *The Wall Street Journal*, August 7, 2007, p.A11.

189 *Ibid.*

190 Karl Marx, *The Communist Manifesto*, David McLellan, Ed., *Karl Marx: Selected Writings* (Oxford: Oxford UP, 1977, p.226.

191 Advertisement, *The Wall Street Journal*, May 6, 2004, p.A15.

192 Lou Cannon, *Official Negligence: How Rodney King and the Riots Changed Los Angeles and the LAPD* (Boulder: Westview Press, 1999), photo caption.

193 *Ibid.*, p.281.

194 "Trial Story: The Rodney King Case: What the Jury Saw in CA v. Powell." Court TV, Broadcast 1992.

195 Lou Cannon, *Official Negligence: How Rodney King and the Riots Changed Los Angeles and the LAPD* (Boulder: Westview Press, 1999), pp.17-18.

196 *Ibid.*, p.18.

197 *Ibid.*, p.373.

198 *Ibid.*, p.587.

199 *Ibid.*, pp.587-88.

200 *Ibid.*, p.591.

201 *Ibid.*, p.592.

202 *Ibid.*, p.588.

203 *Ibid.*

204 *Ibid.*, p.592.

205 *Ibid.*, p.349.

206 "Iran's Icon," *The Wall Street Journal*, March 28, 2006, p.A20.

207 "Pagones v. Maddux [sic], Mason and Sharpton: Tawana Brawley Grand Jury Report," Court TV Online, http://www.courttv.com/archive/legaldocs/newsmakers/tawana/

208 *Ibid.*

209 *Ibid.*, "Conclusions," http://www.courttv.com/archive/legaldocs/newsmakers/tawana/part4.html#conclusions

210 *Ibid.*

211 *Ibid.*

212 *Ibid.*

213 *Ibid.*

214 *Ibid.*

215 *Ibid.*

216 *Ibid.*

217 *Ibid.*

218 Gail Collins, "The Rev. Al Sharpton Thinks the Verdict Over," *The New York Times*, July 15, 1998, p.A18.

219 William Saletan, Ben Jacobs, and Avi Zenilman, "The Worst of Al Sharpton: A Troubling Tale from His Past. Is It True?," *Slate*, September 8, 2003, http://www.slate.com/id/2087557

220 *Ibid.*

221 S. Barrett Hickman, J.S.C., *Pagones v. Maddox, Mason, Sharpton and Brawley*, Decision, Supreme Court of the State of New York, County of Dutchess, Index No. 4595/88, October, 1998. press/old_keep/brawley.htm

222 "Pagones v. Maddux [sic], Mason and Sharpton: Tawana Brawley Grand Jury Report," Court TV Online, http://www.courttv.com/archive/legaldocs/newsmakers/tawana/

223 *Ibid.*

224 Arnold H. Lubasch, "Court Suspends Maddox for Refusal to Testify at Grievance Hearing," *The New York Times*, May 22, 1990, p.B1.

225 William Glaberson, "Once Again, Brawley Declines to Testify," *The New York Times*, July 24, 1998, p.B4.

226 "Pagones v. Maddux [sic], Mason and Sharpton: Tawana Brawley Grand Jury Report," Court TV Online, http://www.courttv.com/archive/legaldocs/newsmakers/tawana/

227 "Judge Orders Brawley to Pay $185,000 for Defamation," *New York Times*, October 10, 1998, p.B7.

228 S. Barrett Hickman, J.S.C., *Pagones v. Maddox, Mason, Sharpton and Brawley*, Decision, Supreme Court of the State of New York, County of Dutchess, Index No. 4595/88, October, 1998. press/old_keep/brawley.htm

229 Gail Collins, "The Rev. Al Sharpton Thinks the Verdict Over," *The New York Times*, July 15, 1998, p.A18.

230 S. Barrett Hickman, J.S.C., *Pagones v. Maddox, Mason, Sharpton and Brawley*, Decision, Supreme Court of the State of New York, County of Dutchess, Index No. 4595/88, http://www.courts.state.ny.us/press/old_keep/brawley.htm

231 Nan Lin, *The Struggle for Tiananmen: Anatomy of the 1989 Mass Movement* (Westport: Praeger Publishers, 1992), p.8.

232 *Ibid.*

233 *Ibid.*, p.10.

234 *Ibid.*, p.11.

235 *Ibid.*, p.17.

236 Zhang Liang, *The Tiananmen Papers: The Chinese Leadership's Decision to Use Force Against Their Own People—in Their Own Words*, Andrew J. Nathan and Perry Link, eds. (New York: PublicAffairs), p.viii.

237 *Ibid.*, pp.187-88.

238 Jack Gray, *Rebellions and Revolutions: China from the 1800s to 2000* (Oxford: Oxford UP, 2002), p.422.

239 Zhang Liang, *The Tiananmen Papers: The Chinese Leadership's Decision to Use Force Against Their Own People—in Their Own Words*, Andrew J. Nathan and Perry Link, eds. (New York: PublicAffairs), pp.117-118.

240 Jack Gray, *Rebellions and Revolutions: China from the 1800s to 2000* (Oxford: Oxford UP, 2002), p.425.

241 Nan Lin, *The Struggle for Tiananmen: Anatomy of the 1989 Mass Movement* (Westport: Praeger Publishers, 1992), p.4.

242 Jack Gray, *Rebellions and Revolutions: China from the 1800s to 2000* (Oxford: Oxford UP, 2002), p.426.

243 *Ibid.*, p.427.

244 Public Broadcasting System, *FRONTLINE: The Tank Man*, http://www.pbs.org/wgbh/pages/frontline/tankman/view/

245 *Ibid.*

246 *Ibid.*

247 Zhang Liang, *The Tiananmen Papers: The Chinese Leadership's Decision to Use Force Against Their Own People—in Their Own Words*, Andrew J. Nathan and Perry Link, eds. (New York: PublicAffairs), p.184.

248 Taylor Branch, "I Have Seen the Promised Land: The untold story of the turbulent final days of Martin Luther King Jr.," *Time*, January 9, 2006, p.51.

249 Andrew Browne, "Bubbling Anger: Blogger Hits Home By Urging Boycott of Chinese Property," *The Wall Street Journal*, June 12, 2006, p.A1.

250 *Ibid.*, p.A11.

251 Rosa Parks, Jim Haskins, *Rosa Parks: My Story* (New York: Puffin Books, 1992), p.126.

252 Donnie Williams, Wayne Greenshaw, *The Thunder of Angels: The Montgomery Bus Boycott and the People Who Broke the Back of Jim Crow* (Chicago: Lawrence Hill Books, 2006), p.116.

253 *Browder v. Gayle*, 142 F. Supp. 707, available at http://www.nps.gov/archive/malu/documents/browder_v_gayle.htm

254 Ronald Reagan, "Remarks at the Brandenburg Gate," West Berlin, Germany June 12, 1987, available at http://www.reaganlibrary.com/reagan/speeches/wall.asp

255 Michel Foucault, *Discipline and Punish: The Birth of the Prison* (New York: Vintage Books, 1995) p.7.

256 *Ibid.*, p.9.

257 *Ibid.*, pp.202-203.

258 *Ibid.*, p.60.

259 Henry Louis Gates, Jr., *The Classic Slave Narratives*, "Introduction" (New York: New American Library, 1987), p.1.

260 Abraham Lincoln, "Second Inaugural Address," Philip Van Doren Stern, ed., *The Life and Writings of Abraham Lincoln* (New York: Random House, 1940), p.841.

261 *Ibid.*

262 Thomas L. Livermore, *Numbers and Losses in the Civil War in America*, 1861-1865 (Boston: Houghton, Mifflin, 1991); also available at www.civilwar.com/casualties

263 Abraham Lincoln, "Letter to A.G. Hodges," Philip Van Doren Stern, ed., *The Life and Writings of Abraham Lincoln* (New York: Random House, 1940), p.807.

264 Abraham Lincoln, "Reply in the First Joint Debate in Ottawa," *Ibid.*, pp.472-3.

265 Abraham Lincoln, "Speech at Springfield, Illinois," *Ibid.*, p.429.

266 Abraham Lincoln, "First Inaugural Address," *Ibid.*, p.657.

267 Abraham Lincoln, "Address at Cooper Institute," *Ibid.*, p.585.

268 *Biography: Frederick Douglass*, A&E Network, 1994.

269 William Finnegan, "A Slave in New York," *The New Yorker*, January 24, 2000, p.56.

270 Olaudah Equiano, *The Interesting Narrative of the Life of Olaudah Equiano, or Gustavo Vassa, the African. Written by Himself*, Henry Louis Gates, Jr., ed., *The Classic Slave Narratives* (New York: New American Library, 1987), pp.47-8.

271 *Ibid.*, p.60.

272 Frederick Douglass, *Narrative of the Life of Frederick Douglass, an American Slave. Written by Himself*, Henry Louis Gates, Jr., ed., *The Classic Slave Narratives* (New York: New American Library, 1987), p.343.

273 Harriett Jacobs, *Incidents in the Life of a Slave Girl, Written by Herself. Linda Brendt*, Henry Louis Gates, Jr., ed., *The Classic Slave Narratives* (New York: New American Library, 1987), p.470.

274 *Biography: Frederick Douglass*, A&E Network, 1994.

275 Lucius C. Matlock, as quoted in Henry Louis Gates, Jr., *The Classic Slave Narratives*, "Introduction" (New York: New American Library, 1987), p.4.

276 *Ibid.*, p.5.

277 Henry Louis Gates, Jr., *The Classic Slave Narratives*, "Introduction" (New York: New American Library, 1987), p.3.

278 *Ibid.*, p.1.

279 *Biography: Frederick Douglass*, A&E Network, 1994.

About the Author

Born in Northern California, Stephen Michael Strager has a B.A. in Political Science from the University of California at Berkeley and a Master's in English from San Francisco State University. He has lived and worked around the world, and his writing has appeared in numerous journals. In 1992, the Manhattan-based law firm for whom he was employed sent him to manage its newly opened office in Prague. There he witnessed first-hand the residue of communism as well as significant events in the country's movement toward freedom. He now works as a writer in New York City, where he lives with his family.

Index

aspirin (acetyl salicylic acid), 183, 186,
187, 193
    patent, 184, 187
    trademark, 188, 189
*Aspirin: The Remarkable Story of a
Wonder Drug* (Jefreys), 186, 187,
188, 193
authoritarianism
    problem, 160
    definition, 121
authority, 54, 73, 80, 103
    definition of, 49
    in relation to cooperation, 126, 127
    clerical/spiritual, 117

B

Bagley, James H., 249
Bank of America Corporation, 172
Bao Dai, 43, 44, 48
Barclays PLC, 172
Barr, William, 231
Batista, Fulgencio, 43, 48
Batson, Andrew
    China Builds Commerce Codes,
    Beijing Fashions Measures
    to Underpin Fast-Changing
    Economy, 135, 176
Bayer Company, 183, 186, 187
    monopoly of aspirin, 186
    ownership of aspirin trademark, 188
*Bayer v. Chemische
Fabrik von Heyden,* 187
Bentham, Jeremy, 253
    Panopticon, 253
Berlin Wall, fall of 266
Bill of Rights (United States). *See*
United States Bill of Rights

Biography: Frederick Douglass (film),
261, 264, 266
*Birth of Tragedy and The Genealogy of
Morals, The* (Nietzsche), 106, 113
Blair, Jayson
    scandal, 220
Blind Injustice (Li et al.), 148
Bloody Sunday (Selma to Montgomery
First March), 247
Boccardi, Louis D.
    Report of the Independent Review
    Panel on the September 8, 2004
    60 Minutes Wednesday Segment
    'For the Record' Concerning
    President Bush's Texas Air Guard
    Service, 217
Bostic, Michael, 31
boycotts (exertion-as-broadcast), 228,
246, 248, *See also* Montgomery bus
boycotts
    deemed revolutionary, 248
    efficacy, 249
Bracton, Henry, 53
    *On The Laws and Customs of
    England*, 53, 54, 105
    perspective on monarchy, 105
Branch, Taylor
    I Have Seen the Promised Land: The
    untold story of the turbulent final
    days of Martin Luther King Jr., 247
Brandenburg v. Ohio, 86
Brawley, Tawana, 235, 237, 238, 250
Brendt, Linda (pseudonym). *See*
Jacobs, Harriet
broadcast
    definition of, 26, 209
    role of, 210, 244
    truth, 217, 220, 223, 224, 227, 235

10366811R0

Made in the USA
Lexington, KY
18 July 2011